TM

BESTSELLING BOOK SERIES

References for the Rest of Us!®

Are you intimidated and confused by computers? Do you find that traditional manuals are overloaded with technical details you'll never use? Do your friends and family always call you to fix simple problems on their PCs? Then the For Dummies® computer book series from Wiley Publishing, Inc. is for you.

For Dummies books are written for those frustrated computer users who know they aren't really dumb but find that PC hardware, software, and indeed the unique vocabulary of computing make them feel helpless. For Dummies books use a lighthearted approach, a down-to-earth style, and even cartoons and humorous icons to dispel computer novices' fears and build their confidence. Lighthearted but not lightweight, these books are a perfect survival guide for anyone forced to use a computer.

Already, millions of satisfied readers agree. They have made For Dummies books the #1 introductory level computer book series and have written asking for more. So, if you're looking for the most fun and easy way to learn about computers, look to For Dummies books to give you a helping hand.

Wiley Publishing, Inc.

5/09

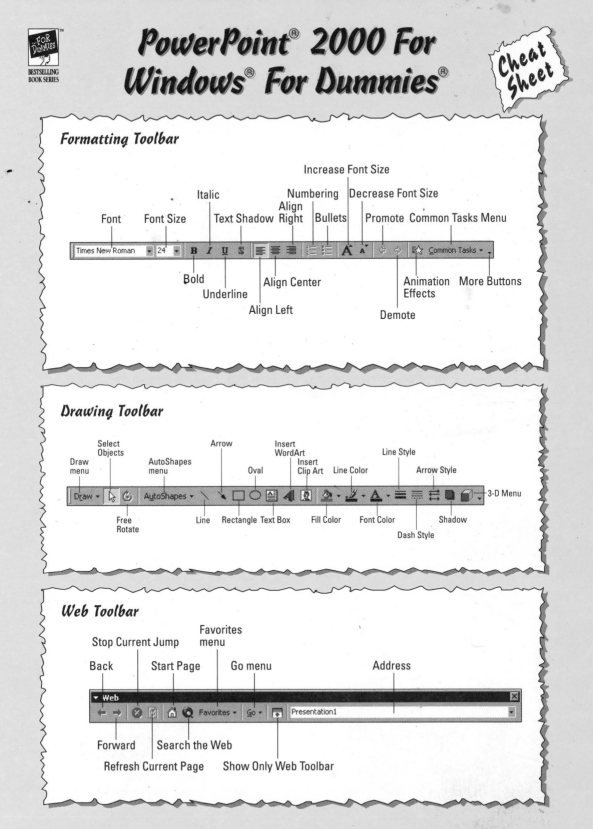

PowerPoint® 2000 For Windows® For Dummies®

Cheat Sheet

Formatting Toolbar

Font • Font Size • Italic • Text Shadow • Align Right • Numbering • Bullets • Increase Font Size • Decrease Font Size • Promote • Common Tasks Menu

Bold • Underline • Align Left • Align Center • Demote • Animation Effects • More Buttons

Drawing Toolbar

Draw menu • Select Objects • AutoShapes menu • Arrow • Insert WordArt • Insert Clip Art • Oval • Line Color • Line Style • Arrow Style • 3-D Menu

Free Rotate • Line • Rectangle • Text Box • Fill Color • Font Color • Dash Style • Shadow

Web Toolbar

Back • Stop Current Jump • Start Page • Favorites menu • Go menu • Address

Forward • Refresh Current Page • Search the Web • Show Only Web Toolbar

Web — Presentation1

For Dummies: Bestselling Book Series for Beginners

PowerPoint® 2000 For Windows® For Dummies®

Cheat Sheet

The PowerPoint 2000 Window

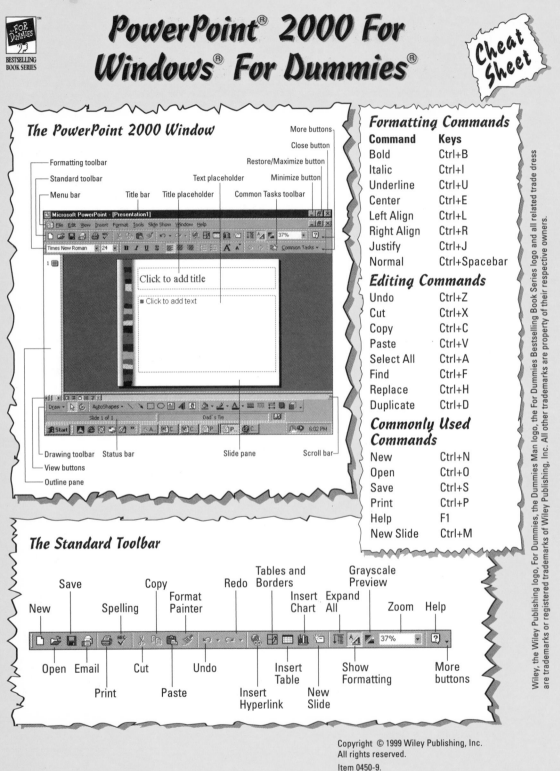

- Formatting toolbar
- Standard toolbar
- Menu bar
- Title bar
- Title placeholder
- Text placeholder
- Common Tasks toolbar
- More buttons
- Close button
- Restore/Maximize button
- Minimize button

Microsoft PowerPoint - [Presentation1]

Click to add title

■ Click to add text

Slide 1 of 1   Dad's Tie

- Drawing toolbar
- Status bar
- View buttons
- Outline pane
- Slide pane
- Scroll bar

Formatting Commands

Command	Keys
Bold	Ctrl+B
Italic	Ctrl+I
Underline	Ctrl+U
Center	Ctrl+E
Left Align	Ctrl+L
Right Align	Ctrl+R
Justify	Ctrl+J
Normal	Ctrl+Spacebar

Editing Commands

Undo	Ctrl+Z
Cut	Ctrl+X
Copy	Ctrl+C
Paste	Ctrl+V
Select All	Ctrl+A
Find	Ctrl+F
Replace	Ctrl+H
Duplicate	Ctrl+D

Commonly Used Commands

New	Ctrl+N
Open	Ctrl+O
Save	Ctrl+S
Print	Ctrl+P
Help	F1
New Slide	Ctrl+M

The Standard Toolbar

- New
- Save
- Spelling
- Copy
- Format Painter
- Redo
- Tables and Borders
- Insert Chart
- Expand All
- Grayscale Preview
- Zoom
- Help
- Open
- Email
- Print
- Cut
- Paste
- Undo
- Insert Hyperlink
- Insert Table
- New Slide
- Show Formatting
- More buttons

For Dummies: Bestselling Book Series for Beginners

POWERPOINT® 2000 FOR WINDOWS® FOR DUMMIES®

by Doug Lowe

with

Grace Jasmine

Wiley Publishing, Inc.

PowerPoint® 2000 For Windows® For Dummies®

Published by
Wiley Publishing, Inc.
909 Third Avenue
New York, NY 10022

www.wiley.com

Copyright © 1999 by Wiley Publishing, Inc., Indianapolis, Indiana

Published by Wiley Publishing, Inc., Indianapolis, Indiana

Published simultaneously in Canada

For general information on our other products and services or to obtain technical support, please contact our Customer Care Department within the U.S. at 800-762-2974, outside the U.S. at 317-572-3993, or fax 317-572-4002.

Wiley also publishes its books in a variety of electronic formats. Some content that appears in print may not be available in electronic books.

Library of Congress Control Number: 98-88796

ISBN: 0-7645-0450-9

Manufactured in the United States of America

20 19 18 17 16 15 14 13 12 11

About the Author

Doug Lowe has written more than 30 computer books, the most recent being *Office 2000 For Dummies Quick Reference* and *Internet Explorer 5 For Windows For Dummies,* published by IDG Books Worldwide, Inc. Although he has yet to win the Pulitzer Prize, he remains hopeful. He is contributing editor to *DOS World* magazine and a frequent contributor to *I-Way* magazine.

Dedication

To Debbie, Rebecca, Sarah, and Bethany.

Author's Acknowledgments

Thanks to project editors Kel Oliver and Nancy DelFavero for whipping this book into shape and bending over backwards to help expedite things when deadlines came and went. Thanks to Grace Jasmine for her great updates, to Paula Lowell for her excellent editorial prowess, and to Garrett Pease for his technical review. I'd also like to thank all the folks who helped out with the previous editions of this book: Rev Mengle, Tina Sims, Pam Mourouzis, Leah Cameron, Jim McCarter, Kezia Endsley, Becky Whitney, and Michael Partington.

Publisher's Acknowledgments

We're proud of this book; please send us your comments through our online registration form located at www.dummies.com/register/.

Some of the people who helped bring this book to market include the following:

Acquisitions, Editorial, and Media Development

Project Editors: Kelly Oliver, Nancy DelFavero

Acquisitions Editor: Steve Hayes

Copy Editor: Paula Lowell

Technical Editor: Garrett Pease

Editorial Manager: Mary P. Corder

Editorial Assistant: Paul E. Kuzmic

Production

Project Coordinator: Valery Bourke

Layout and Graphics: Beth Brooks, Linda Boyer, Angela F. Hunckler, Anna Rohrer, Brent Savage, Janet Seib, Michael A. Sullivan, Brian Torwelle

Proofreaders: Christine Berman, Jennifer Mahern, Nancy Price, Marianne Santy, Rebecca Senninger, Toni Settle

Indexer: Ty Koontz

Special Help: Stephanie Koutek, Jim McCarter, Suzanne Thomas

General and Administrative

Wiley Technology Publishing Group: Richard Swadley, Vice President and Executive Group Publisher; Bob Ipsen, Vice President and Group Publisher; Joseph Wikert, Vice President and Publisher; Barry Pruett, Vice President and Publisher; Mary Bednarek, Editorial Director; Mary C. Corder, Editorial Director; Andy Cummings, Editorial Director

Wiley Manufacturing: Ivor Parker, Vice President, Manufacturing

Wiley Marketing: John Helmus, Assistant Vice President, Director of Marketing

Wiley Composition Services for Branded Press: Debbie Stailey, Composition Services Director

Wiley Sales: Michael Violano, Vice President, International Sales and Sub Rights

Contents at a Glance

Cartoons at a Glance

By Rich Tennant

page 193

page 285

page 103

page 255

page 7

page 347

Fax: 978-546-7747
E-mail: richtennant@the5thwave.com
World Wide Web: www.the5thwave.com

Table of Contents

Introduction

●●

Welcome to *PowerPoint 2000 For Windows For Dummies,* the book written especially for those who are forced to use PowerPoint at gunpoint and want to learn just enough to save their necks.

Do you ever find yourself in front of an audience, no matter how small, flipping through flip charts or shuffling through a stack of handwritten transparencies? You need PowerPoint! Have you always wanted to take your notebook computer with you to impress a client at lunch, but you don't know what to do with it between trips to the salad bar? Have you ever spent an entire afternoon stuck in an airport, realizing that weather conditions were making you miss a major meeting and that if you could phone in your presentation, you would finally get that promotion you have deserved for the past year? You *really* need PowerPoint!

Or maybe you're one of those unfortunate folks who bought Microsoft Office 97 because it was such a bargain and you needed a Windows word processor and spreadsheet anyway, and hey, you're not even sure what PowerPoint is, but it was free. Who can resist a bargain like that?

Whichever way, you're holding the perfect book right here in your formerly magic-marker-stained hands. Help is here, within these humble pages.

This book talks about PowerPoint in everyday — and often irreverent — terms. No lofty prose here; the whole thing checks in at about the fifth-grade reading level. I have no Pulitzer expectations for this book. My goal is to make an otherwise dull and lifeless subject at least tolerable, if not kind of fun.

About This Book

This isn't the kind of book that you pick up and read from start to finish as though it were a cheap novel. If I ever see you reading it at the beach, I'll kick sand in your face. This book is more like a reference, the kind of book you can pick up, turn to just about any page, and start reading. It has 30 chapters, each one covering a specific aspect of using PowerPoint — such as printing, changing colors, or using clip art.

Each chapter is divided into self-contained chunks, all related to the major theme of the chapter.

For example, the chapter on using clip art contains nuggets like these:

- ✔ Dropping in some clip art
- ✔ Moving, sizing, and stretching pictures
- ✔ Boxing, shading, and shadowing a picture
- ✔ Editing a clip art picture
- ✔ Inserting pictures without using the Clip Gallery

You don't have to memorize anything in this book. It's a "need-to-know" book: You pick it up when you need to know something. Need to know how to create an organization chart? Pick up the book. Need to know how to override the Slide Master? Pick up the book. Otherwise, put it down and get on with your life.

How to Use This Book

This book works like a reference. Start with the topic you want to find out about; look for it in the Table of Contents or in the Index to get going. The Table of Contents is detailed enough that you should be able to find most of the topics you look for. If not, turn to the Index, where you find even more detail.

When you find your topic in the Table of Contents or the Index, turn to the area of interest and read as much or as little as you need or want. Then close the book and get on with it.

This book is loaded with information, of course, so if you want to take a brief excursion into your topic, you're more than welcome. If you want to know all about Slide Masters, read the chapter on templates and masters. If you want to know all about color schemes, read the chapter on color schemes. Read whatever you want. This is *your* book, not mine.

On occasion, this book directs you to use specific keyboard shortcuts to get things done. When you see something like

Ctrl+Z

it means to hold down the Ctrl key while pressing the Z key and then release both together. Don't type the plus sign.

Sometimes I tell you to use a menu command, like this:

File⇨Open

This line means to use the keyboard or mouse to open the File menu and then choose the Open command. (The underlined letters are the keyboard *hot keys* for the command. To use them, first press the Alt key. In the preceding example, you press and release the Alt key, press and release the F key, and then press and release the O key.)

Whenever I describe a message or information that you see on-screen, it looks like this:

```
Are we having fun yet?
```

Anything you are instructed to type appears in bold like so: Type **a:setup** in the Run dialog box. You type exactly what you see, with or without spaces.

Another nice feature of this book is that whenever I discuss a certain button that you need to click to accomplish the task at hand, the button appears in the margin. This way, you can easily locate it on your screen.

This book rarely directs you elsewhere for information — just about everything you need to know about using PowerPoint is right here. On occasion, I suggest that you turn to Andy Rathbone's *Windows 98 For Dummies* (IDG Books Worldwide, Inc.) for more specific information about wildebeests and dilithium mining techniques — oops — I mean Windows 98.

What You Don't Need to Read

Some parts of this book are skippable. I carefully place extra-technical information in self-contained sidebars and clearly mark them so that you can give them a wide berth. Don't read this stuff unless you just gots to know. Don't worry; I won't be offended if you don't read every word.

Foolish Assumptions

I make only three assumptions about you:

  ✔ You use a computer.

  ✔ You use Windows 95 or better.

  ✔ You use or are thinking about using PowerPoint 2000 for Windows.

Nothing else. I don't assume that you're a computer guru who knows how to change a controller card or configure memory for optimal use. These types of computer chores are best handled by people who like computers. Hopefully, you are on speaking terms with such a person. Do your best to stay there.

How This Book Is Organized

Inside this book are chapters arranged in six parts. Each chapter is broken down into sections that cover various aspects of the chapter's main subject. The chapters have a logical sequence, so it makes sense to read them in order if you want. But you don't have to read the book that way; you can flip it open to any page and start reading.

Here's the lowdown on what's in each of the six parts:

Part I: Basic PowerPoint 2000 Stuff

In this part, you review the basics of using PowerPoint. This is a good place to start if you're clueless about what PowerPoint is, let alone how to use it.

Part II: Looking Mahvelous

The chapters in this part show you how to make presentations that look good. Most important is the chapter about templates and masters, which control the overall look of a presentation. Get the template right, and everything else falls into place.

Part III: Neat Things You Can Add to Your Slides

The chapters in this part show you how to spice up an otherwise dreary presentation with clip art, graphs, drawings, organization charts, sealing wax, and other fancy stuff. It also shows you how to make your slides grunt like Tim Allen of TV's *Home Improvement*.

Part IV: Oh, What a Tangled Web We Weave

The chapters in this part show you how to use the new Web features of PowerPoint 2000, which are designed to let you create presentations that are connected to one another with special linkages called *hyperlinks*. Such presentations can be saved as Web pages to be used on the Internet's World

Wide Web. Also in this part, you find lots of cool things you can do online. For example, you can collaborate in real time, talking to colleagues and marking up presentations internationally, or you can use the PowerPoint 2000 nifty new Presentation Broadcast to give the same kind of multimedia presentations you give in your conference room, but now, to a worldwide audience.

Part V: Working with Presentations

This part presents several chapters that deal with putting it all together nicely, fine-tuning your presentations and some fairly advanced PowerPoint topics, such as creating 35mm slides.

Part VI: The Part of Tens

This wouldn't be a ...For Dummies book without lists of interesting snippets: ten new features in PowerPoint 2000, ten things that often go wrong, ten PowerPoint shortcuts, and more! Sorry, no Ginsu knives.

Icons Used in This Book

As you are reading all this wonderful prose, you occasionally see the following icons. They appear in the margins to draw your attention to important information. They are defined as follows:

Watch out! Some technical drivel is just around the corner. Read it only if you have your pocket protector firmly attached.

Pay special attention to this icon — it tells you that some particularly useful tidbit is at hand, perhaps a shortcut or a way of using a command that you may not have considered.

Danger! Danger! Danger! Stand back, Will Robinson!

Did I tell you about the memory course I took?

You may already know how to do this stuff if you use any of the other programs in Microsoft Office, specifically Word for Windows or Excel.

This stuff is new to PowerPoint 2000. Cool!

Where to Go from Here

Yes, you can get there from here. With this book in hand, you're ready to charge full speed ahead into the strange and wonderful world of desktop presentations. Browse through the table of contents and decide where you want to start. Be bold! Be courageous! Be adventurous! Above all else, have fun!

Dealing with older versions

I have good news and I have bad news. The good news is that Microsoft added a bunch of new features to PowerPoint 2000 that make the program easier to use and enable you to create flashier presentations. You may remember that in PowerPoint 97, Microsoft changed the file format it used to store presentation files. In the last version of PowerPoint, you couldn't go backwards; in other words, PowerPoint 97 presentations were not compatible with presentations created by earlier versions. Because this had users ripping off their toupees at every turn,

PowerPoint (as well as other applications in the suite) now has backward compatibility. Rest easy, Bill is listening to you.

Not only can PowerPoint 2000 read all your old presentations, but you can also save presentations in earlier versions. With the Pack and Go feature you can also package your entire presentation for another computer, including a viewer.

And for the bad news? Oh yes, I was kidding. There is no bad news.

Part I

Basic PowerPoint 2000 Stuff

The 5th Wave   By Rich Tennant

"NIFTY CHART, FRANK, BUT NOT ENTIRELY NECESSARY."

In this part . . .

*O*nce upon a time, the term *presentation software* meant poster board and marker pens. But now, programs such as Microsoft PowerPoint 2000 enable you to create spectacular presentations on your computer.

The chapters in this part comprise a bare-bones introduction to PowerPoint 2000. You learn exactly what PowerPoint is and how to use it to create simple presentations. More advanced stuff like adding charts or using fancy text fonts is covered in later parts. This part is just the beginning. As a great king once advised, begin at the beginning and go on till you come to the end; then stop.

Chapter 1

PowerPoint 101

*T*his chapter is a grand and gala welcoming ceremony for PowerPoint. It's kind of like the opening ceremony for the Olympics, in which all the athletes march in and parade around the track, and famous people you've never heard of make speeches in French. In this chapter, I parade the PowerPoint features around the track so that you can see what they look like. I may even make a few speeches.

I Give Up . . . What Is PowerPoint?

PowerPoint is the oddball program that comes with Microsoft Office. Most people buy Microsoft Office because it's a great bargain: You get Microsoft Word and Excel for less than it would cost to buy them separately. As an added bonus, you get a bunch of extra stuff thrown in: Outlook, Microsoft Access, PowerPoint, a complete set of Ginsu knives, and a Binford VegaPneumatic Power Slicer and Dicer (always wear eye protection).

You know what Word is — word-processing software, like WordPerfect but trendier. Excel is a spreadsheet, kind of like Lotus 1-2-3 but with more ambition. But what the heck is PowerPoint? Does anybody know or care?

PowerPoint is a *desktop presentation* program, and it's one of the coolest programs I know. If you've ever flipped a flip chart, headed over to an overhead projector, or slipped on a slide, you're going to love PowerPoint. With just a few clicks of the mouse, you can create presentations that bedazzle your audience and instantly sway them to your point of view, even if you're selling real estate on Mars, Ruble futures, or season tickets for the Mets.

PowerPoint is kind of like word-processing software, except that it's geared toward producing *presentations* rather than *documents*. In PowerPoint lingo, a presentation consists of a sequence of *slides*. After you've created the slides, you can print them on plain paper or on transparencies for overhead projection or you can have them made into glorious 35mm color slides, use them as a Web page, or even present your PowerPoint presentation in real time even on the Internet. You can print handouts with two, three, or six slides on each page, notes on the pages to help you bluff your way through your presentation, and a complete outline of your presentation.

Here are a few important features of PowerPoint 2000:

- ✔ PowerPoint is a great time-saver for anyone who makes business presentations, whether you've been asked to speak in front of hundreds of people at a shareholders' convention, to a group of sales reps at a sales conference, or one-on-one with a potential client.

- ✔ PowerPoint is also great for teachers or conference speakers who want to back up their lectures with slides or overheads.

- ✔ You can use PowerPoint to create fancy on-computer presentations in which the slides are displayed on-screen one at a time. You can embellish an on-computer presentation with all sorts of jazzy effects like slides, wipes, dissolves, sound effects, and even rudimentary animations. This process can get a bit theatrical, but it's loads of fun. It is an especially popular feature with insurance reps who own laptop computers.

- ✔ You can also use PowerPoint 2000 to create presentations for the Internet's World Wide Web. Each slide is saved as a separate HTML document, which in a layperson's terms means that each slide becomes a page on the World Wide Web.

- ✔ With PowerPoint, you can broadcast or publish a slide presentation on the World wide Web and increase your influence in the global marketplace, or at least have something interesting to talk about at your next cocktail party.

✔ Okay, not everybody buys PowerPoint as part of Microsoft Office. Some people buy it separately. I figure that if you bought PowerPoint by itself, you probably did it on purpose, so I assume that you already know what PowerPoint is (at least sort of). Heck, you didn't need to read this section anyway. I wrote this little section for the millions of innocent victims who bought Microsoft Office just to get Word and Excel and have no idea what to do with PowerPoint other than to use it as a bookend.

PowerPoint 2000 lingo you can't escape

Sorry, but if you're going to use PowerPoint, you have to get used to its own peculiar little dialect. Here's a quick spin through the PowerPoint lexicon:

Body text: Most slides also have a text object called the body text. The body text usually (but not always) consists of a series of main points set off by bullets. The main points can have subpoints that are indented under the main points. (The subpoints can have sub-subpoints and sub-sub-subpoints, but let's not get ridiculous.) The format of body text is also controlled by the Slide Master.

Object: An element on a slide. Objects can contain text, clip art pictures, charts, organization charts, or other types of graphics. You cannot place text directly on a slide; instead, a slide must contain at least one text object if you want text to appear on the slide.

Presentation: All the supporting materials that you need to present information to an audience. The audience may be small (just one person) or large (63 million people tuned in to watch you in a presidential debate). In PowerPoint, a presentation consists of slides, presenter notes, handouts, and an outline.

Presentation file: A PowerPoint file that contains the presentation materials, the PowerPoint equivalent of a Microsoft Word document file or an Excel spreadsheet file. You can then save and store these files in PPT or HTML format, or several other formats.

Slide: One page of a PowerPoint presentation. You can set up the slide page to fit the dimensions of an overhead transparency, a 35mm film slide, or the actual computer screen.

Slide Master: Sets up elements that appear on all slides, such as a background design, your name, the date, and so on.

Slide Show: Displays slides in sequence on your computer screen. You can use Slide Show to preview the appearance of your slides before you print them, or you can use it to actually present your slides to your audience.

Title: Most slides have a text object called the title. The format of the title text is governed by the Slide Master.

Tri-pane view: How you look at your presentation while working in PowerPoint. The main way you look at your presentation is to pretend you have your Slide, your Outline, and your Notes all sitting there on the table (or desktop). With just a little clicking and dragging, you grab the part of the presentation you feel like working on. By clicking any view pane, you can immediately begin the editing task of your choice. Each view is best at a particular editing task.

Welcome to PowerPoint 2000!

Before I discuss the features in 2000, I want to take a little trip through techno-history. Back in August 1995, Microsoft released its, up to then, latest and greatest version of Windows, called Windows 95. Windows 95 sported many new features, most of which were actual improvements over the older and clunkier Windows 3.1. Now, Bill and his minions have released the new Windows version, Windows 98. You may remember that one of the most important improvements in Windows 95 was that it freed you from the tyranny of eight-character filenames. With Windows 95, you could create long filenames such as "Letter to my Mom.doc" or "Presentation for Spacely Sprockets.ppt." Now, along with this wonderful advantage, a lot more bells and whistles also exist, including greater Web compatibility and better backward capability (which is nice, because who knows what version of Windows anybody is running these days, anyway).

Way back when, Microsoft quickly realized that long filenames were not much use unless you also had programs that could utilize them. So Microsoft hastily threw together a Windows 95 version of its popular Office suite and called it Office 95, which included a new version of PowerPoint, called PowerPoint 95. Although a few nifty features were thrown in, PowerPoint 95 was really just a long filename version of PowerPoint 4.0.

Microsoft rushed it to market as quickly as possible so that users could take advantage of long filenames in Windows 95, and then got back to work on a *real* revision of Microsoft Office, which was released in December 1996 under the name Microsoft Office 97. Thus was born PowerPoint 97. In order to keep up with the time-warp speed of Internet advancements, Microsoft decided to improve upon Office 97, and lo and behold, Office 2000 was born.

Because these events all moved so fast, if you went on a long vacation you may have missed Office 97. So that you won't feel left out in the cold, I review the major changes in Office 97 and then tell you the fabulous news about the Office 2000 major advancement list. (If you're a techie these days, you really don't have to have more than a short-term memory.)

Although all the Office programs, including PowerPoint, received many improvements in Office 97, the biggest improvements fell into two areas:

   ✔ **Macros:** In previous versions of Office, each program had its own way of creating *macros,* those handy little shortcuts that save you time by automatically performing common tasks for you. Excel had a macro language called Visual Basic for Applications, Word had a different macro language called WordBasic, and Access had yet a third macro language called AccessBasic. And poor, lowly PowerPoint had no macros at all. In Office 97, all the Office programs — including PowerPoint — were built with the same macro language: Visual Basic for Applications. So the big news was that for the first time, PowerPoint users could create and use macros to automate routine tasks.

Visual Basic for Applications, or VBA as computer geeks like to call it, is not for the faint of heart. This book doesn't even touch it with a ten-foot pole.

✔ **The Internet:** In Office 97, Microsoft added Internet features to all the Office programs, including PowerPoint. With PowerPoint 97, you could create complete presentations for the World Wide Web with just a few clicks of the mouse. However, the way you saved and used presentations wasn't quite up-to-snuff; pages didn't fit the screen, graphics looked different, and other stuff. In Office 2000, Microsoft comes into its own, utilizing Web technology. These new features are so cool that I devote three entire chapters to them: Chapters 18, 19, and 20.

In Office 2000, some really interesting additions make PowerPoint the ultimate telecommuters dream. In addition to being able to create snazzy presentations, now you don't even have to leave your home to present them. Online collaboration becomes a reality with the expanded ability in 2000 to use the Internet to hold meetings, write documents, and broadcast presentations.

Starting PowerPoint 2000

Here's the procedure for starting PowerPoint 2000:

1. Get ready.

Light some votive candles. Take two Tylenol. Put on a pot of coffee. If you are allergic to banana slugs, take an antihistamine and an allergy pill. Sit in the lotus position facing Redmond, Washington, and recite the Windows creed three times:

Bill Gates is my friend. Resistance is futile. You will be assimilated.

2. Rev up your engines (turn your computer on).

You have to flip only one switch to do that (I hope). But if your computer, monitor, and printer are plugged in separately, you have to turn each one on separately.

3. Click the Start button.

The Start button is ordinarily found at the lower-left corner of the Windows 98 display. After you click it, a menu magically appears out of nowhere. If you are still using Windows 95, you do it the same way. The only difference you notice at first in Windows 98 is how menus zip out kind of like the doors on the starship *Enterprise,* whereas Windows 95 menus kind of open like those automatic doors at supermarkets.

If you can't find the Start button, try moving the mouse pointer all the way to the bottom edge of the screen and holding it there a moment. With luck on your side, you see the Start button appear. If not, try moving the mouse pointer to the other three edges of the screen: top, left, and right. Sometimes the Start button hides behind these edges.

If you're not sure what I mean by *click,* read the sidebar "The mouse is your friend" later in this chapter.

4. Point to Programs on the Start menu.

After you click the Start button to reveal the Start menu, move the mouse pointer up to the word Programs and hold it there a moment. Yet another menu appears, revealing a bevy of commands resembling those shown in Figure 1-1.

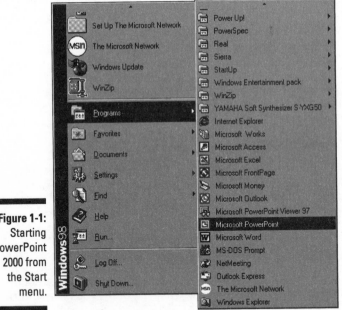

Figure 1-1:
Starting
PowerPoint
2000 from
the Start
menu.

5. Click Microsoft PowerPoint on the Programs menu.

Your computer whirs and clicks and possibly makes other unmentionable noises while PowerPoint comes to life.

The first thing you see as a result of the ongoing efforts of PowerPoint to make you realize that you need to get a life is the innocent-looking dialog box shown in Figure 1-2. Note that the first time you start PowerPoint, you see the Office Assistant, a little animated guy that offers to guide you through the ins and outs of using PowerPoint. The Office Assistant is described in detail in Chapter 7; you can ignore him for now.

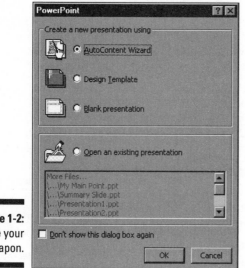

Figure 1-2:
Choose your
weapon.

PowerPoint gives you four options to choose from:

- ✔ **AutoContent Wizard:** This option practically builds a whole presentation for you by asking basic questions about what you want to say. It is
  designed for true beginners who not only know nothing about
  PowerPoint but also know nothing about giving presentations. It's pretty
  limited but can help get you going. It can also be a quick way of getting a
  presentation together for an experienced user who doesn't have time to
  be creative.

  The marketing folks at Microsoft want you to believe that the
  AutoContent Wizard writes your presentation for you, as if you just click
  the button and then go play a round of golf while PowerPoint does your
  research, organizes your thoughts, writes your text, and throws in a few
  good lawyer jokes to boot. Sorry. All the AutoContent Wizard does is
  create an outline for a number of common types of presentations. It
  doesn't do your thinking for you.

- ✔ **Design Template:** This option enables you to pick from one of the many
  predefined templates supplied with PowerPoint. The template that you
  use governs the basic appearance of each slide in your presentation —
  things like the background color, text font, and so on.

- ✔ **Blank presentation:** This option is useful in two situations: (1) You're a
  computer whiz who is insulted by the shortcuts provided by the
  AutoContent or Template options, or (2) You're an incredibly boring
  person, and you *want* your presentations to have a blank sort of look to
  them.

✔ **Open an existing presentation:** You pick this option if you want to work a little more on that presentation that you didn't quite finish yesterday, or if the presentation that you want to create is so similar to the one you gave last month that there's no point in starting all over again.

TECHNICAL STUFF

The mouse is your friend

Remember that scene in *Star Trek IV* when Scotty, having been zapped back into the 1990s and forced to use a primitive computer (it was a Macintosh), picked up the mouse, and talked into it like a microphone? "Computer! Hello computer! Hmmph. How quaint."

You don't get very far with PowerPoint (or any other Windows program) until you learn how to use the mouse. You can try picking it up and talking into it if you want, but you won't get any better results than Scotty did.

Most mice have two buttons on top and a ball underneath. When you move the mouse, the ball rolls. The rolling motion is detected by little wheels inside the mouse and sent to your computer, which responds to your mouse movements by moving the mouse cursor on-screen. What will they think of next?

Here's the lowdown on the various acts of mouse dexterity that you are asked to perform as you use PowerPoint:

✔ To move or point the mouse means to move it without pressing any mouse buttons so that the mouse cursor moves to a desired screen location. Remember to leave the mouse on the mouse pad as you move it; if you pick it up, the ball doesn't roll and your movement doesn't register. As you move the little creature, you should see a little arrow whiz across the screen in the general direction you are moving the mouse.

✔ To click means to press and release the left mouse button. Usually, you are asked to click something, which means to point to the something and then click the left button.

✔ To double-click means to press and release the left mouse button twice, as quickly as you can.

✔ To triple-click means to press and release the left mouse button three times, as quickly as you can. Right.

✔ To right-click means to click the right mouse button instead of the left. Get used to right-clicking: It's a handy action in PowerPoint.

✔ To click and drag something (also simply called drag) with the mouse means to point at it, press the left button (or right button, depending on the task), and move the mouse while holding down the button. When you arrive at your destination, you release the mouse button.

✔ To stay the mouse means to let go of the mouse and give it the command "Stay!" You don't need to raise your voice; speak in a normal but confident and firm tone. If your mouse starts to walk away, say "No," put it back in its original position, and repeat the command "Stay!" (Under no circumstances should you strike your mouse. Remember, there are no bad mice.)

To choose one of these options, click the appropriate radio button, and then click OK. You can bail out of this startup dialog box altogether by clicking the Cancel button or pressing the Esc key. Doing so leaves you with a blank screen but enables you to use the menus or toolbars to create a new presentation or open an existing one. If this little dialog box bothers you, you can click the Don't Show This Dialog Box Again option at the bottom of the dialog box, but I wouldn't advise that new users select this option. It's a good idea to use this dialog box until you are familiar with the PowerPoint set up. You can always click the check box later if you want.

Help Me, Mr. Wizard!

The easiest way to create a new presentation, especially for novice PowerPoint users, is to use the AutoContent Wizard. This wizard asks you for some pertinent information, such as your name, the title of your presentation, and the type of presentation you want to create. Then it automatically creates a skeleton presentation that you can modify to suit your needs.

To create a presentation using the AutoContent Wizard, follow these steps:

1. **Start PowerPoint.**

   You get that annoying "Choose your weapon" dialog box. Hey, get your mouse arrow off that "not again" check box!

2. **Choose AutoContent Wizard from the PowerPoint startup dialog box and click OK.**

   The AutoContent Wizard takes over and displays the dialog box shown in Figure 1-3. You may also notice your office assistant saying something pithy about the AutoContent Wizard; ignore him for now by right-clicking and choosing Hide.

3. **Click Next.**

   The dialog box shown in Figure 1-4 appears.

4. **Select the type of presentation that you want to create by clicking one of the presentation types.**

   A variety of presentation types exist in six different categories. Click the category you find the most useful and select a presentation type.

5. **Click Next.**

   When you click Next, the AutoContent Wizard advances to the dialog box shown in Figure 1-5.

6. **Indicate the type of output that you want to create.**

7. **Click Next.**

   The wizard proceeds to the dialog box shown in Figure 1-6.

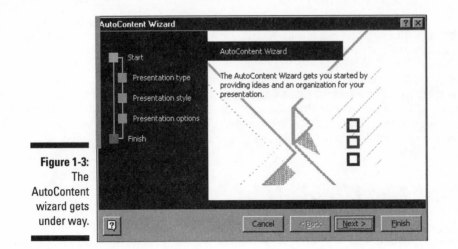

Figure 1-3:
The
AutoContent
wizard gets
under way.

8. **Type the title of your presentation and footer information, such as your name or company.**

   Note that you get the last-updated presentation by default as well as a slide number. (You can click the check box if you don't feel like having those default settings.)

   For example, in Figure 1-6, I typed *Trouble in River City* as the title and *Professor Harold Hill* as footer information.

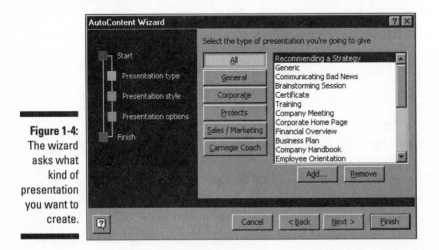

Figure 1-4:
The wizard
asks what
kind of
presentation
you want to
create.

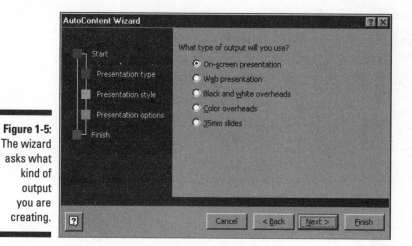

Figure 1-5:
The wizard
asks what
kind of
output
you are
creating.

9. **Click Next.**

When you click Next, the wizard moseys on to the dialog box shown in Figure 1-7.

10. **Click Finish.**

The AutoContent Wizard creates a presentation for you. After the presentation is finished, you can use the editing and formatting techniques described in the rest of this chapter and throughout the book to personalize the presentation.

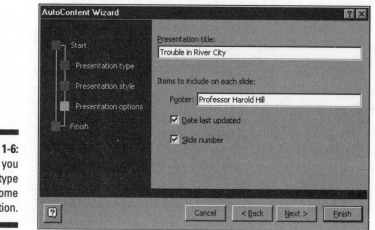

Figure 1-6:
Now you
have to type
in some
information.

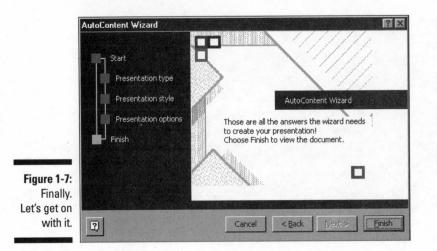

Figure 1-7:
Finally.
Let's get on
with it.

Which Way Is Up? (Or, What Is All That Stuff on the Screen?)

Working with the AutoContent Wizard is easy enough: It presents you with a series of simple, fill-in-the-blank questions and a limited number of buttons you can click. After you finish the questions, the wizard creates a skeleton presentation and dumps you into the *Tri-pane,* or Normal view. As you can see, you have your slide in the right corner and across from it, you have an outline with suggestions about what to do. On the bottom, you have a place to add notes. Now you are free to figure out for yourself how to use the dozens of menu commands and toolbar buttons that make PowerPoint work. Being abandoned like this is maddening enough to drive you to consider newsprint and markers as a viable alternative for your presentation.

Before getting started, it's important for you to be aware of the new toolbar customizing feature in PowerPoint 2000. Get this figured out right now, so that later you won't have to join a newsgroup called alt.PowerPoint.hate. Basically, if you click any little down arrow in your existing toolbar(s), you will see that you have the opportunity to add or subtract toolbar features. Scroll down to the very end of the drop-down menu, and you see that you have a chance to customize your toolbars. Click this option to see the dialog box shown in Figure 1-8.

Notice that the dialog box has a check box to make both your Standard and your Formatting toolbars appear on the same toolbar line. Don't select this check box! If it's already checked, uncheck it. This way, your screen will look like my pictures in the book. Later, if you're comfortable with the toolbars being combined and prefer it that way, come back here and check away. Now that everyone is all together, I'll move on.

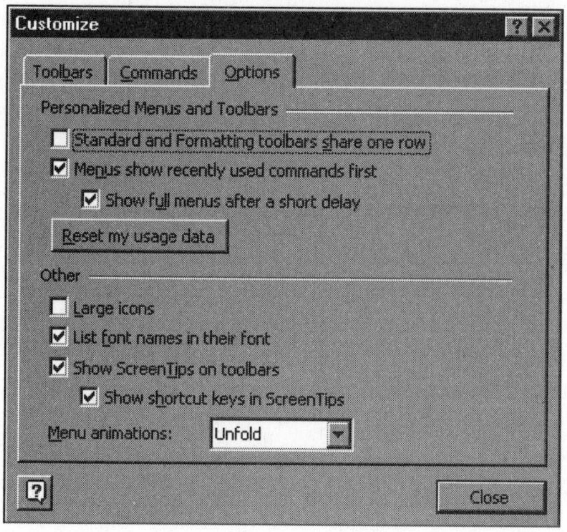

Figure 1-8:
Time to cus-
tomize your
toolbars!

Figure 1-9 shows how the PowerPoint screen appears when working in Tri-
pane view. (For more information about each pane and how they all work
together, refer to the section "The View from Here Is Great" that appears later
in this chapter.)

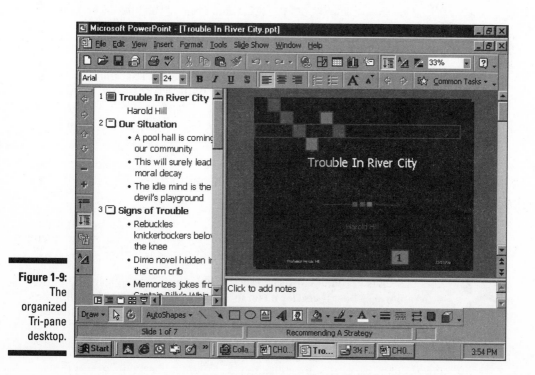

Figure 1-9:
The
organized
Tri-pane
desktop.

Five items on the PowerPoint screen are worthy of your attention:

✔ Across the top of the screen, just below the Microsoft PowerPoint title, is the *menu bar.* The deepest and darkest secrets of PowerPoint are hidden on the menu bar. Wear a helmet when exploring it. Back in the old days, when PowerPoint 97 was born, the menu just sat there. Now, you have a custom toolbar, which means your random acts are recorded for posterity and replayed for you as if they were information from a prophet.

✔ Just below the menu bar are two of the many *toolbars* PowerPoint offers you in an effort to make its most commonly used features easy to use. Each toolbar consists of a bunch of buttons that you can click to perform common functions. The toolbar on the top is the Standard toolbar; immediately beneath it is the Formatting toolbar. Notice at the right of the Formatting toolbar is the Common Tasks toolbar, which has a little down arrow next to it. (In PowerPoint 97, this toolbar was at the bottom right of your screen.) You use the spiffy little down arrow to find all the tasks that you can't locate on the other toolbars. As you use the tasks, they appear in the toolbar itself; thus you have been customized! Down near the bottom of the screen is the Drawing toolbar. Just remember, every time you see a down arrow on a toolbar, click it if you can't find something you need.

If you're not sure about the function of one of the billions and billions of buttons that clutter the PowerPoint screen, place the mouse pointer on the button in question. After a moment, the name of the button appears in a box just below the button.

✔ At the right is where your current slide appears. That thing on the left is the Outline view, and the thing on the bottom is the place where you add your notes. Not so hard yet, huh?

✔ At the bottom of the screen is the *status bar,* which tells you which slide is currently displayed (in this example, Slide 1 of 7).

✔ The salad bar is located . . . well, actually there is no salad bar. I lied. Really only four things are worth noticing in Figure 1-9.

You'll never get anything done if you feel that you have to understand every pixel of the PowerPoint screen before you can do anything. Don't worry about the stuff that you don't understand; just concentrate on what you need to know to get the job done and worry about the bells and whistles later.

Lots of stuff is crammed into the PowerPoint screen, enough stuff that the program works best if you let it run in *Full Screen* mode. If PowerPoint doesn't take over your entire screen, look for the boxy-looking maximize button near the top-right corner of the PowerPoint window (it's the middle of the three buttons clustered in the top-right corner — the box represents a window maximized to its largest possible size). Click it to maximize the PowerPoint screen. Click it again to restore the PowerPoint screen to its smaller size.

The View from Here Is Great

On the bottom-left edge of the Presentation window is a series of View buttons. These buttons enable you to switch among the various *views,* or ways of looking at your presentation. The Tri-pane view is how your desktop normally looks, so it's also called Normal view. Table 1-1 summarizes what each View button does.

Table 1-1	View Buttons
Button	*What It Does*
⊡	Switches to Normal, or Tri-pane view, which shows your slide, outline, and notes all at once. This view is how your desktop normally appears. The line borders between the different views are called *pane borders.*
▤	Switches to Outline view, which enables you to focus on the content of your presentation rather than its appearance.
▢	Switches to Slide view, which shows the slides as they appear when printed or displayed.
▦	Switches to Slide Sorter view, which enables you to easily see what order your slides are in.
▯	Switches to Slide Show view, which displays your slides in an on-screen presentation.

Zooming In

PowerPoint automatically adjusts its zoom factor so that Slide view displays each slide in its entirety. In Normal view, your slide is at 37 percent. You can change the size of your slide in Normal or Slide view, and depending on the size of your computer's monitor and whether you have maximized the PowerPoint window, the slide may end up being too small to see. If this miniaturization happens, you can increase the zoom factor using the View➪Zoom command or the Zoom control on the Standard toolbar.

On the other hand, if you set the zoom so high that the entire slide doesn't fit in the window, PowerPoint calls up a little slide miniature on top of the slide so that you can still see the whole slide. If you don't see this miniature, click View➪Slide Miniature. You will also notice the scroll bars at the right and the bottom of the window. You can use these scroll bars to scoot the slide around so that you can see the slide parts that don't fit in the window.

Editing Text

In PowerPoint, slides are blank areas that you can adorn with various types of objects. The most common types of objects are *text objects,* which are rectangular areas that are specially designated for holding text. Other types of objects include shapes such as circles or triangles, pictures imported from clip-art files, and graphs.

Most slides contain two text objects: one for the slide's title, the other for its body text. However, you can add additional text objects if you want, and you can remove the body text or title text object. You can even remove both to create a slide that contains no text.

 Whenever you move the mouse cursor over a text object, the cursor changes from an arrow to what's lovingly called the *I-beam,* which you can use to support bridges or build aircraft carriers. Seriously, when the mouse cursor changes to an I-beam, you can click the mouse button and start typing text.

When you click a text object, a box appears around the text and an insertion pointer appears right at the spot where you clicked. PowerPoint then becomes like a word processor. Any characters that you type are inserted into the text at the insertion pointer location. You can use the Delete or Backspace keys to demolish text, and you can use the arrow keys to move the insertion pointer around in the text object. If you press the Enter key, a new line of text begins within the text object.

When a text object contains no text, a *placeholder* message appears in the object. For a title text object, the message Click to add title appears. For other text objects, the placeholder message reads Click to add text. Either way, the placeholder message magically vanishes when you click the object and begin typing text.

If you start typing without clicking anywhere, the text that you type is entered into the title text object — assuming that the title text object doesn't already have text of its own. If the title object is not empty, any text that you type (with no text object selected) is simply ignored.

When you're done typing text, press the Esc key or click the mouse anywhere outside the text object.

In Chapter 2, you find many details about playing with text objects, so hold your horses. You have more important things to attend to first.

Moving from Slide to Slide

You have several ways to move forward and backward through your presentation, from slide to slide:

> ✔ Click one of the double-headed arrows at the bottom of the vertical scroll bar. Doing so moves you through the presentation one slide at a time.
>
> ✔ Use the Page Up and Page Down keys on your keyboard. Using these keys also moves one slide at a time.
>
> ✔ Drag the scroll box (the box that appears in the middle of the scroll bar) up or down. As you drag the scroll box, you see a text box that indicates which slide PowerPoint will display when you release the mouse button. Dragging the scroll box is the quickest way to move directly to any slide in your presentation.

Fifty Ways to Add a New Slide

The slides created by the AutoContent Wizard may not be adequate for your presentation. Although you may be able to adapt some of the prebuilt slides by editing their titles and text objects, eventually you'll need to add slides of your own.

You're in luck! PowerPoint gives you about 50 ways to add new slides to your presentation. You see only four of them here:

> ✔ Click the New Slide button on the standard toolbar.
>
> ✔ Click the Common Tasks button and then the New Slide button (shown in the margin) in the formatting toolbar.
>
> ✔ Choose the Insert⇨New Slide command.
>
> ✔ Press Ctrl+M.

In all four cases, PowerPoint displays the New Slide dialog box shown in Figure 1-10. This dialog box enables you to pick from 24 different types of slide layouts. Just click the mouse on the one you want to use and click OK. PowerPoint inserts the new slide into your presentation immediately after the slide currently shown on-screen.

Notice that each slide layout has a name. The one that's highlighted in Figure 1-11 is called _Bulleted List_. The layout name tells you which types of objects are included in the layout. For example, Bulleted List includes a text object that contains a bulleted list. _Text & Clip Art_ layout includes two objects: one for text, the other for a picture from the PowerPoint clip art gallery. You'll probably use the Bulleted List layout most. It's the best format for presenting a topic along with several supporting points. For example, Figure 1-11 shows a typical bulleted list slide, in which a list of bulleted items describes signs that your son is headed down the road towards moral decay.

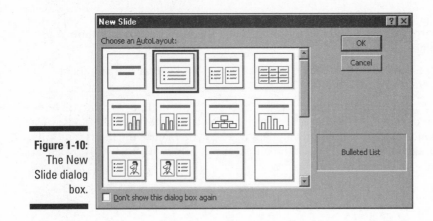

Figure 1-10:
The New
Slide dialog
box.

One of the layouts available in the AutoLayout section of the New Slide dialog box is named *Blank*. This layout doesn't include any objects; it is a blank slate that you can use to create a slide that doesn't fit any of the predefined layouts. All slide layouts except Blank include a single-line text object that serves as a title for the slide. This title is formatted consistently from slide to slide in order to give your presentation a professional look.

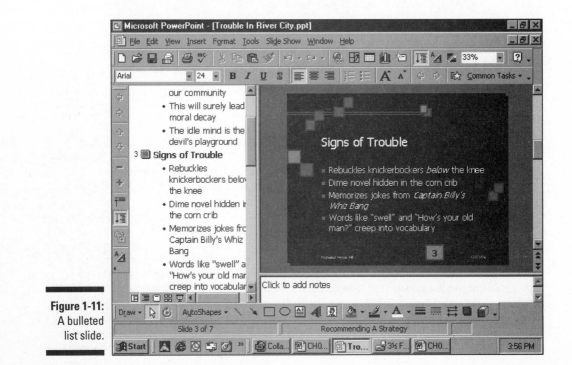

Figure 1-11:
A bulleted
list slide.

Outline That for Me!

So far, you've seen the Normal or Tri-pane view, and you have been working with PowerPoint in *Slide view,* the view mode that shows your presentation slides one at a time, exactly as they appear when you print them. Slide view is useful for tinkering with each slide's appearance, but it's not exactly the most efficient way to dump a bunch of text into PowerPoint for a whole series of slides. To make a series of slides, you need to use PowerPoint's *Outline view.* In Normal or Tri-pane view, you can see the lefthand part of your screen, which is your outline. You can click and drag the pane border of the outline to make it big enough to use on your desktop, or you can click the Outline View button on the bottom-left of your screen.

Figure 1-12 shows a presentation displayed in Outline view. Gone are the glamorous graphics, the fancy fonts, and the cheery colors. Instead, all you get is the text that shows up on each slide in that most boring of all formats: the good old-fashioned outline. The view is not pretty, but it frees you from the tyranny of appearances and enables you to concentrate on your presentation's content, which is what you should be concentrating on (unless your viewers are so gullible that they'd buy the Brooklyn Bridge if your slides were dazzling enough).

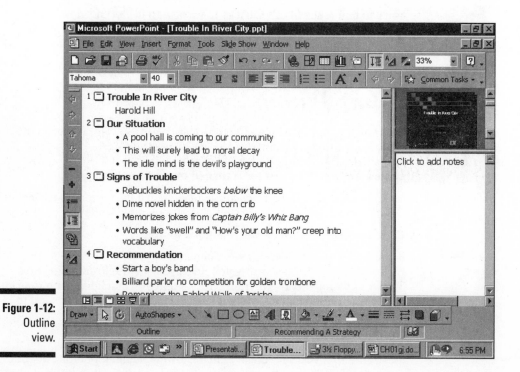

Figure 1-12:
Outline
view.

You will notice that you still see a little picture of your slide and your note area, too. Ignore them, and concentrate on your outline.

You have two ways to change PowerPoint to Outline view:

- ✔ Click the Outline View button on the status bar.
- ✔ Click and drag the pane borders of the Outline in Normal view and make it as big as you like on your desktop.

Once in Outline view, you can zip back to Slide view using either of these methods:

- ✔ Click the Slide View button on the status bar.
- ✔ Click and drag on the pane borders of the Slide View pane and make it as big as you like on your desktop.

A few hints on using Outline view:

- ✔ Once in Outline view, press the Enter key to create a new line. Then use the Tab key at the beginning of a line to indent the line or use the Shift+Tab key to reduce the line's indent.
- ✔ You can find loads of other tricks to work with in Outline view. If you're totally confused but think that Outline view sounds like the greatest thing since sliced bread, you can find more about it in Chapter 3.

Printing That Puppy

After you finish your masterpiece, you probably want to print it. Here's the procedure for printing all the slides in your presentation:

1. **Make sure that your printer is turned on and ready to print.**

   Make sure that the *select* or *on-line* light is on. If it isn't, press the Select or On-line button to make it so. Check the paper supply while you're at it.

2. **Click the Print button on the Standard toolbar.**

   If you prefer, use the File⇨Print command, or press Ctrl+P or Ctrl+Shift+F12. Whichever way you do it, you see the Print dialog box. The Print dialog box has myriad options that you can fiddle with to print your presentation just so, but you can leave them alone if you want to print all the slides in your presentation.

3. **Click the OK button or press the Enter key.**

   Make sure that you say "Engage" in a knowing manner, pointing at your printer as you do so. The secret is to fool your printer into thinking that you know what you're doing.

Printed pages should soon appear on your printer. Check the pages to make sure that they look the way you want. Depending on how complex your slides are and how fast your printer is, your slides may pop right out of your printer before you can say, "I love this program." Or you may be able to take a family vacation to Disneyland while your slides print.

If you're using overhead transparencies, you can load them directly into your laser printer provided that you get transparencies that are designed for laser printers — ordinary transparencies may melt and leave gooey stuff all over your printer's guts and possibly spread radioactive dust throughout the entire tristate area. Bad idea. Laser transparencies are expensive, though, so printing a proof on plain paper before printing on the transparencies is a good idea.

Similarly, if you use transparencies with an inkjet printer, you should get transparencies that are designed for inkjet printers. Such transparencies have a rough coating on one side that's designed to hold the ink that the printer sprays on. If you use the wrong transparencies or use the right transparencies but load them upside down, you may end up with smeared ink on your hands (and everywhere else).

Tune in to Chapter 6 if you want to know more about printing. If you want your output printed on 35mm slides, check out Chapter 25.

Saving Your Work

Now that you've spent hours creating the best presentation since God gave Moses the Ten Commandments, you can just turn your computer off, right? Wrong-o! All your precious work is held in your computer's fleeting RAM *(random access memory)* until you save your work to a disk file. Turn off your computer before you save your work, and *poof!* your work vanishes as if David Copperfield were in town.

Like everything else in PowerPoint, you have at least four ways to save a document:

- ✔ Click the Save button on the Standard toolbar.
- ✔ Choose the File➪Save command.
- ✔ Press Ctrl+S.
- ✔ Press Shift+F12.

If you haven't yet saved the file to disk, the magical Save As dialog box appears. Type the name that you want to use for the file in the Save As dialog box and click the OK button to save the file. After you save the file once, subsequent saves update the disk file with any changes that you made to the presentation since the last time you saved it.

Some notes to keep in mind when saving files:

- Use your noggin when assigning a name to a new file. The filename is how you can recognize the file later on, so pick a meaningful name that suggests the file's contents.

- When you save a document, PowerPoint displays a bar graph at the bottom of the screen to prove that it's really doing something. See how PowerPoint saves. Save, PowerPoint, save!

- After you save a file for the first time, the name in the presentation window's title area changes from *Presentation* to the name of your file. Still more proof that the file has been saved.

- Don't work on your file for hours at a time without saving it. I've learned the hard way to save my work every few minutes. After all, the earth may be hit by a giant asteroid any time now. Get into the habit of saving every few minutes, especially after making a significant change to a presentation, like adding a covey of new slides or making a gaggle of complicated formatting changes. It's also a good idea to save your work before printing your presentation.

When you save a file for the first time, you will get a dialog box asking you for a filename and file type. Type away, and then click OK or Save to save the file. If you try to save a file using a filename you've already used for another presentation, PowerPoint asks whether you're sure you want to replace the existing disk file. If you made a mistake and didn't really mean to assign a filename that's already in use, click No and save the file under a different name. Consult Chapter 23 for more information about filenames and file management.

Retrieving a Presentation from a Disk

After you save your presentation to a disk file, you can retrieve it later when you want to make additional changes or to print it. As you may guess, PowerPoint gives you about 40 ways to accomplish the retrieval. Here are the four most common:

- Click the Open button on the Standard toolbar.
- Use the File⇨Open command.
- Press Ctrl+O.
- Press Ctrl+F12.

All four retrieval methods pop up the Open dialog box, which gives you a list of files to choose from. Click the file that you want; then click the OK button or press the Enter key. PowerPoint reads the file from disk and puts it into your computer's RAM, where you can work on it.

The Open dialog box has controls that enable you to rummage through the various folders on your hard disk in search of your files. If you know how to open a file in any Windows 95 application, you know how to do it in PowerPoint (because the Open dialog box is pretty much the same in any Windows program). If you seem to have lost a file, rummage around in different folders to see whether you can find it. Sometimes you can save a file in the wrong folder by accident. Also, check the spelling of the filename. Maybe your fingers weren't on the home row when you typed the filename, so instead of BRODART.PPT, you saved the file as NTPFSTY.PPT. I hate it when that happens.

The fastest way to open a file from the Open dialog box is to double-click the file you want to open. Point to the file and click the mouse twice, as fast as you can. This spares you from having to click the file once and then clicking the OK button. Double-clicking also exercises the fast-twitch muscles in your index finger.

PowerPoint keeps track of the last few files you've opened and displays them on the File menu. To open a file you've recently opened, click the File menu and inspect the list of files at the bottom of the menu. If the file you want is in the list, click it to open it.

Closing a Presentation

Having finished your presentation and printed it just right, you have come to the time to close it. Closing a presentation is kind of like gathering up your papers, putting them neatly in a file folder, and returning the folder to its proper file drawer. The presentation disappears from your computer screen. Don't worry: It's tucked safely away on your hard disk where you can get to it later if you need to.

To close a file, use the File⇨Close command. You also can use the keyboard shortcut Ctrl+W, but you need a mind like a steel trap to remember that Ctrl+W stands for Close.

You don't have to close a file before exiting PowerPoint. If you exit PowerPoint without closing a file, PowerPoint graciously closes the file for you. The only reason you may want to close a file is that you want to work on a different file and you don't want to keep both files open at the same time.

If you've made changes since the last time you saved the file, PowerPoint offers to save the changes for you. Click Yes to save the file before closing or click No to abandon any changes you've made to the file.

If you close all the open PowerPoint presentations, you may discover that most of the PowerPoint commands have been rendered useless (they are grayed on the menu). Fear not. Open a presentation or create a new one, and the commands return to life.

Exiting PowerPoint

Had enough excitement for one day? Use any of these techniques to shut PowerPoint down:

- ✔ Choose the File➪Exit command.
- ✔ Click the X box at the top-right corner of the PowerPoint window.
- ✔ Press Alt+F4.

Bammo! PowerPoint is history.

You should know a few things about exiting PowerPoint (or any application):

- ✔ PowerPoint doesn't enable you to abandon ship without first considering to save your work. If you've made changes to any presentation files and haven't saved them, PowerPoint offers to save the files for you. Lean over and plant a fat kiss right in the middle of your monitor — PowerPoint just saved you your job.

- ✔ Never, never, never, ever, never turn off your computer while PowerPoint or any other program is running. Naughty! Always exit PowerPoint and all other programs that are running before you turn off your computer.

- ✔ In fact, you'd best get clean out of Windows before shutting down your computer. Exit all of your programs the same way you exited PowerPoint. Then click the Windows Start button and choose the Shut Down command. Select the Shut down your computer option and click Yes. Then wait for Windows to display the message It's now safe to turn off your computer before turning off your computer.

Chapter 2

Editing Slides

● ●

In This Chapter

▶ Moving around in a presentation

▶ Working with objects

▶ Editing text

▶ Undoing a mistake

▶ Deleting slides

▶ Finding and replacing text

▶ Rearranging slides

● ●

*I*f you're like Mary Poppins ("Practically Perfect in Every Way"), you can skip this chapter. Perfect people never make mistakes, so everything they type in PowerPoint 2000 comes out right the first time. They never have to press Backspace to erase something they typed incorrectly, go back and insert a line to make a point they left out, or rearrange their slides because they didn't add them in the right order to begin with.

If you're more like Jane ("Rather Inclined to Giggle; Doesn't Put Things Away") or Michael ("Extremely Stubborn and Suspicious"), you probably make mistakes along the way. This chapter shows you how to go back and correct those mistakes.

Reviewing your work and correcting it if necessary is called *editing*. It's not a fun job, but it has to be done. A spoonful of sugar usually helps.

This chapter focuses mostly on editing text objects. Many of the techniques apply to editing other types of objects, such as clip art pictures or drawn shapes. For more information about editing other types of objects, see Part III.

Moving from Slide to Slide

The most common way to move around in a PowerPoint presentation is to press the Page Up and Page Down keys on your keyboard:

- ✔ **Page Down:** Moves forward to the next slide in your presentation
- ✔ **Page Up:** Moves backward to the preceding slide in your presentation

If you press Page Up or Page Down in Normal or Tri-pane view, nothing happens, so make sure that you're in Slide view before you drive yourself crazy. Just click the slide in Normal view, or click Slide view.

Alternatively, you can move forward or backward through your presentation by clicking the double-headed arrows at the bottom of the vertical scroll bar on the right edge of the presentation window. You also can use the vertical scroll bar on the right edge of the presentation window to move forward or backward through your presentation.

Another way to move quickly from slide to slide is to click the scroll box within the vertical scroll bar on the right side of the window and drag it up or down by holding down the left mouse button. As you drag the box, a little text box pops up next to the slide bar to tell you which slide will be displayed if you release the button at that position.

Dragging the scroll box to move from slide to slide is just one example of the many Windows tasks that are much harder to explain than to actually do. After you read this, you probably will say to yourself, "Huh?" But after you try it, you'll say, "Oh, I get it! Why didn't he just say so?"

Working with Objects

In the beginning, the User created a slide. And the slide was formless and void, without meaning or content. And the User said, "Let there be a Text Object." And there was a Text Object. And there was evening and there was morning, one day. Then the User said, "Let there be a Picture Object." And there was a Picture Object. And there was evening and there was morning, a second day. This continued for forty days and forty nights, until there were forty objects on the slide, each after its own kind. And the User was laughed out of the auditorium by the audience who could read the slide not.

I present this charming little parable solely to make the point that PowerPoint slides are nothing without objects. Objects are the lifeblood of PowerPoint. Objects give meaning and content to otherwise formless and void slides.

Most slide objects are simple text objects, which you don't have to worry much about. If you're interested, read the sidebar titled "I object to this meaningless dribble about PowerPoint objects" in this chapter. Otherwise, just plow ahead.

When you add a new slide to your presentation, the slide layout that you choose determines which objects are initially placed on the new slide. For example, if you choose the Title layout, PowerPoint creates a new slide with two text objects. You can add more objects to the slide later; or you can delete objects, move them around, or resize them if you want. Most of the time, though, you can be content to leave the objects where they are.

Each object occupies a rectangular region on the slide. The contents of the object may or may not visually fill the rectangular region, but you can see the outline of the object when you select it (see the section "Selecting objects" later in this chapter).

Objects can overlap. Usually, you don't want them to, but sometimes doing so creates a jazzy effect. You may lay some text on top of some clip art, for example.

I object to this meaningless drivel about PowerPoint objects

I don't really want to do this to you, but I feel compelled to point out that you can use several distinct types of objects on a PowerPoint slide. They're shown in this list:

- **Text object:** The first and most common type of object. Most of the objects you create are probably text objects. Text objects contain, uh, text.

- **Shape objects:** Contain shapes such as rectangles, circles, and arrowheads. Odd as it may seem, shape objects can also contain text. To confuse the issue even more, PowerPoint uses the term *text object* to refer to both text objects and shape objects.

- **Line objects:** Lines and freeform drawing objects made up of line segments. Unlike shapes, lines can't contain text.

- **Embedded objects:** Beasties created by some other program. Embedded objects can be clip art pictures, organization charts, graphs, sounds, movies, or other types of ornaments. PowerPoint comes with a handful of programs for creating embedded objects, and it can also work with Microsoft Word and Excel to create embedded tables and spreadsheets in a slide.

Forget about everything except text objects for now. All these other types of objects are covered in later chapters.

Selecting objects

Before you can edit anything on a slide, you have to select the object that contains whatever it is you want to edit. For example, you can't start typing away to edit text on-screen. Instead, you must first select the text object that contains the text you want to edit. Likewise, you must select other types of objects before you can edit their contents.

Here are some guidelines to keep in mind when selecting objects:

✔ Before you can select anything, make sure that the cursor is shaped like an arrow. If it isn't, click the arrow button on the Drawing toolbar. (This button is officially called the *Selection button,* but it sure looks like an arrow to me.)

✔ To select a text object so that you can edit its text, move the arrow pointer over the text you want to edit and click the left button. A rectangular box appears around the object, and the background behind the text changes to a solid color to make the text easier to read. A text cursor appears so that you can start typing away.

✔ Other types of objects work a little differently. Click an object, and the object is selected. The rectangular box appears around the object to let you know that you have hooked it. After you have hooked the object, you can drag it around the screen or change its size, but you cannot edit it. To edit a nontext object, you must double-click it. (Selecting the object first is not necessary. Just point to it with the arrow pointer and double-click.)

✔ Another way to select an object — or more than one object — is to use the arrow pointer to drag a rectangle around the objects that you want to select. Point to a location above and to the left of the object or objects that you want to select, and click and drag the mouse down and to the right until the rectangle surrounds the objects. When you release the button, all the objects within the rectangle are selected.

✔ Also, you can press the Tab key to select objects. Press Tab once to select the first object on the slide. Press Tab again to select the next object. Keep pressing Tab until the object that you want is selected.

Pressing Tab to select objects is handy when you can't easily point to the object you want to select. This problem can happen if the object that you want is buried underneath another object or if the object is empty or otherwise invisible and you're not sure of its location.

Resizing or moving an object

When you select an object, an outline box appears around it, as shown in Figure 2-1. If you look closely at the box, you can see that it has *love handles,* one on each corner and one in the middle of each edge. You can use these love handles to adjust the size of an object. And you can grab the box between the love handles to move the object around on the slide.

To change the size of an object, click it to select it and then grab one of the love handles by clicking it with the arrow pointer. Hold down the mouse button and move the mouse to change the object's size.

Why so many handles? To give you different ways to change the object's size. The handles at the corners allow you to change both the height and the width of the object. The handles on the top and bottom edges allow you to change just the object's height, and the handles on the right and left edges change just the width.

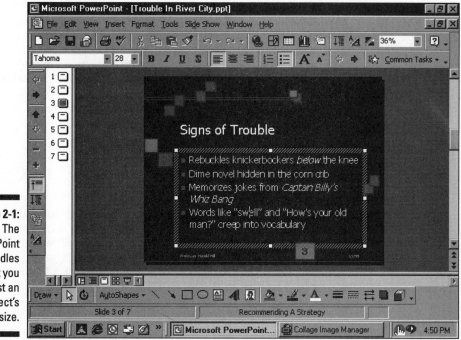

Figure 2-1:
The
PowerPoint
love handles
let you
adjust an
object's
size.

Changing a text object's size doesn't change the size of the text in the object; it changes only the size of the "frame" that contains the text. Changing the width of a text object is equivalent to changing margins in a word processor: It makes the text lines wider or narrower. To change the size of the text within a text object, you must change the font size. Chapter 8 has the exciting details.

If you hold down the Ctrl key while you drag one of the love handles, the object stays centered at its current position on the slide. Try it, and you can see what I mean. Also, try holding down the Shift key as you drag an object using one of the corner love handles. This combination maintains the object's proportions as you resize it.

To move an object, click anywhere on the outline box except on a love handle; then drag the object to its new locale.

The outline box can be hard to see if you have a fancy background on your slides. If you select an object and have trouble seeing the outline box, try squinting or cleaning your monitor screen. Or, in severe weather, try clicking the Black and White View button in the Standard toolbar. This button switches to Black and White view, in which the slide is displayed without its colors. Viewing the slide in this mode may make the love handles easier to spot. To switch back to full-color view, click the Black and White View button again. (Sometimes, PowerPoint calls Black and White view Grayscale Preview, but it's the same thing.) Notice, however, that when you change to Black and White, the slide miniature retains its color. Nifty!

Editing a Text Object: The Baby Word Processor

When you select a text object for editing, PowerPoint transforms itself into a baby word processor. If you're familiar with just about any other Windows word-processing software, including Microsoft Word or even WordPad (the free word processor that comes with Windows 98), you will have no trouble working in baby word-processor mode. This section presents some of the highlights, just in case.

PowerPoint automatically splits lines between words so that you don't have to press the Enter key at the end of every line. Press Enter only when you want to begin a new paragraph.

Text in a PowerPoint presentation is usually formatted with a *bullet character* at the beginning of each paragraph. The default bullet character is usually a simple square box, but you can change it to just about any shape that you can imagine (see Chapter 8). In PowerPoint 2000, you notice that bullets have suddenly become a lot more interesting! The point to remember here is that the bullet character is a part of the paragraph format, not a character you have to type in your text.

Most word-processing software enables you to switch between *insert mode* and *typeover mode* by pressing the Insert key on the right side of your keyboard. In insert mode, characters that you type are inserted at the cursor location; in typeover mode, each character that you type replaces the character at the cursor location. However, PowerPoint always works in insert mode, so any text that you type is inserted at the cursor location. Pressing the Insert key has no effect on the way text is typed.

Using the arrow keys

You can move around within a text object by pressing the *arrow keys*. I looked at my computer's keyboard and saw that 13 of the keys have arrows on them — 16, if you count the greater-than (>) and less-than (<) signs and the ubiquitous caret (^), which look sort of like arrows. So I have included Figure 2-2, which shows you the arrow keys I'm talking about.

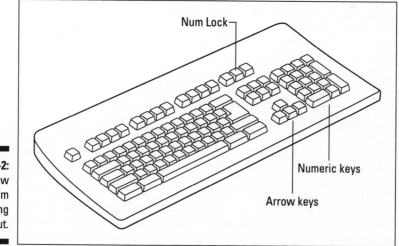

Figure 2-2:
The arrow keys I'm talking about.

The arrow keys are sometimes called the *cursor keys* because they move the cursor around the screen. Each key moves the cursor in the direction in which the arrow points, as shown in Table 2-1.

Table 2-1	The Arrow Keys
Keystroke	*Where the Cursor Moves*
↑	Up one line
↓	Down one line
←	One character to the left
→	One character to the right

The arrow keys are duplicated on the 2, 4, 6, and 8 numeric keys on the right side of the keyboard. The function of these keys alternates between numeric keys and cursor-control keys, depending on whether you have pressed the Num Lock key. When you press Num Lock once, the Num Lock light comes on, indicating that the numeric keys create numerals when you press them. When you press Num Lock again, the Num Lock light goes off, which indicates that these keys control the cursor.

Using the mouse can be the fastest way to get somewhere. Point at the exact spot in the text where you want the cursor to appear and click the left button. The cursor magically jumps to that spot.

The left-arrow key looks just like the Backspace key. This evil plot is designed to fool computer novices into fearing that the arrow keys will erase text, just as the Backspace key does. Not so! Pay no attention to those fearmongers! The arrow keys are completely docile. All they do is move the cursor around; they do not destroy text.

Moving around faster

The arrow keys can get you anywhere within a text object, but sometimes they're as slow as molasses. Table 2-2 shows a few tricks for moving around faster.

For the Ctrl+key combinations listed in Table 2-2, first press and hold the Ctrl key and then press the arrow key, the End key, or the Home key. Then release both keys.

Table 2-2	Keyboard Tricks for Moving Around Faster
Keystroke	*Where the Cursor Moves*
Ctrl+↑	To the start of the current paragraph, and then up one paragraph
Ctrl+↓	Down one paragraph
Ctrl+←	Left one word
Ctrl+→	Right one word
End	To end of line
Home	To beginning of line
Ctrl+End	To end of text object
Ctrl+Home	To beginning of text object

Your keyboard has two Ctrl keys, a lefty and a righty. Either one works. I usually press the one on the left with my little finger and press the arrow key with my right hand. Whatever feels good is okay by me.

As long as the Ctrl key is pressed, you can press any of the arrow keys repeatedly. To move three words to the right, for example, hold down the Ctrl key and press the right-arrow key three times. Then release the Ctrl key. If the cursor is in the middle of a word, pressing Ctrl+← moves the cursor to the beginning of that word. Pressing it again moves the cursor to the beginning of the preceding word.

Deleting text

You delete text by pressing the Delete or Backspace key, both of which work, as shown in Table 2-3.

Table 2-3	Deleting Text
Keystroke	*What It Deletes*
Delete	The character immediately to the right of the cursor
Backspace	The character immediately to the left of the cursor
Ctrl+Delete	Characters from the cursor all the way to the end of the current word
Ctrl+Backspace	Characters from the cursor all the way to the beginning of the current word

You can press Ctrl+Delete to delete an entire word by first pressing Ctrl+← or Ctrl+→ to move the cursor to the beginning of the word you want to delete. Then press Ctrl+Delete.

If you first select a block of text, the Delete and Backspace keys delete the entire selection. If you don't have a clue about what I'm talking about, skip ahead to the following section, "Marking text for surgery."

Another way to delete a word is to double-click anywhere in the middle of the word and then press the Delete key. The double-click marks the entire word, and then the Delete key deletes the marked word.

You can also use the Edit⇨Clear command to delete text permanently. The Delete key is simply a keyboard shortcut for the Edit⇨Clear command.

Marking text for surgery

Some text-editing operations — such as amputations and transplants — require that you first mark the text on which you want to operate. This list shows you the methods for doing so:

✔ When you use the keyboard, hold down the Shift key while you press any of the cursor-movement keys to move the cursor.

✔ When you use the mouse, point to the beginning of the text you want to mark and then click and drag the mouse over the text. Release the button when you reach the end of the text you want to mark.

The PowerPoint Automatic Word Selection option tries to guess when you intend to select an entire word. If you use the mouse to mark a block of text, you notice that the selected text jumps to include entire words as you move the mouse. If you don't like this feature, you can disable it by using the Tools⇨Options command (click the Edit tab and then uncheck the Automatic Word Selection check box).

- ✔ To mark a single word, point the cursor anywhere in the word and double-click. Click-click.

- ✔ To mark an entire paragraph, point anywhere in the paragraph and triple-click. Click-click-click.

- ✔ To delete the entire block of text you have marked, press the Delete key or the Backspace key.

- ✔ To replace an entire block of text, mark it and then begin typing. The marked block vanishes and is replaced by the text you are typing.

- ✔ You can use the Cut, Copy, and Paste commands from the Edit menu with marked text blocks. The following section describes these commands.

Using Cut, Copy, and Paste

Like any good Windows program, PowerPoint uses the standard Cut, Copy, and Paste commands. These commands work on the *current selection*. When you're editing a text object, the current selection is the block of text that you have marked. But if you select an entire object, the current selection is the object itself. In other words, you can use the Cut, Copy, and Paste commands with bits of text or with entire objects.

Cut, Copy, and Paste all work with one of the greatest mysteries of Windows, the *Clipboard*. The Clipboard is where Windows stashes stuff so that you can get to it later. In PowerPoint 2000, the Clipboard has become so useful that it even has its own toolbar. It used to be that after you placed an item on the Clipboard, it stayed there until you replaced it with another item by using another Cut or Copy command or until you exited Windows. Now you can cut or copy up to 12 chunks of text or objects, such as clip art, and then paste whichever one strikes your fancy. Access the Clipboard toolbar (shown in Figure 2-3) by choosing the View⇨Toolbar menu commands and clicking Clipboard.

The Cut and Copy commands add stuff to the Clipboard, which you can later retrieve by using the Paste command.

Figure 2-3:
The Office
Clipboard
toolbar.

The keyboard shortcuts for Cut, Copy, and Paste are the same as they are for other Windows programs: Ctrl+X for Cut, Ctrl+C for Copy, and Ctrl+V for Paste. Because these three keyboard shortcuts work in virtually all Windows programs, memorizing them pays off.

The Copy and Paste commands are often used together to duplicate information. If you want to repeat an entire sentence, for example, you copy the sentence to the Clipboard, place the cursor where you want the sentence duplicated, and then use the Paste command.

The Cut and Paste commands are used together to move stuff from one location to another. To move a sentence to a new location, for example, select the sentence and cut it to the Clipboard. Then place the cursor where you want the sentence moved and choose the Paste command.

Cutting or copying a text block

When you cut a block of text, the text is removed from the slide and placed on the Clipboard, where you can retrieve it later if you want. Copying a text block stores the text in the Clipboard but doesn't remove it from the slide.

To cut a block, first mark the block you want to cut by using the keyboard or the mouse. Then conjure up the Cut command by using any of these three methods:

 ✓ Choose the Edit⇨Cut command from the menu bar.

 ✓ Click the Cut button on the Standard toolbar (shown in the margin).

 ✓ Press Ctrl+X.

Using any method causes the text to vanish from your screen. Don't worry, though. It's safely nestled away on the Clipboard.

To copy a block, mark the block and invoke the Copy command by using one of these methods:

    ✔ Choose the Edit⇨Copy command.

    ✔ Click the Copy button on the Standard toolbar (shown in the margin).

    ✔ Press Ctrl+C.

The text is copied to the Clipboard, but this time the text doesn't vanish from the screen. To retrieve the text from the Clipboard, use the Paste command, as described in the following section.

Pasting text

To paste text from the Clipboard, first move the cursor to the location where you want to insert the text. Then invoke the Paste command by using whichever of the following techniques suits your fancy:

    ✔ Choose the Edit⇨Paste command from the menu bar.

    ✔ Click the Paste button on the Standard toolbar.

    ✔ Press Ctrl+V.

Cutting, copying, and pasting entire objects

The use of Cut, Copy, and Paste isn't limited to text blocks; the commands work with entire objects also. Just select the object, copy or cut it to the Clipboard, move to a new location, and paste the object from the Clipboard.

To move an object from one slide to another, select the object and cut it to the Clipboard. Then move to the slide where you want the object to appear and paste the object from the Clipboard.

To duplicate an object on several slides, select the object and copy it to the Clipboard. Then move to the slide that you want the object duplicated on and paste the object.

You can duplicate an object on the same slide by selecting the object, copying it to the Clipboard, and then pasting it. The only glitch is that the pasted object appears exactly on top of the original object, so you can't tell that you now have two copies of the object on the slide. Never fear! Just grab the newly pasted object with the mouse and move it to another location on the slide. Moving the object uncovers the original so that you can see both objects.

An easier way to duplicate an object is to use the Edit⇨Duplicate command. It combines the functions of Copy and Paste but doesn't disturb the Clipboard. The duplicate copy is offset slightly from the original so that you can tell them apart. (The keyboard shortcut for the Edit⇨Duplicate command is Ctrl+D.)

If you want to blow away an entire object permanently, select it and press the Delete key or use the Edit⇨Clear command. This step removes the object from the slide but doesn't copy it to the Clipboard. It's gone forever. Well, sort of — you can still get it back by using the Undo command, but only if you act fast. See the next section, "Oops! I Didn't Mean It (The Marvelous Undo Command)".

To include the same object on each of your slides, you can use a better method than copying and pasting: Add the object to the *slide master,* which governs the format of all the slides in a presentation (see Chapter 9).

Oops! I Didn't Mean It (The Marvelous Undo Command)

Made a mistake? Don't panic. Use the Undo command. Undo is your safety net. If you mess up, Undo can save the day.

You have three ways to undo a mistake:

- ✔ Choose the Edit⇨Undo command from the menu bar.
- ✔ Click the Undo button on the Standard toolbar (shown in the margin). If you can't find it, use the down arrow on the standard toolbar to access it the first time; it will then become a customized toolbar feature.
- ✔ Press Ctrl+Z.

Undo reverses whatever you did last. If you deleted text, Undo adds it back in. If you typed text, Undo deletes it. If you moved an object, Undo puts it back where it was. You get the idea.

Undo remembers up to 20 of your most recent actions. However, as a general rule, you should correct your mistakes as soon as possible. If you make a mistake, feel free to curse, kick something, or fall on the floor in a screaming tantrum if you must, *but don't do anything else on your computer!* If you use Undo immediately, you can reverse your mistake and get on with your life.

PowerPoint also offers a Redo command, which is sort of like an Undo for Undo. In other words, if you undo what you thought was a mistake by using the Undo command and then decide that it wasn't a mistake after all, you can use the Redo command. Following are three ways to use the Redo command:

✔ Choose the Edit➪Redo command from the menu bar.

✔ Click the Redo button on the Standard toolbar (shown in the margin).

✔ Press Ctrl+Y.

Deleting a Slide

Want to delete an entire slide? No problem. Move to the slide that you want to delete and use the Edit➪Delete Slide command. Zowie! The slide is history.

No keyboard shortcut for deleting a slide exists, nor does the Standard toolbar have a button for it. Sorry — you have to use the menu for this one.

You can also delete a slide in Outline or Slide Sorter view. Chapter 3 covers Outline view, and this chapter discusses Slide Sorter view.

Duplicating a Slide

PowerPoint 97 sported a new feature that let you duplicate an entire slide, text, formatting, and everything else included. That way, after you toiled over a slide for hours to get its formatting just right, you could create a duplicate to use as the basis for another slide. Well, 2000 lets you do the same thing!

To duplicate a slide, move to the slide that you want to duplicate. Then choose the Insert➪Duplicate Slide. A duplicate of the slide is inserted into your presentation.

Sorry, no keyboard shortcut or toolbar button exists for this command.

Finding Text

You know that buried somewhere in that 60-slide presentation is a slide that lists the options available on the Vertical Snarfblat, but where is it? This sounds like a job for the PowerPoint Find command!

The Find command can find text buried in any text object on any slide. These steps show you the procedure for using it:

1. **Think of what you want to find.**

   Snarfblat will do in this example.

2. **Summon the Edit➪Find command.**

The keyboard shortcut is Ctrl+F. Figure 2-4 shows the Find dialog box, which contains the secrets of the Find command.

Figure 2-4:
The Find
dialog box.

3. **Type the text that you want to find.**

   It shows up in the Find What box.

4. **Press the Enter key.**

   Or click the Find Next button. Either way, the search begins.

If the text that you type is located anywhere in the presentation, the Find command zips you to the slide that contains the text and highlights the text. Then you can edit the text object or search for the next occurrence of the text within your presentation. If you edit the text, the Find dialog box stays on-screen to make it easy to continue your quest.

Here are some facts to keep in mind when using the Find command:

✔ To find the next occurrence of the same text, press Enter or click the Find Next button again.

✔ To edit the text you found, click the text object. The Find dialog box remains on-screen. To continue searching, click the Find Next button again.

✔ You don't have to be at the beginning of your presentation to search the entire presentation. When PowerPoint reaches the end of the presentation, it automatically picks up the search at the beginning and continues back to the point at which you started the search.

✔ You may receive the message:

```
PowerPoint has finished searching the presentation. The
          search item was not found.
```

This message means that PowerPoint has given up. The text you typed just isn't anywhere in the presentation. Maybe you spelled it wrong, or maybe you didn't have a slide about Snarfblats after all.

✔ If the right mix of uppercase and lowercase letters is important to you, check the Match Case box before beginning the search. This option is handy when you have, for example, a presentation about Mr. Smith the Blacksmith.

✔ Use the Find Whole Words Only check box to find your text only when it appears as a whole word. If you want to find the slide on which you talked about Smitty the Blacksmith's mitt, for example, type **mitt** for the Find What text and check the Find Whole Words Only box. That way, the Find command looks for *mitt* as a separate word. It doesn't stop to show you the *mitt* in *Smitty.*

✔ If you find the text you're looking for and decide that you want to replace it with something else, click the Replace button. This step changes the Find dialog box to the Replace dialog box, which is explained in the following section.

✔ To make the Find dialog box go away, click the Close button or press the Esc key.

Replacing Text

Suppose that the Rent-a-Nerd company decides to switch to athletic consulting, so it wants to change the name of its company to Rent-a-Jock. Easy. Just use the handy Replace command to change all occurrences of the word *Nerd* to *Jock.* The following steps show you how:

1. Invoke the Edit⇨Replace command.

The keyboard shortcut is Ctrl+H. I have no idea why. In any case, you see the Replace dialog box, shown in Figure 2-5.

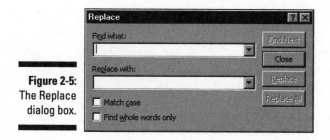

Figure 2-5:
The Replace
dialog box.

2. In the Find What box, type the text that you want to find.

Enter the text that you want to replace with something else (*Nerd,* in the example).

3. Type the replacement text in the Replace With box.

Enter the text that you want to use to replace the text you typed in the Find What box (*Jock,* in the example).

4. Click the Find Next button.

PowerPoint finds the first occurrence of the text.

5. **Click the Replace button to replace the text.**

   Read the text first to make sure that it found what you were looking for.

6. **Repeat the Find Next and Replace sequence until you're finished.**

   Click Find Next to find the next occurrence, click Replace to replace it, and so on. Keep going until you have finished.

If you're absolutely positive that you want to replace all occurrences of your Find what text with the Replace with text, click the Replace All button. This step dispenses with the Find Next and Replace cycle. The only problem is that you're bound to find at least one spot where you didn't want the replacement to occur. Replacing the word *mitt* with *glove,* for example, results in *Sglovey* rather than *Smitty.* Don't forget that you can also use the Find whole words only option to find and replace text only if it appears as an entire word.

If you totally mess up your presentation by clicking Replace All, you can use the Undo command to restore sanity to your presentation.

Rearranging Your Slides in Slide Sorter View

Slide view is the view you normally work in to edit your slides, move things around, add text or graphics, and so on. But Slide view has one serious limitation: It doesn't enable you to change the order of the slides in your presentation. To do that, you have to switch to Slide Sorter view or Outline view.

Outline view is useful enough — and complicated enough — to merit its own chapter, so I cover it in Chapter 3. But Slide Sorter view is easy enough to discuss here.

You can switch to Slide Sorter view in two easy ways:

- ✔ Click the Slide Sorter view button in the bottom-left corner of the screen.
- ✔ Choose the View⇨Slide Sorter command.

The PowerPoint Slide Sorter view is shown in Figure 2-6.

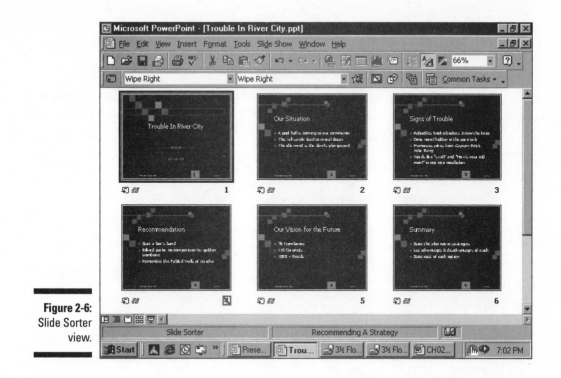

Figure 2-6:
Slide Sorter
view.

The following list tells you how to rearrange, add, or delete slides from Slide Sorter view:

✔ To move a slide, click and drag it to a new location. Point to the slide and then press and hold down the left mouse button. Drag the slide to its new location and release the button. PowerPoint adjusts the display to show the new arrangement of slides.

✔ To delete a slide, click the slide to select it and then press the Delete key. The Delete key works on an entire slide only in Slide Sorter view. You also can use the Edit⇨Delete Slide command.

✔ To add a new slide, click the slide you want the new slide to follow and then click the New Slide button. The New Slide dialog box appears so that you can choose the layout for the new slide. To edit the contents of the slide, return to Slide or Outline view by using the view buttons (located at the bottom-left corner of the screen) or the View command.

If your presentation contains more slides than fit on-screen at one time, you can use the scroll bars to scroll through the display. Or you can change the zoom factor to make the slides smaller. Click the down arrow next to the zoom size in the Standard toolbar and choose a smaller zoom percentage, or just type a new zoom size into the toolbar's zoom control box. (The zoom control is shown in the margin.)

Slide Sorter view may seem kind of dull and boring, but it's also the place where you can add jazzy transitions, build effects, and cool animation effects to your slides. For example, you can make your bullets fall from the top of the screen like bombs and switch from slide to slide by using strips, wipes, or blinds. Chapter 17 describes all this cool stuff.

Chapter 3

Outlining Your Presentation

● ●

In This Chapter

▶ Understanding Outline view

▶ Focusing on substance, not form

▶ Adding a slide in Outline view — the many ways

▶ Promoting, demoting, and the lateral arabesque

▶ Collapsing and expanding the outline

▶ Expanding a slide

▶ Creating a summary slide

▶ Busting up a humongous slide and using the Presentation Assistant

● ●

*Y*ou probably have already noticed that most presentations consist of slide after slide of bulleted lists. You may see a chart here or there and an occasional bit of clip art thrown in for comic effect, but the bread and butter of presentations is the bulleted list. It sounds boring, but it's the best way to make sure that your message gets through.

For this reason, presentations lend themselves especially well to outlining. Presentations are light on prose but heavy in the point and subpoint department — and that's precisely where outlines excel. The PowerPoint Outline view enables you to focus on your presentation's main points and subpoints. In other words, it enables you to focus on content without worrying about appearance. You can always switch back to Slide view to make sure that your slides look good. But when you want to make sure that your slides make sense, Outline view is the way to go.

Switching to Outline View

You have already figured out that in PowerPoint 2000 Slide view, Outline view, and Notes view are all part of the Normal or Tri-pane desktop. This is what you see most of the time, and you can click and drag the pane borders of each pane to focus on the specific view you want. (You can also click the Outline View button or the Slide View button on the status bar at the bottom-left corner of the desktop.)

When you click the Slide view section of the Tri-pane desktop, you notice that Slide view displays slides one at a time in a *what-you-see-is-what-you-get* (WYSIWYG) manner. Outline view shows the same information, but in the form of an outline. You can switch to Outline view in two ways:

- ✔ Click the Outline view button on the status bar near the bottom-left corner of the PowerPoint window.

- ✔ Click and drag the pane border until you think the Outline view is big enough to work in comfortably.

Figure 3-1 shows an example of a presentation in Outline view.

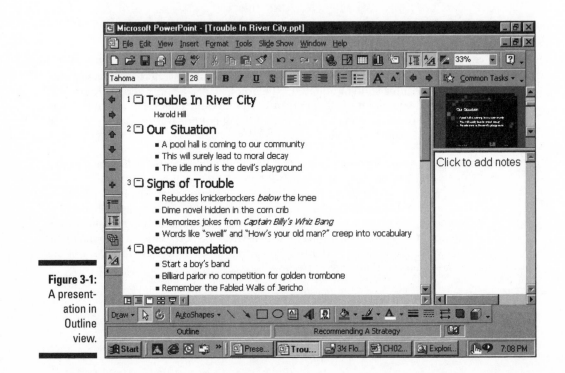

Figure 3-1:
A present-
ation in
Outline
view.

Understanding Outline View

The key to understanding the PowerPoint Outline view is realizing that Outline view is just another way of looking at your presentation. The outline is not a separate entity from the presentation. This is easy to see when you look at the Normal or Tri-pane desktop. In fact, as you add to your outline, you can see your slides change and vice versa. Outline view takes the data from your slides and redisplays it in the form of an outline. Any changes that you make to the presentation while in Outline view are automatically reflected in the presentation when you return to Slide view, and any changes that you make while in Slide view automatically appear in Outline view. The reason that changes made in one view also appear in the other view is that Slide view and Outline view are merely two ways of displaying the content of your presentation.

The following list highlights a few important things to notice about Outline view:

- ✔ The outline is made up of the titles and body text of each slide. Any other objects that you add to a slide — such as pictures, charts, and so on — are not included in the outline. Also, if you add any text objects to the slide in addition to the basic title and body text objects that are automatically included when you create a new slide, the additional text objects are not included in the outline.

- ✔ Each slide is represented by a high-level heading in the outline. The text of this heading is drawn from the slide's title, and a button that represents the entire slide appears next to the heading. Also, the slide number appears to the left of the slide button.

- ✔ Each text line from a slide's body text appears as an indented heading, subordinate to the slide's main title heading.

- ✔ As Figure 3-1 shows, an outline can contain subpoints that are subordinate to the main points on each slide. PowerPoint enables you to create as many as five heading levels on each slide, but your slides probably will get too complicated if you go beyond two headings. You can find more about working with heading levels in the section "Promoting and Demoting Paragraphs" later in this chapter.

- ✔ When you expand Outline view, you will find it easier to use the Outlining toolbar. You may notice that in Normal or Tri-pane view that the Outlining toolbar is not yet activated. Just click Outline view, and the toolbar is instantly activated. Each button on this toolbar is explained in detail later in this chapter. Table 3-1 summarizes what each button does.

Table 3-1		Buttons on the Outlining Toolbar
Button	**Name**	**What It Does**
←	Promote	Promotes the paragraph to a higher outline level
→	Demote	Demotes the paragraph to a lower outline level
↑	Move Up	Moves the paragraph up
↓	Move Down	Moves the paragraph down
−	Collapse	Collapses the selected slide or slides
+	Expand	Expands the selected slide or slides
	Collapse All	Collapses an entire presentation
	Expand All	Expands an entire presentation
	Summary Slide	Creates a summary slide
	Show Formatting	Shows or hides formatting

✔ Figure 3-1 shows several complete slides in Outline view. In Slide view, you can see only one slide at a time. By presenting your content more concisely, Outline view enables you to focus on your presentation's structure and content. Of course, only the smallest of presentations fits entirely on-screen even in Outline view, so you still have to use the scroll bars to view the entire presentation.

Selecting and Editing an Entire Slide

When you work in Outline view, you often have to select an entire slide. PowerPoint provides three ways to do that:

✔ Click the slide's Slide icon.

✔ Click the slide's number.

✔ Triple-click anywhere in the slide's title text.

When you select an entire slide, the slide title and all of its body text are highlighted. In addition, any extra objects such as graphics that are on the slide are selected as well.

To delete an entire slide, select it and then press the Delete key.

To cut or copy an entire slide to the Clipboard, select it and then press Ctrl+X (Cut) or Ctrl+C (Copy). You can then move the cursor to any location in the outline and press Ctrl+V to paste the slide from the Clipboard.

To duplicate a slide, select it and then either invoke the Edit⇨Duplicate command or press Ctrl+D. This step places a copy of the selected slide immediately in front of the selection.

Selecting and Editing One Paragraph

You can select and edit an entire paragraph along with all of its subordinate paragraphs. Just click the bullet next to the paragraph that you want to select or triple-click anywhere in the text. To delete an entire paragraph along with its subordinate paragraphs, select it and then press the Delete key.

To cut or copy an entire paragraph to the Clipboard along with its subordinates, select it and then press Ctrl+X (Cut) or Ctrl+C (Copy). You can then press Ctrl+V to paste the paragraph anywhere in the presentation. To duplicate a paragraph, select it and then either invoke the Edit⇨Duplicate command or press Ctrl+D.

Promoting and Demoting Paragraphs

To *promote* a paragraph means to move it up one level in the outline. If you promote the "Remember the Fabled Walls of Jericho" line in Figure 3-1, for example, that line becomes a separate slide rather than a bullet paragraph under "Recommendation."

To *demote* a paragraph is just the opposite: The paragraph moves down one level in the outline. If you demote the "This will surely lead to moral decay" paragraph in Figure 3-1, it becomes a subpoint under "A pool hall is coming to our community" rather than a separate main point.

Promoting paragraphs

To promote a paragraph, place the cursor anywhere in the paragraph and then perform any of the following techniques:

- ✔ Click the Promote button (shown in the margin) on the Outlining toolbar (this button also appears on the right side of the Formatting toolbar).
- ✔ Press the Shift+Tab key.
- ✔ Use the keyboard shortcut Alt+Shift+←.

The paragraph moves up one level in the outline pecking order.

You can't promote a slide title. Slide title is the highest rank in the outline hierarchy.

If you want to promote a paragraph and all of its subordinate paragraphs, click the point's bullet or triple-click anywhere in the paragraph, and then promote it. You can also promote text by dragging it with the mouse. See the section "Dragging paragraphs to new levels" later in this chapter.

Demoting paragraphs

To demote a paragraph, place the cursor anywhere in the paragraph and then do one of the following:

- ✔ Click the Demote button (shown in the margin) on the Outline toolbar (this button also appears at the right side of the Formatting toolbar).
- ✔ Press the Tab key.
- ✔ Use the keyboard shortcut Alt+Shift+→.

The paragraph moves down one level in the outline pecking order.

If you demote a slide title, the entire slide is subsumed into the preceding slide. In other words, the slide title becomes a main point in the preceding slide.

To demote a paragraph and all of its subparagraphs, click the paragraph's bullet or triple-click anywhere in the paragraph text and then demote it. You can also demote text by dragging it with the mouse. See the following section, "Dragging paragraphs to new levels."

Be sensitive when you demote paragraphs. Being demoted can be an emotionally devastating experience.

Dragging paragraphs to new levels

When you move the mouse pointer over a bullet (or the slide button), the pointer changes from a single arrow to a four-cornered arrow. This arrow is your signal that you can click the mouse to select the entire paragraph (and any subordinate paragraphs). Also, you can use the mouse to promote or demote a paragraph along with all of its subordinates.

To promote or demote with the mouse, follow these steps:

1. **Point to the bullet that you want to demote or promote.**

   The mouse pointer changes to a four-cornered arrow. To demote a slide, point to the slide button. (Remember that you can't promote a slide. It's already at the highest level.)

2. **Click and hold the mouse button down.**

3. **Drag the mouse to the right or left.**

   The mouse pointer changes to a double-pointed arrow, and a vertical line appears that shows the indentation level of the selection. Release the button when the selection is indented the way you want. The text is automatically reformatted for the new indentation level.

If you mess up, press Ctrl+Z or click the Undo button to undo the promotion or demotion. Then try again.

Adding a New Paragraph

To add a new paragraph to a slide, move the cursor to the end of the paragraph that you want the new paragraph to follow and then press the Enter key. PowerPoint creates a new paragraph at the same outline level as the preceding paragraph.

If you position the cursor at the beginning of a paragraph and press the Enter key, the new paragraph is inserted to the left of the cursor position. If you position the cursor in the middle of a paragraph and press the Enter key, the paragraph is split in two.

After you add a new paragraph, you may want to change its level in the outline. To do that, you must promote or demote the new paragraph. To create a subpoint for a main point, for example, position the cursor at the end of the main point and press the Enter key. Then demote the new paragraph. For details about how to promote or demote a paragraph, refer to the section "Promoting and Demoting Paragraphs" earlier in this chapter.

Adding a New Slide

You can add a new slide in many ways when you're working in Outline view. This list shows the most popular methods:

- ✔ Promote an existing paragraph to the highest level. This method splits a slide into two slides. In Figure 3-1, for example, you can create a new slide by promoting the "The idle mind is the devil's playground" paragraph. That step splits the "Our Situation" slide into two slides.

- ✔ Add a new paragraph and then promote it to the highest level.

- ✔ Place the cursor in a slide's title text and press the Enter key. This method creates a new slide before the current slide. Whether the title text stays with the current slide, goes with the new slide, or is split between the slides depends on the location of the cursor within the title when you press Enter.

- ✔ Place the cursor anywhere in a slide's body text and press Ctrl+Enter. This method creates a new slide immediately following the current slide. The position of the cursor within the existing slide doesn't matter; the new slide is always created after the current slide. (The cursor must be in the slide's body text for this method to work, though. If you put the cursor in a slide title and press Ctrl+Enter, the cursor jumps to the slide's body text without creating a new slide.)

- ✔ Place the cursor anywhere in a slide and click the New Slide button (shown in the margin). If you can't find the New Slide button, look for it on the Common Tasks toolbar located at the right side of the Formatting toolbar.

- ✔ Place the cursor anywhere in a slide and click the New button (shown in the margin) in the Standard toolbar. (This will create a new slide in a new blank presentation.)

- ✔ Place the cursor anywhere in the slide and invoke the Insert⇨New Slide command or its keyboard shortcut, Ctrl+M.

- ✔ Select an existing slide by clicking the slide button or triple-clicking the title and then duplicate it by using the Edit⇨Duplicate command or its keyboard shortcut, Ctrl+D.

Because Outline view focuses on slide content rather than on layout, new slides always receive the basic Bulleted List layout, which includes title text and body text formatted with bullets. If you want to change the layout of a new slide, you must click the Slide Layout button to select a new slide layout. You can also find this button on the Common Tasks toolbar. Remember, if you can't find something on a toolbar, it's that new PowerPoint 2000 customization feature. So, go ahead and click those cute little down-arrows, and you will find all the missing buttons. Wa-laa!

Moving Text Up and Down

Outline view is also handy for rearranging your presentation. You can easily change the order of individual points on a slide, or you can rearrange the order of the slides.

Moving text the old-fashioned way

To move text up or down, first select the text that you want to move. To move just one paragraph (along with any subordinate paragraphs), click its bullet. To move an entire slide, click its slide button.

To move the selected text up, use either of the following techniques:

- ✔ Click the Move Up button (shown in the margin) on the Outline toolbar on the left side of the screen.
- ✔ Press Alt+Shift+↑.

To move the selected text down, use either of the following techniques:

- ✔ Click the Move Down button (shown in the margin) on the Outline toolbar on the left side of the screen.
- ✔ Press Alt+Shift+↓.

Moving text the dragon drop way

To move text up or down by using the mouse, follow these steps:

1. **Point to the bullet next to the paragraph that you want to move.**

   The mouse pointer changes to a four-cornered arrow. To move a slide, point to the slide button.

2. **Click and hold the mouse button down.**

3. **Drag the mouse up or down.**

   The mouse pointer changes again to a double-pointed arrow, and a horizontal line appears, showing the horizontal position of the selection. Release the mouse when the selection is positioned where you want it.

Be careful when you're moving text in a slide that has more than one level of body text paragraphs. Notice the position of the horizontal line as you drag the selection; the entire selection is inserted at that location, which may split up subpoints. If you don't like the result of a move, you can always undo it by pressing Ctrl+Z or clicking the Undo button.

Expanding and Collapsing the Outline

If your presentation has many slides, you may find that grasping its overall structure is difficult, even in Outline view. Fortunately, PowerPoint enables you to *collapse* the outline so that only the slide titles are shown. Collapsing an outline doesn't delete the body text; it merely hides the body text so that you can focus on the order of the slides in your presentation.

Expanding a presentation restores the collapsed body text to the outline so that you can once again focus on details. You can collapse and expand an entire presentation, or you can collapse and expand one slide at a time.

Collapsing an entire presentation

To collapse an entire presentation, you have two options:

> ✔ Click the Collapse All button (shown in the margin) on the Outlining toolbar on the left side of the screen.
>
> ✔ Press Alt+Shift+1.

Expanding an entire presentation

To expand an entire presentation, try one of these methods:

> ✔ Click the Expand All button (shown in the margin) on the Outlining toolbar on the left side of the screen.
>
> ✔ Press Alt+Shift+A.

Collapsing a single slide

To collapse a single slide, position the cursor anywhere in the slide that you want to collapse. Then do one of the following:

> ✔ Click the Collapse button (shown in the margin) on the Outline toolbar on the left side of the screen.
>
> ✔ Press Alt+Shift+− (the minus sign).

Expanding a single slide

To expand a single slide, position the cursor anywhere in the title of the slide that you want to expand. Then perform one of the following techniques:

✔ Click the Expand button (shown in the margin) on the Outlining toolbar on the left side of the screen.

✔ Press Alt+Shift++ (the plus sign).

Showing and Hiding Formats

The idea behind Outline view is to give you the opportunity to focus on the content of your presentation, rather than how it looks. With PowerPoint, you can take this idea one step further by removing the text formatting from your outline. The outline shown in Figure 3-1 includes text formatting. As you can see, the text for slide titles appears larger than the body text, and the bullet character varies depending on its level in the outline hierarchy.

Figure 3-2 shows the same outline with text formatting hidden. All text appears in the same vanilla font, and simple bullets replace fancy bullet characters.

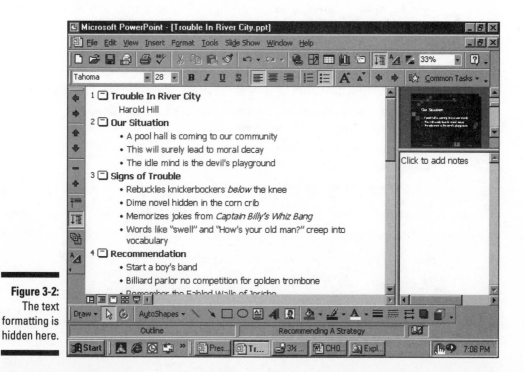

Figure 3-2:
The text formatting is hidden here.

To hide character formatting in Outline view, do one of the following:

✔ Click the Show Formatting button (shown in the margin) on the Outline toolbar or the Standard toolbar on the left side of the screen.

✔ Press the slash key (/), the one on the numeric keypad, just above the number 8.

To restore formatting, just click the Show Formatting button or press the slash key again.

Hiding character formatting doesn't remove the formatting attributes from your presentation. It simply hides them while you're in Outline view so that you can concentrate on your presentation's content rather than on its appearance. Hiding character formatting removes not only character fonts and fancy bullets but also basic character styles, such as italics, bold, and underlining. Too bad. Hiding formats would be more useful if it still showed these basic character styles.

Creating a Summary Slide

A nifty feature that was first introduced in PowerPoint 97 and is still around for PowerPoint 2000 is the Summary Slide button, which automatically creates a summary slide that shows the titles of some or all of the slides in your presentation. To use the Summary Slide feature, follow these steps:

1. **Select the slides whose titles you want to appear on the summary slide.**

   To include the entire presentation, press Ctrl+A to select all the slides.

2. **Click the Summary Slide button. You can find the Summary Slide button on the Outlining toolbar.**

   A summary slide is created for the selected slides, as shown in Figure 3-3.

3. **Type a title for the summary slide.**

To use the Summary Slide button, you must be in Outline view or Slide Sorter view.

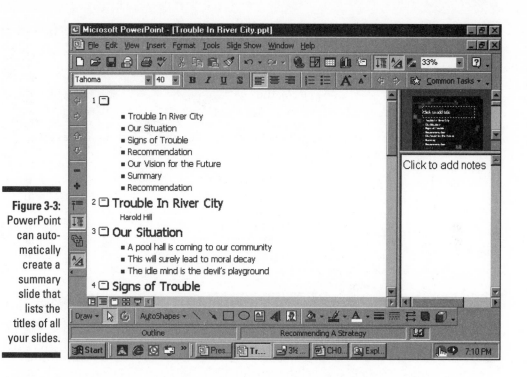

Figure 3-3:
PowerPoint
can auto-
matically
create a
summary
slide that
lists the
titles of all
your slides.

Busting Up a Humongous Slide and Using the Presentation Assistant

If you have a slide that has gotten out of hand, with far too many points and subpoints, you need to break the slide up so that its points are spread out over several slides. You can do this in Outline view by manually inserting a new slide and promoting or demoting text as necessary. One interesting and new feature of PowerPoint 2000 is the Office Assistant (which may already annoy you), which once again adds his/her/its two cents about this issue. When you err and ramble on and on and on and on, the Office Assistant flashes a light bulb. This light bulb hovers until you click it or until you move on to some other task. Heck, why not click it, just to see what this busybody has to say?

When you finally break down and click it, the Office Assistant tells you that you have too many bullets! You can see what I mean in Figure 3-4.

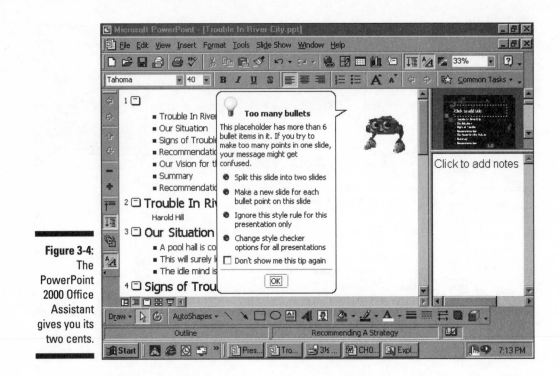

Figure 3-4:
The
PowerPoint
2000 Office
Assistant
gives you its
two cents.

Here is where you should be careful not to be too hasty. You have the option of clicking a selection that says, "Don't show me this tip again." If you click this option, the Office Assistant, in its ultimate wisdom and glory, alters the setup in your AutoFit text controls area. The IntelliSense feature of this little Assistant is actually changing your setup, and that's kinda scary. So, be careful before you wildly click things in an effort to get the Assistant to leave you alone.

If you were a PowerPoint 97 user, you were probably familiar with a feature called Expand Slide. This feature allowed you to click an existing slide that was too big and expand it so that it broke into additional slides. This feature is gone in PowerPoint 2000, but you can learn to cope elegantly with a few easy tricks.

Say you are faced with a humongous slide like the one shown in Figure 3-5.

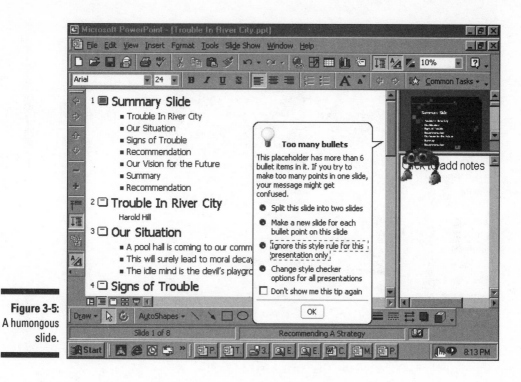

Figure 3-5:
A humongous
slide.

By using the Office Assistant, you can expand a huge slide. Follow these steps:

1. **Click the Office Assistant's little light bulb.**

   The Assistant asks you if you want to break the slide in to two slides, or break it up by bulleted points or ignore this suggestion for this presentation only. It also asks if you don't want to be given this tip again. If you check this selection, the Assistant deactivates your AutoFit text setup, and turns it off. And that leads to the important dialog box shown in Figure 3-6.

2. **Select Tools⇨Options.**

3. **Click the Spelling and Style command.**

   Good.

4. **Click the button on the bottom of the dialog box that says Style Options.**

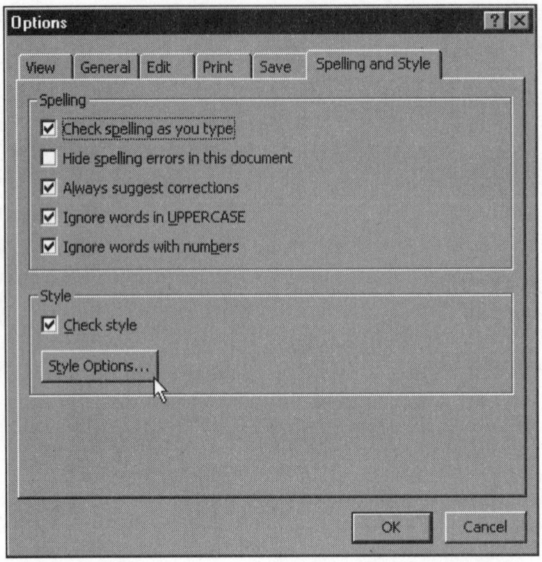

Figure 3-6:
HAL: The
Humongous
Altering
Life-force,
or the place
where you
change the
set-up stuff.

Suddenly, you are transported to another dialog box.

5. **Click the tab that says Visual Clarity.**

   Here is where it gets down and dirty. See that check box that says, "Number of bullets should not exceed . . ." and the text box that allows you to select a perfect number? This is it. This is the place the Assistant altered.

6. **Change it back.**

   Make the number of bullets whatever you feel is best for you, and you are done. Perfect.

By the way, unless you have the Office Assistant on, none of this works.

Chapter 4

Doing It with Style

· ·

In This Chapter

▶ Checking your presentation for embarrassing stylistic mistakes

▶ Checking your spelling

▶ Capitalizing correctly

▶ Placing periods consistently

· ·

I was voted Worst Speller in the sixth grade. Not that that qualifies me to run for vice president or anything, but it shows how much I appreciate computer spell checkers. Spelling makes no sense to me. I felt a little better after watching *The Story of English* on public television. Now at least I know whom to blame for all the peculiarities of English spelling — the Angles, the Norms (including the guy from *Cheers*), and the Saxophones.

Fortunately, PowerPoint has a pretty decent spell checker. In fact, the spelling checker in PowerPoint 2000 is so smart that it knows that you've made a spelling mistake almost before you make it. The spell checker watches over your shoulder as you type and helps you correct your spelling errors as you work.

PowerPoint also has two other nifty features to help catch innocent typographical errors before you show your presentation to a board of directors: a capitalization whirligig that fixes your capitalization (capital idea, eh?) and a period flinger that ensures that each line either does or does not end with a period. You can perform many stylistic checks automatically using a cool PowerPoint feature called Style Options. (See more about this at the end of the chapter.)

The Over-the-Shoulder Spell Checker

Spelling errors in a word-processing document are bad, but at least they're small. In a PowerPoint presentation, spelling errors are small only until you put the transparency in the projector, or publish your presentation on the Internet. Then they get all blown out of proportion. Nothing is more embarrassing than a 2-foot-tall spelling error. And if you're like me, you probably try to look for mistakes in people's Web pages just for yuks. Thank goodness for PowerPoint's new on-the-fly spelling checker.

The PowerPoint spell checker doesn't make you wait until you finish your presentation and run a special command to point out your spelling errors. It boldly points out your mistakes right when you make them by underlining any mistake that you make with a wavy colored line, as shown in Figure 4-1.

In Figure 4-1, two words have been marked as misspelled: *Troible* and *Rebuckles*. When you see the tell-tale wavy colored line, you have several options:

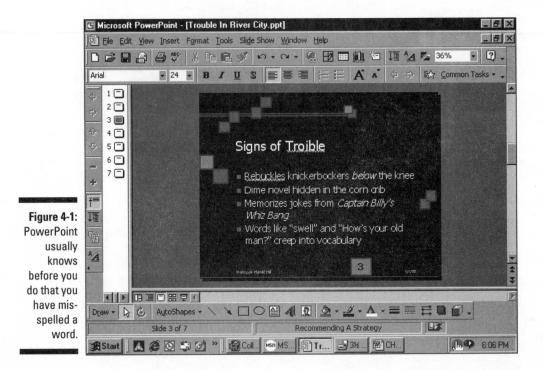

Figure 4-1: PowerPoint usually knows before you do that you have misspelled a word.

✔ You can retype the word using the correct spelling.

✔ You can click the word with the right mouse button to call up a menu that lists any suggested spellings for the word, as shown in Figure 4-2. In most cases, PowerPoint can figure out what you meant to type and suggests the correct spelling. To replace the misspelled word with the correct spelling, just click the correctly spelled word in the menu.

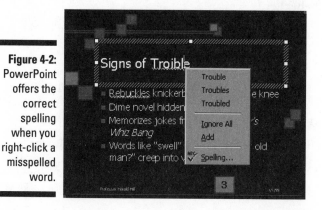

Figure 4-2: PowerPoint offers the correct spelling when you right-click a misspelled word.

✔ You can ignore the misspelling. Sometimes, you want to misspell a word on purpose (for example, if you run a restaurant named "The Koffee Kup"). More likely, the word is correctly spelled, but PowerPoint just doesn't know about the word (for example, *Rebuckles* in Figure 4-1).

After-the-Fact Spell Checking

If you prefer to ignore the constant nagging by PowerPoint about your spelling, you can always check your spelling the old-fashioned way: by running the spell checker after you have finished your document. The spell checker works its way through your entire presentation, looking up every word in its massive list of correctly spelled words and bringing any misspelled words to your attention. It performs this task without giggling or snickering. As an added bonus, the spell checker even gives you the opportunity to tell it that you are right and it is wrong and that it should learn how to spell words the way you do.

The following steps show you how to check the spelling for an entire presentation:

1. **If the presentation that you want to spell check is not already open, open it.**

   It doesn't matter which view you're in. You can spell check from any of these views: Slide, Outline, Notes Pages, or Slide Sorter.

2. **Fire up the spell checker.**

   Click the Spelling button on the Standard toolbar, press F7, or choose the Tools⇨Spelling command.

3. **Tap your fingers on your desk.**

   PowerPoint is searching your presentation for embarrassing spelling errors. Be patient.

4. **Don't be startled if PowerPoint finds a spelling error.**

   If PowerPoint finds a spelling error in your presentation, it switches to the slide that contains the error, highlights the offensive word, and displays the misspelled word along with a suggested correction, as shown in Figure 4-3.

Figure 4-3:
The PowerPoint spell checker points out a boo-boo.

Spelling			? ☒
Not in Dictionary:	Troible		
Change to:	Troible	Ignore	Ignore All
Suggestions:	Trouble	Change	Change All
	Troubles		
	Troubled	Add	Suggest
Add words to:	CUSTOM.DIC ▾	AutoCorrect	Close

5. **Choose the correct spelling or laugh in PowerPoint's face.**

   If you agree that the word is misspelled, scan the list of corrections that PowerPoint offers and click the one you like. Then click the Change button. If you like the way that you spelled the word in the first place (maybe it's an unusual word that isn't in the PowerPoint spelling dictionary, or maybe you like to spell like Chaucer did), click the Ignore button. Watch as PowerPoint turns red in the face.

6. **Repeat Steps 4 and 5 until PowerPoint gives up.**

   When you see the following message:

   ```
   The spelling check is complete
   ```

   You're finished.

PowerPoint always checks spelling for the entire presentation, beginning with the first slide unless you specify a single word or group of words by highlighting them first. PowerPoint checks the spelling of titles, body text, notes, and text objects added to slides. It doesn't check the spelling for embedded objects, however, such as charts or graphs.

If PowerPoint cannot come up with a suggestion or if none of its suggestions are correct, you can type your own correction and click the Change button. If the word you type isn't in the dictionary, PowerPoint asks you whether you're sure that you know what you're doing. Double-check and click OK if you really mean it.

If you want PowerPoint to ignore all occurrences of a particular misspelling, click the Ignore All button. Likewise, if you want PowerPoint to correct all occurrences of a particular misspelling, click the Change All button.

If you get tired of PowerPoint always complaining about a word that's not in its standard dictionary (such as *rebuckles*), click Add to add the word to the custom dictionary. If you cannot sleep at night until you know more about the custom dictionary, read the sidebar titled "Don't make me tell you about the custom dictionary" later in this chapter.

The speller cannot tell the difference between *your* and *you're, ours* and *hours, angel* and *angle,* and so on. In other words, if the word is in the dictionary, PowerPoint passes it by regardless of whether you used the word correctly. The PowerPoint spell checker is no substitute for good, old-fashioned proofing. Print your presentation, sit down with a cup of cappuccino, and *read* it.

Capitalizing Correctly

The PowerPoint Change Case command enables you to capitalize the text in your slides properly. These steps show you how to use it:

1. **Select the text that you want to capitalize.**

2. **Choose the Format➪Change Case command.**

   The Change Case dialog box appears, as shown in Figure 4-4.

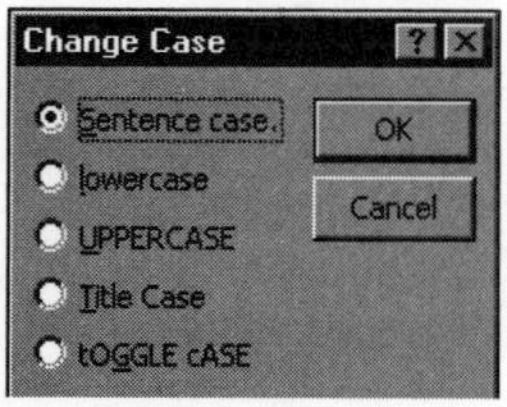

Figure 4-4:
The Change
Case dialog
box.

Change Case	? X
● Sentence case.	OK
○ lowercase	
○ UPPERCASE	Cancel
○ Title Case	
○ tOGGLE cASE	

Don't make me tell you about the custom dictionary

The PowerPoint spell checker uses two spelling dictionaries: a standard dictionary, which contains untold thousands of words all reviewed for correctness by Noah Webster himself (just kidding), and a *custom dictionary*, which contains words you have added by clicking the Add button when the spell checker found a spelling error.

The custom dictionary lives in a file named CUSTOM.DIC, which makes its residence in the \WINDOWS\APPLICATION DATA\MICROSOFT\PROOF folder. Other Microsoft programs that use spell checkers — most notably Microsoft Word — share the same

custom dictionary with PowerPoint. So if you add a word to the custom dictionary in Word, the PowerPoint spell checker knows about the word, too.

What if you accidentally add a word to the dictionary? Then you have a serious problem. You have two alternatives. You can petition Noah Webster to have your variant spelling officially added to the English language, or you can edit the CUSTOM.DIC file, search through the file until you find the bogus word, and delete it. CUSTOM.DIC will automatically default to Notepad, the jiffy editor that comes free with Windows.

3. **Study the options for a moment and then click the one you want.**

   The case options follow:

   - **Sentence case:** The first letter of the first word in each sentence is capitalized. Everything else is changed to lowercase.

   - **lowercase:** Everything is changed to lowercase.

   - **UPPERCASE:** Everything is changed to capital letters.

   - **Title Case:** The first letter of each word is capitalized. PowerPoint is smart enough to leave certain words, such as "a" and "the," lowercase, but you should double-check to ensure that it worked properly.

   - **tOGGLE cASE:** This option turns capitals into lowercase and turns lowercase into capitals, for a ransom-note look.

4. **Click OK or press Enter and check the results.**

Always double-check your text after using the Change Case command to make sure that the result is what you intended.

Slide titles almost always should use title case. The first level of bullets on a slide can use either title or sentence case. Lower levels usually should use sentence case.

Avoid uppercase if you can. It's harder to read and looks like you're shouting.

Using Style Checker Options

Now, if you got used to the PowerPoint 97 Style Checker feature that checked your presentation's spelling, verified the consistency of punctuation and capitalization, and also warned you about slides that were difficult to read because they contained too many bullets or text that is too small, never fear. It is all still here in PowerPoint 2000, it just looks kind of different.

To use the elements of the now absent Style Checker command, follow these simple steps:

1. **Choose the Tools⇨Options command.**

   The dialog box shown in Figure 4-5 appears.

2. **Click the Spelling and Style tab.**

   Notice that the default settings in the Spelling section check your spelling as you go along. Check or uncheck any boxes that please you.

3. **Click the Style Options button.**

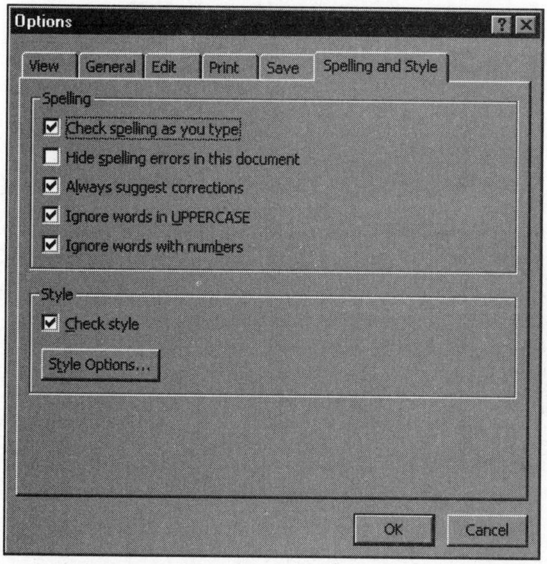

Figure 4-5:
The Options
dialog box.

The Style Options dialog box has two tabs with options for checking the following style element.

- **Case and end punctuation:** These default settings make sure that your capitalization and punctuation are consistent.

- **Visual clarity:** These default options check for visual clarity and warn you about slides that have too many different fonts, titles, and body text that are too small to read or too long, slides that have too many bullets, or slides that have text that runs off the page. Note that there are default numbers here. It's up to you if you prefer to change maximum font sizes or whatever, but realize these defaults usually work pretty well.

4. **Click OK if you like all this stuff and move on!**

   Now that little person/guy/thing you know as the Office or Presentation Assistant acts as your presentation assistant and informs you and makes suggestions about all of these style-related issues. (Spelling is brought to your attention by the red wavy line as you recall.) Make sure he is turned on if you want his advice.

5. **Refer to the "After-the-Fact Spell Checking" section if you're not sure how to use the spell checker.**

Chapter 5

Don't Forget Your Notes!

• •

• •

*E*ver had the fear — or maybe the actual experience — of showing a beautiful slide, complete with snappy text and perhaps an exquisite chart, and suddenly forgetting why you included the slide in the first place? You stumble for words. "Well, as you can see, this is a beautiful chart, and, uh, this slide makes the irrefutable point that, uh, well, I'm not sure — are there any questions?"

Fear not! One of the slickest features in PowerPoint 2000 is its capability to create speaker notes in Tri-pane view to help you get through your presentation. You can make these notes as complete or as sketchy as you want or need. You can write a complete script for your presentation or just jot down a few key points to refresh your memory.

The best part about speaker notes is that you are the only one who sees them. They don't actually show up on your slides for all the world to see. Instead, notes pages are printed separately. There's one notes page for each slide in the presentation, and each notes page includes a reduced version of the slide so that you can keep track of which notes page belongs to which slide.

One great feature of the new PowerPoint 2000 Tri-pane view is the ease with which you can add speaker notes to your presentation. In PowerPoint 97, you had to select Notes Page view to add notes; now you can simply click and drag on the Notes Page pane border in the Tri-pane view. You can actually see your notes without messing around with the Zoom function. In this chapter, I go over both because there are still reasons why you may want to use Notes Page view. However, try adding notes in the Tri-pane view, and you will save money on new glasses!

If you were a PowerPoint 97 user, you may have already noticed that in PowerPoint 2000, the icon on the status bar for Notes Page view is gone. Just as well! Adding your notes in Tri-pane or Normal view is much easier, and the notes are more readable. After you have done this, you can still see the way your notes pages will appear when printed by selecting View➪Notes Page.

To add speaker notes to a presentation, just click and drag on the pane border of the Notes Page pane. In Normal view, in the lower-right corner of the desktop, click the white space that says, "Click to add notes." The Notes Page pane magically appears. Click, and then just type away.

Don't you think that it's about time for a short chapter? Although notes pages are one of the slickest features in PowerPoint, creating notes pages isn't all that complicated — hence the brevity of this chapter.

Understanding the Notes Page View

If you were a user of PowerPoint 97, you may remember that the Notes Page view is found on the View menu and shows the speaker notes pages that are created for your presentation. There is one notes page for each slide in a presentation. Each notes page consists of a reduced version of the slide and an area for notes. Figure 5-1 shows an example of presentation notes in Notes Page view. This is how your finished notes pages will look after you write your notes in Tri-pane view. (Using Tri-pane view makes the notes easier to read, and the view is simple to use.)

You can switch to Notes Page view by choosing View➪Notes Page.

Unfortunately, no keyboard shortcut is available to switch directly to Notes Page view.

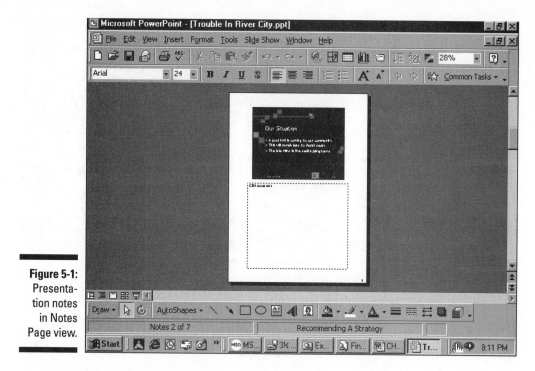

Figure 5-1:
Presenta-
tion notes
in Notes
Page view.

Adding Notes to a Slide

To add notes to a slide, follow this procedure:

1. **In Tri-pane, Slide, or Outline view, move to the slide to which you want to add notes.**

2. **Click and drag the Notes Page pane border if necessary to bring the notes text into view.**

3. **Click the notes text object, where it reads** `Click to add notes`.

4. **Type away.**

The text you type appears in the notes area. As you create your notes, you can use any of the PowerPoint standard word-processing features, such as cut, copy, and paste. Press the Enter key to create new paragraphs.

Figure 5-2 shows a notes page displayed as it appears when you enter notes.

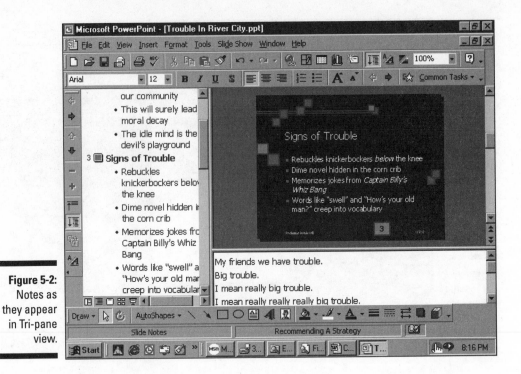

Figure 5-2:
Notes as
they appear
in Tri-pane
view.

After you have switched to the Notes Page pane, you can change notes pages
by either clicking up or down on the scroll bar or clicking the slide you want
to select in the Outline pane. Now you can check your notes pages to see
how they will appear when printed.

If your notes don't fit in the area provided on the notes page, you have two
options: Increase the size of the text area on the notes page or create a
second notes page for a slide.

Include page numbers on both your slides and your notes pages to help keep
them in sync or type each slide's title at the top of the notes page. (You can
set up page numbers for slides and notes pages by using the View⇔Header
and Footer command.)

Adding an Extra Notes Page for a Slide

PowerPoint doesn't provide a way to add more than one page of notes for each slide. But these steps show a trick that accomplishes essentially the same thing:

1. **Create a new slide immediately following the slide that requires two pages of notes.**

   Do this step in Tri-pane, Slide, Outline, or Notes Page view.

2. **Switch to the Notes Page view and move to the notes page for the slide you just created.**

   Delete the slide object at the top of this notes page by clicking it and pressing the Delete key. Then extend the notes text area up so that it fills the page by clicking it and then dragging the top-center love handle up.

3. **Type the additional notes for the preceding slide on this new notes page.**

   Add a heading, such as "Continued from slide 23," at the top of the text to help you remember that this portion is a continuation of notes from the preceding slide.

4. **Use the Slide Show⇨Hide Slide command to hide the slide.**

   You can use this command from any view. The Hide Slide command hides the slide, which means that it isn't included in an on-screen slide show.

The result of this trick is that you now have two pages of notes for a single slide, and the second notes page doesn't have an image of the slide on it and is not included in your slide show.

If you're printing overhead transparencies, you may want to uncheck the Print Hidden Slides check box in the Print dialog box. That way, the hidden slide isn't printed. Be sure to recheck the box when you print the notes pages, though. Otherwise, the notes page for the hidden slide isn't printed either — and the reason you created the hidden slide in the first place was so that you can print a notes page for it!

Think twice before creating a second page of notes for a slide. Do you really have that much to say about a single slide? Maybe the slide contains too much to begin with and should be split into two slides.

Adding a New Slide from Notes Page View

If you're working on the notes for a slide and realize that you want to create a new slide, you don't have to return to the Tri-pane, Slide pane, or Outline pane. Just click the New Slide button on the Standard toolbar or use the Insert⇨New Slide menu command to add the new slide.

If you want to work on the slide's appearance or contents, however, you must switch back to Tri-pane, Slide pane, or Outline pane. You can't modify a slide's appearance or contents from the Notes Page pane or Notes Page view.

To revert quickly to the Slide pane from Notes Page pane, click the Slide icon on the Status toolbar.

Printing Notes Pages

Notes pages don't do you much good if you can't print them. These steps show you how to do so:

1. **Choose the <u>File</u>⇨<u>P</u>rint command.**

   The Print dialog box appears.

2. **Use the Print W<u>h</u>at list box to choose the Notes Pages option.**

3. **Make sure that the Print <u>H</u>idden Slides box is checked if you want to print notes pages for hidden slides.**

4. **Click the OK button or press the Enter key.**

Figure 5-3 shows the Print dialog box with the Notes Pages option selected so that notes pages rather than slides are printed.

If you have just printed slides on overhead transparencies, don't forget to reload your printer with plain paper. You probably don't want to print your speaker notes on transparencies!

More information about printing is in Chapter 6.

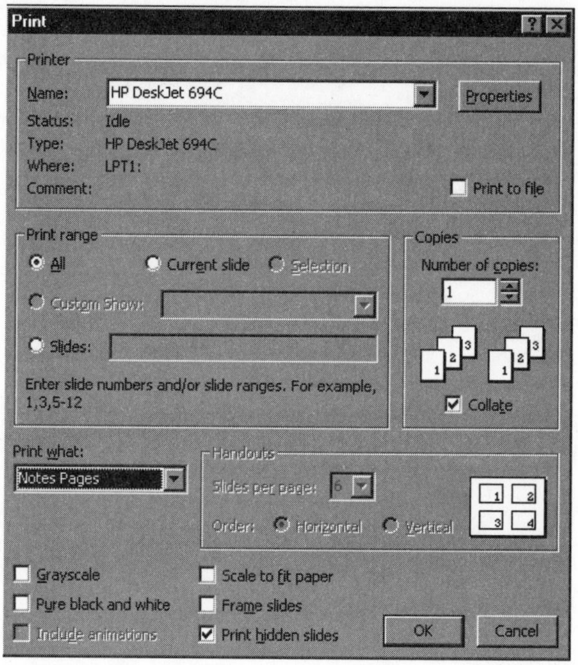

Figure 5-3:
The Print
dialog box.

Random Thoughts about Speaker Notes

This section provides some ideas that may help you make the most of your notes pages.

If you're giving an important presentation for a large audience, you may want to consider using notes pages to write a complete script for your presentation. For less formal presentations, more succinct notes are probably better.

Use notes pages to jot down any anecdotes, jokes, or other asides you want to remember to use in your presentation.

If you prefer to hand-write your notes, you can print blank notes pages. Don't bother adding notes to your presentation, but use the File⇨Print command to print notes pages. The resulting notes pages have a reduced image of the slide at the top and a blank space in which you can hand-write your notes later.

You may also consider providing blank notes pages for your audience. The File⇨Print command can print audience handouts that contain two, three, or six slides per page, but these handout pages leave no room for the audience members to write notes.

Chapter 6

Printing Your Presentation

● ●

In This Chapter

▶ Printing slides

▶ Printing handouts

▶ Printing speaker notes

▶ Printing an outline

▶ Troobleshooting

● ●

The Print command. The Printmeister. Big presentation comin' up. Printin' some slides. The Printorama. The Mentor of de Printor. Captain Toner of the Good Ship Laseroo.

Don't worry — no one's waiting to ambush you with annoying one-liners like that guy who used to be on *Saturday Night Live* when you print a PowerPoint 2000 presentation. Just a handful of boring dialog boxes with boring check boxes. Point-point, click-click, print-print. (Hey, humor me, okay? The French think that I'm a comic genius!)

The Quick Way to Print

 The fastest way to print your presentation is to click the Print button found in the Standard toolbar. Clicking this button prints your presentation without further ado, using the current settings for the Print dialog box, which I explain in the remaining sections of this chapter. Usually, this results in printing a single copy of all the slides in your presentation. But if you have altered the Print dialog box settings, clicking the Print button uses the altered settings automatically.

Using the Print Dialog Box

For precise control over how you want your presentation printed, you must conjure up the Print dialog box. You can do so in more ways than the government can raise revenue without calling it a tax, but the three most common are shown in this list:

- ✔ Choose the File⇨Print command.
- ✔ Press Ctrl+P.
- ✔ Press Ctrl+Shift+F12.

Any of these actions summons the Print dialog box, shown in Figure 6-1. Like the genie in the Disney movie *Aladdin,* this box grants you three wishes, but with two limitations: It can't kill anyone ("ix-nay on the illing-kay"), and it can't make anyone fall in love with you.

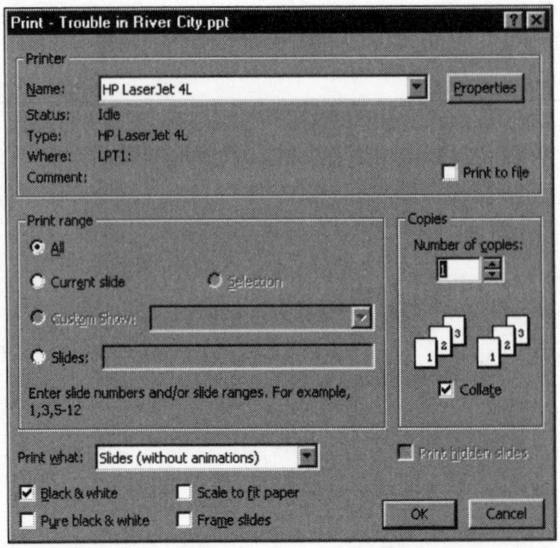

Figure 6-1:
The Print
dialog box.

After you unleash the Print dialog box, click OK or press Enter to print all the slides in your presentation. Or fiddle around with the settings to print a select group of slides, print more than one copy, or print handouts, speaker notes, or an outline. This chapter shows you the treasures that lie hidden in this dialog box.

Printing can be es-el-oh-double-ewe. PowerPoint politely displays a status box to keep you informed of its progress, so at least you know that the darn program hasn't gone AWOL on you.

Don't panic if your printer doesn't start spewing forth pages immediately after the Print dialog box goes away. PowerPoint printouts tend to demand a great deal from the printer, so sometimes the printer has to work for a while before it can produce a finished page. Be patient. The Printer wizard has every intention of granting your request.

Oh, by the way, if you see a vague error message that says something like "Put paper in the printer, silly," try putting paper in the printer.

Changing printers

If you're lucky enough to have two or more printers at your disposal, you can use the Name field to pick which printer you want to use. Each printer must first be successfully installed in Windows 98 — a topic that's beyond the reach of this humble book, but that you will find plenty of information about in Andy Rathbone's *Windows 98 For Dummies* (IDG Books Worldwide, Inc.).

Even if your computer doesn't have two printers physically attached to it, your computer may be connected to a computer network that does have two or more printers. In that case, you can use the Name field to select one of these networked printers to print your presentation.

The Properties button calls forth the Windows 98 Printer Properties dialog box, which lets you futz with various printer settings. Avoid it if you can.

Printing part of a presentation

When you first use the Print command, the All option is checked so that your entire presentation prints. The other options in the Print Range portion of the Print dialog box enable you to tell PowerPoint to print just part of your presentation. In addition to All, you have four options:

- ✔ **Current slide:** Prints just the current slide. Before you invoke the Print command, you should move to the slide you want to print. Then check this option in the Print dialog box and click OK. This option is handy when you make a change to one slide and don't want to reprint the entire presentation.

- ✔ **Selection:** Prints just the portion of the presentation that you selected before invoking the Print command. This option is easiest to use in Outline or Slide Sorter view. First, select the slides you want to print by dragging the mouse to highlight them. Then invoke the Print command, click the Selection box, and click OK. (Note that if you don't select anything before you call up the Print dialog box, this field is grayed out, as shown in Figure 6-1.)

- ✔ **Custom Show:** If you have used the Slide Show⇨Custom Shows command to create custom slide shows, you can use this option to select the show you want to print.

✓ **Slides:** Enables you to select specific slides for printing. You can print a range of slides by typing the beginning and ending slide numbers, separated by a hyphen, as in *5-8* to print slides 5, 6, 7, and 8. Or you can list individual slides, separated by commas, as in *4,8,11* to print slides 4, 8, and 11. And you can combine ranges and individual slides, as in *4,9-11,13* to print slides 4, 9, 10, 11, and 13.

To print a portion of a presentation, first call up the Print dialog box. Next, select the Slide Range option you want. Then click OK or press Enter.

Printing more than one copy

The Number of Copies field in the Print dialog box enables you to tell PowerPoint to print more than one copy of your presentation. You can click one of the arrows next to this field to increase or decrease the number of copies, or you can type directly in the field to set the number of copies.

Below the Number of Copies field is a check box labeled Collate. If this box is checked, PowerPoint prints each copy of your presentation one at a time. In other words, if your presentation consists of ten slides and you select three copies and check the Collate box, PowerPoint first prints all ten slides of the first copy of the presentation, and then all ten slides of the second copy, and then all ten slides of the third copy. If you don't check the Collate box, PowerPoint prints three copies of the first slide, followed by three copies of the second slide, followed by three copies of the third slide, and so on.

The Collate option saves you from the chore of manually sorting your copies. If your presentation takes forever to print because it's loaded down with heavy-duty graphics, however, you probably can save time in the long run by unchecking the Collate box. Why? Because many printers are fast when it comes to printing a second or third copy of a page. The printer may spend ten minutes figuring out how to print a particularly complicated page, but after it figures it out, the printer can chug out umpteen copies of that page without hesitation. If you print collated copies, the printer must labor over each page separately for each copy of the presentation it prints.

What do you want to print?

The Print What field in the Print dialog box enables you to select which type of output that you want to print. The following choices are available:

✓ **Slides:** Prints slides. Note that if you have used build effects in the presentation, this option doesn't appear. Instead, it's replaced with two similar options: *Slides (with Builds)* and *Slides (without Builds)*. If you don't know what builds are — and there's no reason you should, unless you've been reading ahead — just ignore the next two options.

- **Notes pages:** Prints speaker notes pages, which are covered in Chapter 5.

- **Handouts (With Slides per Page):** Prints audience handout pages. Select the number of slides you would like to appear on each handout page by clicking the Slides per page box. You can also order the slides to appear horizontally or vertically on the handout.

- **Outline view:** Prints an outline of your presentation.

Select the type of output that you want to print and then click OK or press Enter. Off you go!

When you're printing slides to be used as overhead transparencies, print a proof copy of the slides on plain paper before committing the output to transparencies. Transparencies are too expensive to print on until you're sure that your output is just right.

To change the orientation of your printed output from Landscape to Portrait mode (or vice versa), use the File⇨Slide Setup command.

To print handouts with two, three, or six slides per page, PowerPoint naturally must shrink the slides to make them fit. Because slides usually have outrageously large type, the handout slides are normally still readable, even at their reduced size.

What are all those other check boxes?

The Print command has six additional check boxes, which hide out near the bottom of the dialog box, hoping to slip by unnoticed. This list shows you what they do:

- **Print hidden slides:** You can hide individual slides by way of the Tools⇨Hide Slide command. After a slide is hidden, it does not print unless you check the Print Hidden Slides option in the Print dialog box.

    In Figure 6-1, this option is shaded, which indicates that it is not available. That happens when the presentation being printed doesn't have any hidden slides. The Print Hidden Slides option is available only when the presentation has hidden slides.

- **Scale to fit paper:** Adjusts the size of the printed output to fit the paper in the printer. Leave this option unchecked to avoid bizarre printing problems.

- **Grayscale:** Check this option if you have a black-and-white printer; it improves the appearance of color slides when printed in black and white.

- **Pure black & white:** Prints slides in black and white only; colors and shades of gray are converted to either black or white.

✔ **Frame slides:** Draws a thin border around the slides.

✔ **Include Animations:** If you used animation effects to build slide show text and you check the Include Animations box, a separate page prints for each bulleted item on the slide. The first page has just the first bulleted item; the second page shows the first and second bullets; and so on. (I cover Animation in Chapter 17.)

Note: Microsoft considered licensing TurnerVision technology to colorize slides printed with the Black & White option, but decided against it when it was discovered that most audiences dream in black and white when they fall asleep during a boring presentation.

Printing Boo-Boos

On the surface, printing seems as though it should be one of the easiest parts of using PowerPoint. After all, all you have to do to print a presentation is click the Print button, right? Well, usually. Unfortunately, all kinds of things can go wrong between the time you click the Print button and the time gorgeous output bursts forth from your printer. If you run into printer trouble, check out the things discussed in this section.

Your printer must be ready and raring to go before it can spew out printed pages. If you suspect that your printer is not ready for action, this list presents some things to check:

✔ Make sure that the printer's power cord is plugged in and that the printer is turned on.

✔ The printer cable must be connected to both the printer and the computer's printer port. If the cable has come loose, turn off both the computer and the printer, reattach the cable, and then restart the computer and the printer. (You know better, of course, than to turn off your computer without first saving any work in progress, exiting from any active application programs, and shutting down Windows. So I won't say anything about it. Not even one little word.)

✔ If your printer has a switch labeled *On-line* or *Select,* press it until the corresponding On-line or Select light comes on.

✔ Make sure that the printer has plenty of paper. (I have always wanted to write a musical about a printer that ate people rather than paper. I think that I'll call it *Little DOS of Horrors.*)

✔ If you're using a dot-matrix printer, make sure that the ribbon is okay. For a laser printer, make sure that the toner cartridge has plenty of life left in it.

Chapter 7

Help!

*T*he ideal way to use PowerPoint 2000 would be to have a PowerPoint expert sitting patiently at your side, answering your every question with a straightforward answer, gently correcting you when you make silly mistakes, and otherwise minding his or her own business. All you'd have to do is occasionally toss the expert a Twinkie and let him or her outside once a day.

The good news is that PowerPoint has such an expert built in. This expert is referred to as the Office Assistant, and he works not just with PowerPoint, but with other Microsoft Office programs, including Word, Excel, Access, and Outlook. You don't even have to feed the Office Assistant, unlike a real guru.

Meet the Assistant

Alexander Graham Bell had Watson, Batman had Robin, and Dr. Frankenstein had Igor. Everybody needs an Assistant, and Office users are no exception. That's why Microsoft decided to update and improve the feature it introduced in Office 97 — the Office Assistant. Naturally, the changes to the Assistant in Office 2000 span across the entire Office suite.

The Office Assistant is an animated persona who suddenly morphs onto your desktop with sage advice and suggestions and even a little idea light that gives you a clue that you could use a clue! You can also ask the Office Assistant a question when you're not sure what to do, and the Assistant thoroughly searches the PowerPoint online Help database to provide the answer.

When you first start up PowerPoint, the Office Assistant appears, as shown in Figure 7-1. As you can see, my Office Assistant resembles a cute little pooch. As it turns out, this one — named Rocky — is but one of eight Assistants that you can choose from. See the section "Changing Assistants" later in this chapter for instructions on how to switch to a different Assistant.

The fun thing about the Assistant is that he is animated. Watch the Assistant on-screen as you work. Every once in a while he blinks, and on occasion he dances or makes a face. The Assistant often responds to commands that you choose in PowerPoint. For example, if you call up the Find command (Edit⇨Find or Ctrl+F), the Assistant makes a gesture as if he is searching for something. And when you print your presentation, the Assistant does some cute little printer schtick. Microsoft went to a lot of trouble to make sure that the Assistant is entertaining, and the results are sometimes amusing. When you ask the Assistant for help, he sits down, plops his feet up on a desk, and takes copious notes — don't you wish real Assistants cared so much!

Notice that the Assistant has a special type of dialog box called a balloon, which includes an area for you to type a question and several buttons that you can click. The balloon functions like any other dialog box, but it has a special appearance that's unique to the Assistant.

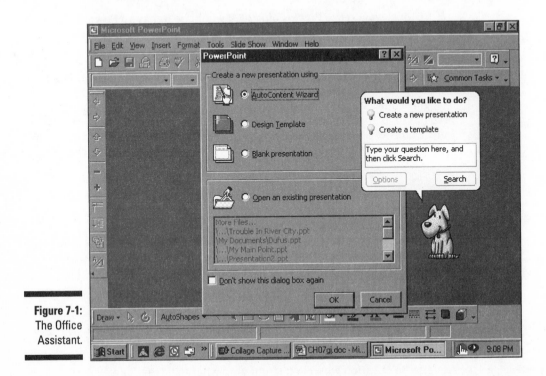

Figure 7-1:
The Office
Assistant.

PowerPoint used to have Help topics that you simply clicked and used, but now Help is driven by the user interacting with the Assistant. Most of the time, if you type in your question nicely and ask pretty-please, the Assistant answers with information on the appropriate Help subject.

When you click any topic presented by the Assistant, you see two boxes at the bottom of the Assistant's word balloon — one that says Options, and another that says Search. If you choose Options, a dialog bo appears that allows you to turn off the Assistant. If you do turn off the Assistant, the Help functions behave differently (a topic I cover later in this chapter in "Help the Old-Fashioned Way).

Summoning the Assistant

You can summon the Assistant in several ways when you need help. In many cases, the Assistant is already on the screen, so all you need to do to get his attention is click the Assistant. This action pops up the balloon dialog box so that you can ask a question.

If the Assistant isn't visible on-screen, you can summon him quickly by using one of the following three methods:

- Choose the Help⇨Microsoft PowerPoint Help command from the menu.
- Press F1, the magic Help key.
- Click the Help button in the Standard toolbar.

When you summon the Assistant while you're working with PowerPoint, the Assistant tries to figure out what you need help with based on what you were doing when you called upon the Assistant. For example, if you open a presentation, choose the Edit⇨Find command, and then summon the Assistant, the Assistant may offer help with topics related to opening documents and finding text, as shown in Figure 7-2.

If you're lucky enough that one of the topics listed in the Assistant's balloon dialog box is exactly what you're looking for, click the topic and help is displayed. For example, Figure 7-3 shows the help that displays when you click Replace text. As you can see, the Help topic in Figure 7-3 lists a simple step-by-step procedure that you can follow to replace text in a PowerPoint presentation.

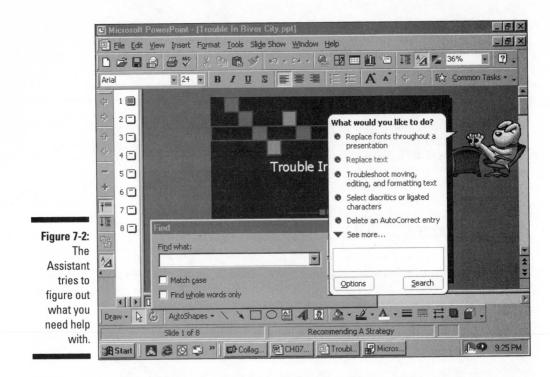

Figure 7-2:
The Assistant tries to figure out what you need help with.

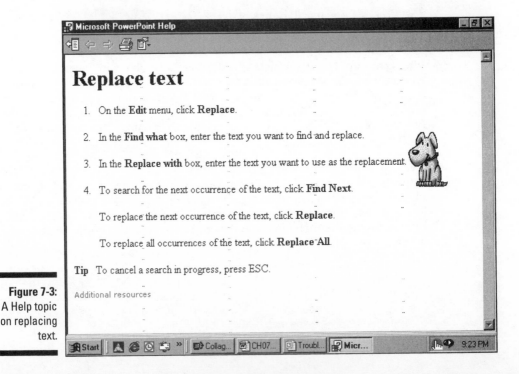

Figure 7-3:
A Help topic on replacing text.

After you get yourself this deep into Help, you need to heed the following advice to find your way around and get out when you find out what you want to know:

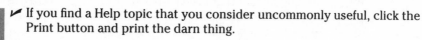

- ✔ If you find a Help topic that you consider uncommonly useful, click the Print button and print the darn thing.

- ✔ If you see an underlined word or phrase, you can click it to zip to a Help page that describes that word or phrase. By following these underlined words, you can bounce your way around from Help page to Help page until you eventually find the help you need.

- ✔ Sometimes, Help offers several choices under a heading such as "What do you want to do?" Each choice is preceded by a little button; click the button to display step-by-step help for that choice.

- ✔ You can retrace your steps by clicking the Help window's Back button. You can use Back over and over again, retracing all of your steps if necessary.

- ✔ Help operates as a separate program, so you can work within PowerPoint while the Help window remains on-screen. The Help window appears as a minimized window you can open which remains visible even when you're working in the PowerPoint window. If the Help window gets in the way, you can move it out of the way by dragging it by the title bar. Or you can minimize it by clicking the minimize button in the top-right corner of the window.

- ✔ When you've had enough of Help, you can dismiss it by pressing Esc or clicking the close button in the upper-right corner of the Help window.

Take-You-by-the-Hand Help

Many PowerPoint Help screens include a special Show Me buton. Click this button and the Assistant actually helps you accomplish the task at hand. For example, if you click the Show Me button from the Change the Way Text Looks topic page, the Assistant delivers you straight to the Font dialog box, where you can select the text options you want.

Asking a Question

If none of the Help topics offered by the Assistant seem to be what you're looking for, you can type a question right in the Assistant's balloon dialog box to look for help on a specific dialog box. For example, if you want to know how to change the background color of a slide, type **How do I change the background color of a slide?** in the text box and then click the Search button or press Enter. The Assistant responds by displaying Help topics that relate to your question, as shown in Figure 7-4. In PowerPoint 2000, as well as all the other applications in Office, Microsoft attempted to make the Assistant more able to understand common language — but not too common! Unlike the cute little animation feature that makes Rocky the dog wag his tail, asking him a pithy question will not engender a cute little response. Microsoft assumes we are all a little more down-to-business than that!

If one of the topics looks promising, click it. Or click See more to see whether the Assistant can come up with other topics related to your question.

If none of the topics seem related to the question you asked, try rephrasing the question and clicking Search again.

 You don't actually have to phrase your question as a question. You can eliminate words such as How do I, and you can also usually eliminate "noise words" such as a, an, the, of, in, and so on. Thus, the brief question "change background color" yields exactly the same result as the more verbose "How do I change the background color of a slide?"

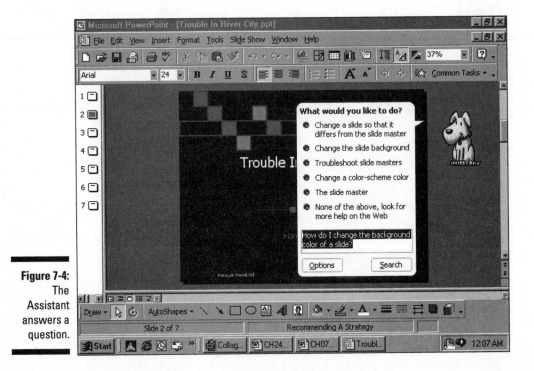

Figure 7-4:
The Assistant answers a question.

Getting a Tip

As I mention earlier, every once in a while, a light bulb appears in the Assistant's word balloon, or even in the middle of your slide. When this light bulb appears, you can click it to see a tip that the Assistant thinks may be useful. If the tip is worthwhile, plant a big fat kiss on the Assistant (not literally!) and be thankful. If not, feel free to roll your eyes and act annoyed.

Changing Assistants

Rocky, the friendly and loyal cyberpup Assistant, is but one of eight Assistants that you can choose from. To select a different Assistant, summon the Assistant by clicking the Help button or pressing F1. Then click the Options button to display the Office Assistant dialog box. Click the Gallery tab located at the top of this dialog box. The Assistant Gallery is displayed, as shown in Figure 7-5.

To change to a different Assistant, click the Next button. Keep clicking the Next button to work your way through all the Assistants; when you find the one that you want to use, click OK.

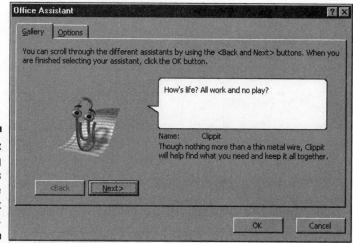

Figure 7-5:
Changing
Assistants
with the
Assistant
Gallery.

After you have clicked the Next button once, you can use the Back button to move backwards through the list of Assistants.

These Assistants differ only in appearance, not in their ability to offer assistance with using PowerPoint features.

Setting Assistant Options

You can configure the Assistant with several options that alter the way it works. To change these options, summon the Assistant and click the Options button to summon the dialog box shown in Figure 7-6. Change whatever options you want to change and then click OK.

The following paragraphs describe each of the Office Assistant options:

- **Use the Office Assistant:** Turns the Assistant on or off until further notice.

- **Respond to F1 key:** Summons the Office Assistant whenever you press F1.

- **Help with wizards:** Activates the Office Assistant whenever you use a PowerPoint Wizard.

- **Display alerts:** Uses the Assistant to display warnings about saving your file before exiting PowerPoint and so on.

- **Move when in the way:** Automatically moves the Assistant dialog box whenever it obscures what you're working on.

- **Guess Help topics:** Attempts to guess what topics you need help with.

- **Make sounds:** If you want the Assistant to make noises to get your attention, select this option.

- **Search for both product and programming help when programming:** If you're a programmer, check this option. Otherwise, leave it blank.

- **Show tips about:** Offers five categories of tips that Assistant can provide: using features, using the mouse, using keyboard shortcuts showing only high priority tips, (so that minor tips don't appear), and showing a Tip of the Day automatically when you start PowerPoint.

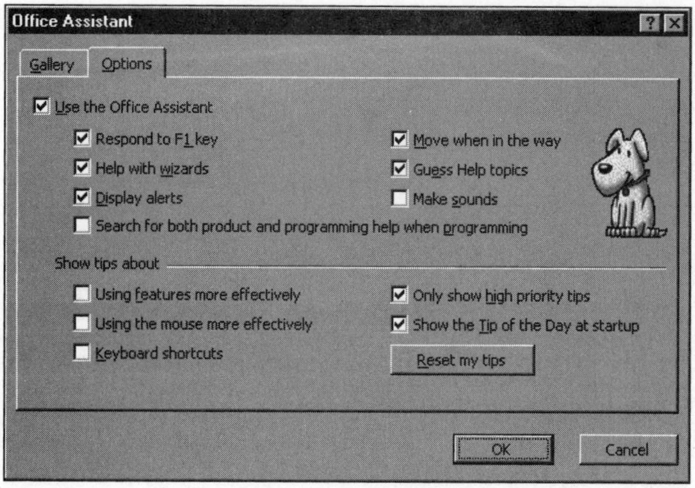

Figure 7-6:
Office
Assistant's
options.

Help the Old-Fashioned Way

The Assistant isn't the only way to get help in PowerPoint 2000. PowerPoint 2000 still offers help the old-fashioned Windows way through the traditional Help interface.

To summon old-fashioned topic menu Help, deselect the Assistant (uncheck the Use the Office Assistant box in the Assistant Options dialog box, described in the previous section). Then press F1 or choose the Help⇨ Microsoft PowerPoint Help command. This summons the Help table of contents, shown in Figure 7-7.

To display help on one of the topics listed in the Help table of contents, just double-click the topic. Doing so expands the Help Contents to show the help that's available for a specific topic. For example, Figure 7-8 shows the expanded Help Contents for Adding Clip Art and Other Pictures.

To display a particular Help topic, double-click the topic title in the contents list.

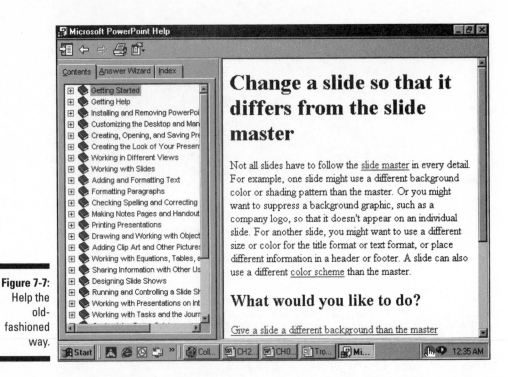

Figure 7-7:
Help the
old-
fashioned
way.

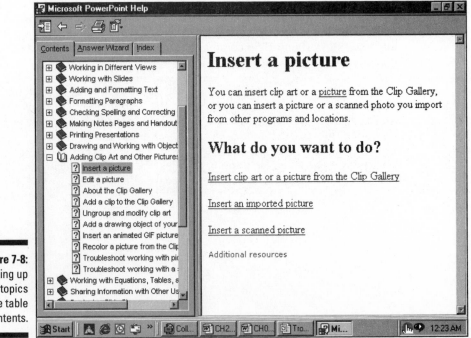

Figure 7-8:
Looking up
Help topics
in the table
of contents.

Searching for Lost Help Topics

If you can't find help for a nasty problem by browsing through the Help Contents, try using the Help Index. It lets you browse through an alphabetical listing of all the Help topics that are available. With luck, you can quickly find the help you're looking for.

When you click the Index tab in the Help topics dialog box, the screen shown in Figure 7-9 appears. Here you can type the text that you want to search for to zip quickly through the list to the words that you want to find.

If you see a match that looks as if it may be helpful, double-click it. Doing so takes you directly to help for that topic or displays a list of related topics. Double-click the topic that you want to display.

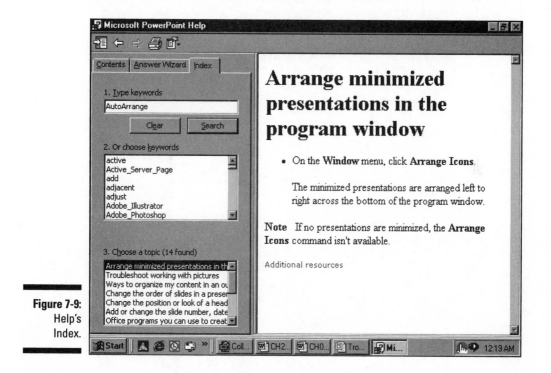

Figure 7-9:
Help's
Index.

Getting Help on the Internet

In addition to the help that's built in to PowerPoint, you can also get help about PowerPoint from the Internet. All you need is an Internet connection. (If you don't have an Internet connection, get a copy of my book, *Internet Explorer 4 For Windows For Dummies,* published by IDG Books Worldwide, Inc. That book shows you how to access the Internet using the popular Microsoft Internet Explorer program.)

Although the Help menu has several links to the Internet, the one you'll use the most is Help⇨Office on the Web. When you choose this command, PowerPoint launches Internet Explorer, the Microsoft program for accessing the Internet, provided free with PowerPoint and Office. Internet Explorer, in turn, connects to the Internet and then displays the Microsoft support page. On the PowerPoint support page, you can ask your question through a search engine.

You may want to check out Microsoft's home page for the variety of down-loads and bells and whistles that can make your PowerPoint application the Master of the Universe. (You can even find tie-dyed template backgrounds for your presentation if you're a throwback or just artistic.)

Part II
Looking Mahvelous

The 5th Wave   By Rich Tennant

"NO, THAT'S NOT A PIE CHART, IT'S JUST A CORN CHIP
THAT GOT SCANNED INTO THE DOCUMENT."

In this part . . .

*I*t is widely believed that Californians indulge in cosmetic surgery more often than Americans from the Midwest add cream of mushroom soup to casseroles. The chapters in this part are all about cosmetic surgery for your presentations. You learn how to perform such procedures as typosuction, clip art lifts, and color tucks.

Chapter 8

Fabulous Text Formats

• •

• •

A good presentation should be like a fireworks show: At every new slide, the audience gasps, "O-o-o-h. A-a-a-h." The audience is so stunned by the spectacular appearance of your slides that no one really bothers to read them.

This chapter gets you on the road toward ooohs and aaahs by showing you how to format text. If you use the AutoContent Wizard or base your new presentations on a template, your text is already formatted acceptably. But to really pull out the pyrotechnic stops, you have to know a few basic formatting tricks.

Many PowerPoint 2000 text-formatting capabilities work the same as Microsoft Word. If you want to format text a certain way and you know how to do it in Word, try formatting the same way in PowerPoint. Odds are that it works.

You may have noticed (if you have played around in an earlier version of Office, especially Office 97) that the toolbars have a brand new appearance. Microsoft, in its effort to make sure computers take over the world, has given Office something called "IntelliSense," which means Bill Gates believes that someday he won't have to interact with humans at all. This kind of "thinking" stuff allows you to inadvertently customize your toolbars based on your normal or usual choices. Let's just hope you are a creature of habit! Now, don't let this scare you, you can find a Reset toolbars option by clicking View➪Toolbars➪Customize➪Reset. It will be interesting to see how well this new custom feature catches on.

In any case, if you can't find an editing or formatting button that you recall on a toolbar in a previous version, just click the little down arrows located periodically on the toolbar and you will see a wealth of button selections. Additionally, on the drop-down menus you may be startled to see things seem to be missing; but if you wait a minute your menu will stretch out like magic. Wa-laa!

As I mentioned in Chapter 1, you have the option of making your standard and formatting toolbars display on the same toolbar line by clicking on View➪Toolbars➪Customize➪Standard and Formatting Toolbars share one row. (You can also click on Tools➪Customize➪Standard and Formatting Toolbars share one row if you crave variety.)

Changing the Look of Your Characters

PowerPoint enables you to change the look of individual characters in subtle or drastic ways. You can control all character attributes by way of the Font dialog box, which you summon by using the Format➪Font command (see Figure 8-1).

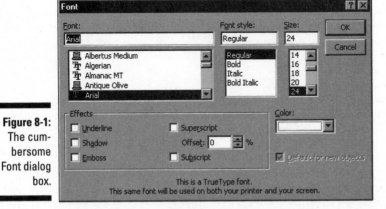

Figure 8-1:
The cumbersome Font dialog box.

The Font dialog box is a bit cumbersome to use, but fortunately PowerPoint provides an assortment of shortcuts for your formatting pleasure. These shortcuts are listed in Table 8-1; the procedures for using them are described in this section.

Table 8-1	Character-Formatting Shortcuts	
Button	*Keyboard Shortcut*	*Format*
B	Ctrl+B	**Bold**
I	Ctrl+I	*Italic*
U	Ctrl+U	Underline
(none)	Ctrl+spacebar	Normal
Times New Roman ▾	Ctrl+Shift+F	Font
24 ▾	Ctrl+Shift+P	Change font size
A^	Ctrl+Shift+>	Increase font size
A˅	Ctrl+Shift+<	Decrease font size
A		Font color
S		Text shadow

It's true — PowerPoint has many keyboard shortcuts for character formatting. You don't have to learn them all, though. The only ones I know and use
routinely are for bold, italic, underline, and normal. Learn those and you'll be
in good shape. You get the added bonus that these keyboard shortcuts are
the same as the shortcuts that many other Windows programs use. And, if
you are mouse-happy and keyboard-annoyed, click away for goodness sakes.
What matters most is that you can find and use what you need easily.

If you want, you can instruct these formats to gang-tackle some text. In other
words, text can be bold, italic, and underlined for extra, extra emphasis. You
can gang-tackle text with any combination of formats that you want.

You also can remove all text formats in one fell swoop by highlighting the text
and pressing Ctrl+spacebar.

Most of the formatting options covered in this chapter are available only in
Tri-pane, Slide or Outline view. If you try to apply a format in Notes Page view
you will notice you can't. However, just double-click on your slide in Notes
Page view and you will instantly be back in Slide view. This is also true in
Slide Sorter view.

Another way to summon the Font dialog box is to highlight the text you want
to format and right-click the mouse. A menu appears. Choose the Font option
from the menu and voilà! — the Font dialog box appears.

To boldly go . . .

Want to emphasize a point? Make it bold. Remember: Martin Luther said that if you must sin, sin boldly.

To make existing text bold, follow these steps:

1. **Highlight the text you want to make bold.**

 2. **Press Ctrl+B or click the Bold button (shown in the margin) on the Formatting toolbar.**

To type new text in boldface, follow these steps:

 1. **Press Ctrl+B or click the Bold button on the Formatting toolbar.**

2. **Type some text.**

    Make a bold effort.

3. **Press Ctrl+B or click the Bold button to return to typing normal text.**

You can use the Format⇨Font command to make text bold, but who wants to mess with a cumbersome dialog box when you can click the Bold button or press Ctrl+B instead? The rule is to use whatever is easiest for you.

 You can remove the bold attribute also by highlighting the bold text and pressing Ctrl+spacebar. This technique removes not only the bold attribute but also other character attributes, such as italics and underlining. In other words, Ctrl+spacebar returns the text to normal.

Italics

Another way to emphasize a word is to italicize it. To italicize existing text, follow these steps:

1. **Highlight the text you want to italicize.**

2. **Press Ctrl+I or click the Italic button (shown in the margin) on the Formatting toolbar.**

To type new text in italics, follow these steps:

1. **Press Ctrl+I or click the Italic button on the Formatting toolbar.**

2. **Type some text.**

    Don't be afraid, Luke.

3. Press Ctrl+I or click the Italic button to return to typing normal text.

The cumbersome Format⇔Font command has an italic option, but why bother? Ctrl+I and the Italic button are too easy to ignore.

Pressing Ctrl+spacebar removes italics along with any other character formatting that you applied. Use this key combination to return text to normal or, as NASA would say, to "re-establish nominal text."

Underlines

Back in the days of typewriters, underlining was the only way to add emphasis to text. You can underline text in PowerPoint, but you wouldn't want to appear antiquated. Also, in these Web-savvy days folks might think the underline is actually a hyperlink, (especially if you are publishing your PowerPoint presentation on the Web). Underlining usually looks out of place in today's jazzy presentations, unless you're shooting for a nostalgic effect.

To underline existing text, follow these steps:

1. Highlight the text you want to underline.

2. Press Ctrl+U or click the Underline button (shown in the margin) on the Formatting toolbar.

To type new text and have it automatically underlined, follow these steps:

1. Press Ctrl+U or click the Underline button on the Formatting toolbar.

2. Type some text.

3. Press Ctrl+U or click the Underline button to return to typing normal text.

The Format⇔Font command enables you to underline text, but Ctrl+U or the Underline button is easier to use.

You can remove the underlines and all other character formats by highlighting the text and pressing Ctrl+spacebar.

Big and little characters

If text is hard to read or you simply want to draw attention to it, you can make part of the text bigger than the surrounding text.

To increase or decrease the font size for existing text, follow these steps:

1. **Highlight the text whose size you want to change.**

2. **To increase the font size, press Ctrl+Shift+> or click the Increase Font Size button (shown in the margin) on the Formatting toolbar.**

   To decrease the font size, press Ctrl+Shift+< or click the Decrease Font Size button (shown in the margin) on the Formatting toolbar.

   To set the font to a specific size, press Ctrl+Shift+P or click the Font Size text box (shown in the margin) on the Formatting toolbar and type the point size you want.

To type new text in a different font size, change the font size by using a method from Step 2. Then type away. Change back to the original font size when you are finished.

Again, you can use the Format⇨Font command to change the point size, but why bother when the controls are right there on the Formatting toolbar? Only a masochist would mess with the Format⇨Font command.

In older versions of PowerPoint, Ctrl+spacebar could clear font attributes, such as bold and italic, but it could not reset the font size. This made PowerPoint perform differently than Word at the time. The good folks at Microsoft finally fixed this "feature" in this new release. Ctrl+spacebar restores text formatting completely.

Text fonts

If you don't like the looks of a text font, you can easily switch to a different font. To change the font for existing text, follow these steps:

1. **Highlight the text that is in the font you can't stand.**

2. **Click the arrow next to the Font control on the Formatting toolbar. A list of available fonts appears. Click the one you want to use.**

   Or press Ctrl+Shift+F and then press the down-arrow key to display the font choices.

If you have combined the Formatting toolbar with your Standard toolbar, you may not see the Font Type dialog box and will get no reaction from the keyboard shortcut. Don't forget to look for more buttons by checking the down arrows on the toolbar or by separating the two toolbars when you run PowerPoint. If you read this book in beginning-to-end order, you will remember that I advised you to separate those toolbars while working through this book.

To type new text in a different font, change the font as described in Step 2 and begin typing. Change back to the original font when you are finished.

Yes, yes, yes — with the Format⇨Font command, you can change the font. One try with this other dialog box will make it obvious why the other method is preferred. The font style options from the toolbar appear in WYSIWYG (pronounced "wiz zee wig") style. WYSIWYG is an acronym that stands for "What You See Is What You Get." With the formatting toolbar font type dialog box you can see what the font will look like before you select it. This will save many lost hours experimenting with every single choice just to see what it is and if you will like it.

If you want to change the font for all the slides in your presentation, you should switch to Slide Master view and then change the font. Details on how to do so are covered in Chapter 9.

PowerPoint automatically moves the fonts you use the most to the head of the font list. This feature makes picking your favorite font even easier.

Don't overdo it with fonts! Just because you have many different font choices doesn't mean that you should try to use them all on the same slide. Don't mix more than two or three typefaces on a slide, and use fonts consistently throughout the presentation. The PowerPoint Assistant reminds you if you use too many fonts.

The color purple

Color is an excellent way to draw attention to text in a slide if, of course, your slides print in color or you can display them on a color monitor or plan to publish on the Web. Follow this procedure for changing text color:

1. **Highlight the text that is in the color you want to change.**

2. **Click the Font Color button (shown in the margin) on the Formatting toolbar.**

   A little box with color choices appears. Click the color you want to use.

To type new text in a different color, change the color and then begin typing. When you have had enough, change back to the original color and continue.

If you don't like any color that the Font Color button offers, click where it reads *More Font Colors*. A bigger dialog box with more color choices appears. If you still cannot find the right shade of teal, click the Custom tab and have at it. Check out Chapter 10 if you need still more color help.

If you want to change the text color for your entire presentation, do so on the Slide Master (see Chapter 9 for details).

The shadow knows

Adding a shadow behind your text can make the text stand out against its background, which makes the entire slide easier to read. For that reason, many of the templates supplied with PowerPoint use shadows. These steps show you how to apply a text shadow:

1. **Highlight the text you want to shadow.**

2. **Click the Shadow button (shown in the margin).**

Embossed text

When you choose to emboss text, PowerPoint adds a dark shadow below the text and a light shadow above it to produce an embossed effect, as shown in Figure 8-2. Try it. It's very cool. Many Web sites use embossed text as part of the background.

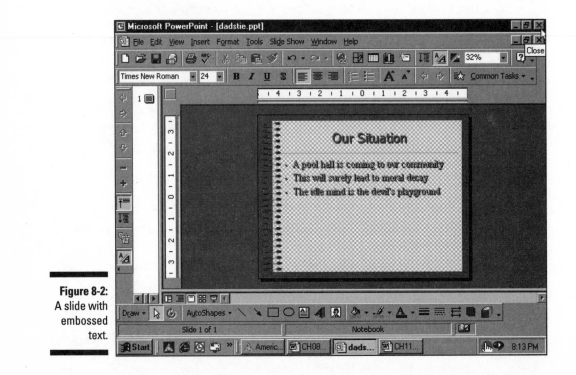

Figure 8-2:
A slide with embossed text.

To create embossed text, follow these simple steps:

1. **Highlight the text you want to emboss.**
2. **Use the Format⇨Font command to pop up the Font dialog box.**

   Sorry — PowerPoint has no keyboard shortcut or toolbar button for embossing. You have to do it the hard way.
3. **Check the Emboss option.**
4. **Click the OK button.**

When you emboss text, PowerPoint changes the text color to the background color to enhance the embossed effect.

Embossed text is hard to read in smaller font sizes. This effect is best reserved for large titles.

Also, embossed text is nearly invisible with some color schemes. You may have to fiddle with the color scheme or switch templates to make the embossed text visible.

Biting the Bullet

Most presentations have at least some slides that include a bulleted list — a series of paragraphs accented by special characters lovingly known as *bullets*. In the old days, you had to add bullets one at a time. Nowadays, PowerPoint comes with a semiautomatic bullet shooter that is illegal in 27 states.

PowerPoint 2000 has made bullets techno-cool by giving you the opportunity to use bitmap or graphic bullets to enhance your presentations or Web sites. Before you go crazy with picture bullets, take a look at the basic way to bite the bullet below.

To add bullets to a paragraph or series of paragraphs:

1. **Highlight the paragraphs to which you want to add bullets.**

   To add a bullet to just one paragraph, you don't have to highlight the entire paragraph. Just place the cursor anywhere in the paragraph.

 2. **Click the Bullet button (shown in the margin).**

   PowerPoint adds a bullet to each paragraph that you select.

The Bullet button works like a toggle: Press it once to add bullets and press it again to remove bullets. To remove bullets from previously bulleted text, therefore, you select the text and click the Bullet button again.

If you don't like the appearance of the bullets that PowerPoint uses, you can choose a different bullet character, picture, or even a motion clip by using the Format⇨Bullet command. This command displays the Bullets and Numbering dialog box, shown in Figure 8-3. From this dialog box, you can choose a different bullet character, change the bullet's color, or change its size relative to the text size.

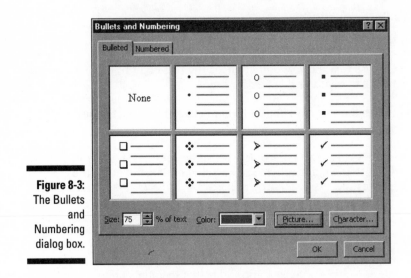

Figure 8-3:
The Bullets
and
Numbering
dialog box.

This list shows you some pointers for using the Bullets and Numbering dialog box. (If you are an old, world-weary PowerPoint user and not new to the application, you probably notice that bullets have come into their own. No longer bullets, but media darlings, these little guys are destined for greatness, or at least their own TV talk show.)

✔ Several collections of characters are available for choosing bullet characters. If you don't like any of the bullet characters displayed for you in the dialog box, click Character in the lower-right-hand corner of the dialog box. Change the option in the Bullets from drop-down list box. The Wingdings collection contains such useful bullets as pointing fingers, a skull and crossbones, and a time bomb. You may see other collections in the Bullets from list box as well.

✔ If the bullet characters don't seem large enough, increase the Size value in the Bullets and Numbering dialog box. The size is specified as a percentage of the text size.

✔ To change the bullet color, use the drop-down Color list box to choose the color you want to use. Colors from the current color scheme appear in the drop-down menu that appears when you use the Color list box. For additional color choices, click More Colors to call forth a dialog box offering a complete range of color choices. For more information about using colors, see Chapter 10.

✔ To use a picture bullet, close the Character section of the dialog box by clicking on the close box (X) in the right-hand corner, and then select picture by clicking Picture. Notice that this new section of the dialog box is getting pretty snazzy. Take a look at it in Figure 8-4.

Notice the pretty bitmap, graphic bullets! You can also add Motion clips as bullets and import clips from the Internet or on your hard drive. Notice the "Web-page-looking" interface of the dialog box. An arrow lets you go backward or forward, and a button that lets you go Home. Or, if you want to use a keystroke for "home," it's (Alt+Home), also known as going to your "old home." There *is* no place like home — Right Dorothy?

You can use certain bullet characters for good comic effect in your presentations. Be creative, but also be careful. A thumbs-down bullet next to the name of your boss may get a laugh, but it may also get you fired. One cool thing to do with bullets when you pitch a product or service is to use your logo as a bullet. It subliminally grinds your image in their brains until they submit to your will.

And another thing — I found that the dialog box for picture bullets has gotten so big and deluxe here that I have to click and drag it around a little bit to see it all. Don't worry, it's all there.

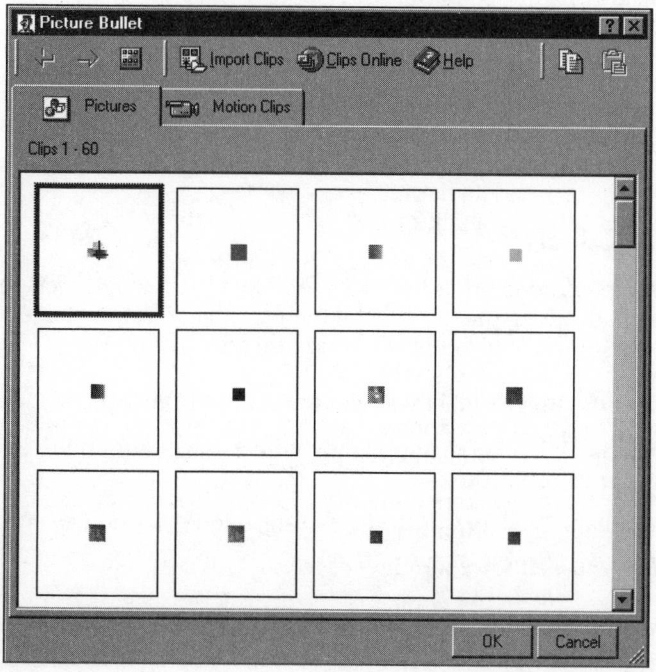

Figure 8-4:
The Picture
Bullet dialog
box.

Lining Things Up

PowerPoint enables you to control the way your text lines up on the slide. You can center text, line it up flush left or flush right, or justify it. You can change these alignments by using the Format⇨Alignment command, or you can use the convenient toolbar buttons and keyboard shortcuts.

Centering text

Centered text lines up right down the middle of the slide. (Actually, down the middle of the text object that contains the text; a text line appears centered on the slide only if the text object is centered on the slide.)

To center existing text, follow this procedure:

1. **Select the line or lines you want to center.**

2. **Click the Center button (shown in the margin) on the Formatting toolbar or press Ctrl+E.**

   It's true that E doesn't stand for *center.* Ctrl+C was already taken (for Copy, remember?), so the Microsoft jocks decided to use Ctrl+E. They consider it to be some sort of demented practical joke.

3. **Admire your newly centered text.**

To type new centered text, skip Step 1; just click the Center button or press Ctrl+E and begin typing.

Flush to the left

Centered text is sometimes hard to read. Align the text *flush left*, and the text lines up neatly along the left edge of the text object. All the bullets line up too. These steps show you how to make text flush left:

1. **Select the line or lines you want to scoot to the left.**

2. **Click the Align Left button (shown in the margin) on the Formatting toolbar or press Ctrl+L.**

   Hallelujah! The L in Ctrl+L stands for — you guessed it — *left.*

3. **Toast yourself for your cleverness.**

If you want to type new flush-left text, just click the Align Left button or press Ctrl+L and begin typing.

Other terms for flush left are *left justified* and *ragged right.* Just thought you may want to know.

Flush to the right

Yes, you can align text against the right edge, too. I don't know why you want to, but you can.

1. **Select the line or lines you want to shove to the right.**

2. **Click the Align Right button (shown in the margin) on the Formatting toolbar or press Ctrl+R.**

   R equals right — get it?

3. **Have a drink on me.**

If you want to type new flush-right text, just click the Align Right button or press Ctrl+R and continue.

Other terms for flush right are _right justified_ and _ragged left_. With this extra cocktail party verbiage to add to your vocabulary, you'll be the hit at any nerd party.

Stand up, sit down, justify!

You also can tell PowerPoint to _justify_ text: to line up both the left and right edges. The keyboard shortcut is Ctrl+J (J is for _justified_). And although there is no Justify button in the Formatting toolbar, you can add such a button via the Tools⇨Customize command.

Messing with Tabs and Indents

PowerPoint enables you to set tab stops to control the placement of text within a text object. For most presentations, you don't have to fuss with tabs. Each paragraph is indented according to its level in the outline, and the amount of indentation for each outline level is preset by the template you use to create the presentation.

Although there's little need to, you can mess with the indent settings and tab stops if you're adventurous and have no real work to do today. Here's how you do it:

1. **Click the Slide button to switch to Slide view.**

   You cannot mess with tabs or indents in Outline view. You can make changes in Notes Pages view, but Slide view is more convenient.

Don't even bother with this stuff about tab types

PowerPoint isn't limited to just boring left-aligned tabs. In all, it has four distinct types of tabs: left, right, center, and decimal. The square button at the far left side of the ruler tells you which type of tab is added when you click the ruler. Click this button to cycle through the four types of tabs:

✔ **Standard left-aligned tab.** Press Tab to advance the text to the tab stop.

✔ **Right-aligned tab.** Text is aligned flush right with the tab stop.

✔ **Centered tab.** Text lines up centered over the tab stop.

✔ **Decimal tab.** Numbers line up with the decimal point centered over the tab stop.

2. **Activate the ruler by using the <u>V</u>iew⇨<u>R</u>uler comma**

   Rulers appear above and to the left of the presentation window and show the current tab and indentation settings. You must activate the ruler if you want to change tab stops or text indents.

   Figure 8-5 shows a PowerPoint presentation with the ruler activated.

3. **Select the text object whose tabs or indents you want to change.**

   Each text object has its own tabs and indents setting. After you click a text object, the ruler shows that object's tabs and indents.

4. **Click the ruler to add a tab stop.**

   Move the mouse pointer to the ruler location where you want to add a tab stop and then click. A tab stop appears.

5. **Grab the indentation doohickey and drag it to change the indentation.**

   Try dragging the different parts of the indentation doohickey to see what happens. Have fun. Good luck.

Tabs and indents can be pretty testy, but fortunately you don't have to mess with them for most presentations. If you're one of the unlucky ones, keep these pointers in mind:

✔ Each text object has its own tab settings. The tab settings for an object apply to all the paragraphs within the object, so you can't change tab settings for individual paragraphs within a text object.

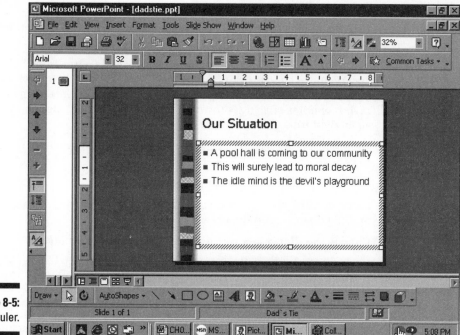

Figure 8-5:
The ruler.

> ✔ The ruler shows as many as five different indentation levels, one for each outline level. Only those levels used in the text object are shown, so if the object has only one outline level, only one indent is shown. To see additional indents, demote text within the object by pressing the Tab key.

If all this stuff about outline levels and demotions upsets you, refer to Chapter 3, where you can find a comforting explanation of PowerPoint outlines.

Each text object is set up initially with default tab stops set at every inch. When you add a tab stop, any default tab stops to the left of the new tab stop disappear.

To remove a tab stop, use the mouse to drag the stop off the ruler (click the tab stop, drag it off the ruler, and then release the mouse button).

Spacing Things Out

Feeling a little spaced out? Try tightening the space between text lines. Feeling cramped? Space out the lines a little. These steps show you how to do it all:

1. **Switch to Slide view.**

   You can change line spacing in Tri-pane view, Slide view, or Outline view, Notes Page view only. Slide view is more convenient.

   Although you can change the line spacing of slide notes from Tri-pane view, you can't see the effect of the spacing until you print your handouts or examine the results in Notes Pages view. The Notes Pages view review of notes spacing is the best because you can change the spacing again right from the same view.

2. **Highlight the paragraph or paragraphs whose line spacing you want to change.**

3. **Use the Format⇨Line Spacing command.**

   Sorry, PowerPoint has no keyboard shortcut for this step. The Line Spacing dialog box suddenly appears.

4. **Change the dialog box settings to adjust the line spacing.**

   Line spacing refers to the space between the lines within a paragraph. Before paragraph adds extra space before the paragraph, and After paragraph adds extra space after the paragraph.

   You can specify spacing in terms of lines or points. The size of a line varies depending on the size of the text font. If you specify spacing in terms of points, PowerPoint uses the exact spacing you specify, regardless of the size of the text font.

5. **Click the OK button or press Enter.**

You can also increase or decrease the spacing between paragraphs by clicking the Increase Paragraph Spacing or Decrease Paragraph Spacing buttons found in the Formatting toolbar. If you can't find the buttons, remember to try the down arrow.

Chapter 9

Masters of the Universe Meet the Templates of Doom

*W*ant to add a bit of text to every slide in your presentation? Or maybe add your name and phone number at the bottom of your audience handouts? Or place a picture of Rush Limbaugh at the extreme right side of each page of your speaker notes?

Masters are the surefire way to add something to every slide. No need to toil separately at each slide. Add something to the Master and it automatically shows up on every slide. Remove it from the Master and — poof! —it disappears from every slide. Very convenient.

Masters govern all aspects of a slide's appearance: its background color, objects that appear on every slide, text that appears on all slides, and more.

Although tinkering with the Masters lets you fine-tune the appearance of a presentation, changing the presentation's template allows you to make drastic changes to a presentation's appearance. A *template* is a special type of presentation file that holds Masters. When you apply a template to an existing presentation, the presentation's existing Masters are replaced with the Masters from the template, thus completely changing the appearance of the presentation without changing its content.

With templates, you can easily try on different looks for your presentation before settling on a final design.

Working with Masters

In PowerPoint 2000, a Master governs the appearance of all the slides or pages in a presentation. Each presentation has four Masters:

✔ **Slide Master:** Dictates the format of your slides. You work with this Master most often as you tweak your slides to cosmetic perfection.

✔ **Title Master:** Prescribes the layout of the presentation's title slide. This Master allows you to give your title slides a different look from the other slides in your presentation.

✔ **Handout Master:** Controls the look of printed handouts.

✔ **Notes Master:** Determines the characteristics of printed speaker notes.

Each Master specifies the appearance of text (font, size, and color, for example), the slide's background color, and text or other objects you want to appear on each slide or page.

Each presentation has just one of each type of Master. The Master governs the appearance of all slides or pages in the presentation.

Masters are not optional. Every presentation has them. You can, however, override the formatting of objects contained in the Master for a particular slide. This capability enables you to vary the appearance of slides when it's necessary.

The quick way to call up a Master is to hold down the Shift key while you click one of the view buttons at the left side of the status bar at the bottom of the screen. Clicking the Slide View icon takes you to the Title Master if your title slide is active in the Slide view pane or is highlighted in Slide Sorter view. Clicking the Slide View icon takes you to Slide Master if any other slide is active. Clicking either the Slide Sorter View icon or the Outline View icon takes you to the Handout Master. Pick an icon — any icon. The results are the same. For Notes Master, you have to do it the old-fashion way: View➪Master➪Notes Master. You can also get to Notes Master by holding down the Shift key and choosing View➪Notes Page. Holding down the Shift key and clicking the Normal View icon puts you in regular old Normal View (none of the Masters). Go ahead. Try it. I'll wait here until you come back.

Do *not* hold down the Shift key and press the Slide Show icon. Doing so takes you into the Set Up Show dialog box. This territory is strictly reserved for those who read Chapter 26.

Changing the Slide Master

If you don't like the layout of your slides, call up the Slide Master and do something about it, as shown in these steps:

1. **Choose the View⇨Master⇨Slide Master command or hold down the Shift key while clicking the Slide View button.**

   If you use the View⇨Master command, a submenu pops up with a listing of the four Masters. Choose Slide Master to call up the Slide Master.

   If this is your first time with the View⇨Master command, you may only see one of the four Masters listed. This is a feature, not a bug! Do not be frightened. In a calm but firm voice tell your monitor, "I am your true Master. Show me the others who would call themselves Masters." Then carefully slide your pointer over the little double down arrow, and the other Masters appear on the submenu. You will intimidate them, so they will appear faded and shy.

2. **Behold the Slide Master in all its splendor.**

   Figure 9-1 shows a typical Slide Master. You can see the placeholders for the slide title and body text in addition to other background objects. Note also that the Slide Master includes placeholders for three objects that appear at the bottom of each slide: the Date Area, Footer Area, and Number Area. These special areas are used by the View⇨Header and Footer command and are described later in this chapter, under the heading "Using Headers and Footers."

   Notice the cute little Slide Miniature in the upper-right corner. You can click on the "X" and make it go away if you want. You can also dump the Slide Miniature by toggling the Slide Miniature icon on the Master toolbar.

3. **Make any formatting changes you want.**

   Select the text you want to apply a new style to and make your formatting changes. If you want all the slide titles to be in italics, for example, select the title text and press Ctrl+I or click the Italic button on the Formatting toolbar.

   If you're not sure how to change text formats, consult Chapter 8.

4. **Click the Normal View button on the status toolbar to return to your slide.**

   The effect of your Slide Master changes should be apparent immediately.

PowerPoint applies character formats such as bold, italics, font size, and font to entire paragraphs when you work in Slide Master view. You don't have to select the entire paragraph before you apply a format; just click anywhere in the paragraph.

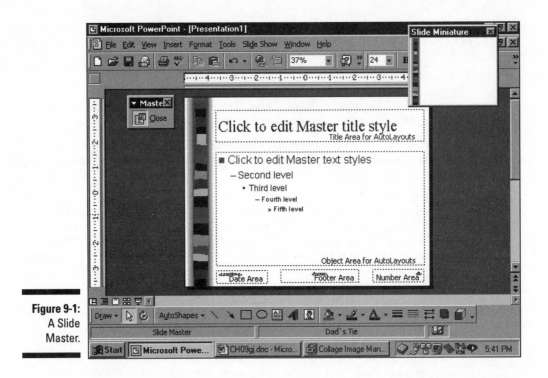

Figure 9-1:
A Slide
Master.

Notice that the body object contains paragraphs for five outline levels formatted with different point sizes, indentations, and bullet styles. If you want to change the way an outline level is formatted, this is the place.

You can type all you want in the title or object area placeholders, but the text you type doesn't appear on the slides. The text that appears in these placeholders is provided only so that you can see the effect of the formatting changes you apply. (To insert text that appears on each slide, see the next section, "Adding recurring text.")

You can edit any of the other objects on the Master by clicking them. Unlike the title and object area placeholders, any text you type in other Slide Master objects appears exactly as you type it on each slide.

Adding recurring text

To add recurring text to each slide, follow this procedure:

1. Call up the Slide Master if it's not displayed already.

The menu command is View➪Master➪Slide Master. Or you can Shift+click the Slide View button.

2. **Click the Text Box button (shown in the margin) on the Drawing toolbar.**

   This step highlights the Text Box button. The mouse cursor turns into an upside-down cross.

3. **Click where you want to add text.**

   PowerPoint places a text object at that location.

4. **Type the text that you want to appear on each slide.**

   For example: **Call 1-800-555-NERD today! Don't delay! Operators standing by!**

5. **Format the text however you want.**

   For example, if you want bold, press Ctrl+B.

6. **Click the Normal or Tri-pane View button to return to your presentation.**

   Now's the time to gloat over your work. Lasso some coworkers and show 'em how proud you are.

You can add other types of objects to the Slide Master, too. You can click the Insert Clip Art button (shown in the margin) on the Drawing toolbar, for example, to insert any of the clip art pictures supplied with PowerPoint. Or you can use the Insert⇨Movies and Sounds command to add a video or sound clip. (Clip art is described in detail in Chapter 11, and movies and sounds are covered in Chapter 16.) Anything you can add to an individual slide can be added to the Slide Master.

After you place an object on the Slide Master, you can grab it with the mouse and move it around or resize it any way you want. The object appears in the same location and size on each slide.

To delete an object from the Slide Master, click it and press the Delete key. To delete a text object, you must first click the object and then click again on the object frame. Then press Delete.

If you can't highlight the object no matter how many times you click it, you probably have returned to Slide view. Shift+click the Slide View button or choose the View⇨Master⇨Slide Master command again to call up the Slide Master.

Changing the Master color scheme

You can use the Slide Master to change the color scheme used for all slides in a presentation. To do that, follow these steps:

1. **Choose the <u>V</u>iew⇨<u>M</u>aster⇨<u>S</u>lide Master command or Shift+click the Slide button to summon the Slide Master.**

2. **Choose the F<u>o</u>rmat⇨Slide <u>C</u>olor Scheme command to change the color scheme.**

   Treat yourself to a bag of Doritos if it works the first time.

PowerPoint color schemes are hefty enough that I have devoted an entire chapter to them. Skip to Chapter 10 now if you can't wait.

If you don't have a color printer, don't waste your time messing with the color scheme unless you're going to make your presentation on-screen. If, however, you are going to broadcast your presentation over the Internet, generating millions of dollars in additional revenue and a raise for yourself, color away. Mauve, teal, azure, and cerulean all look like gray when they're printed on a noncolor laser printer.

The PowerPoint color schemes were chosen by professionals who are color-blind in no more than one eye. Stick to these schemes to avoid embarrassing color combinations! (I wish that my sock drawer came with a similar color-scheme feature.)

If you want to adjust the shading that's applied to the background slide color, choose the F<u>o</u>rmat⇨Background command. Chapter 10 walks you through this feature.

Changing the Title Master

PowerPoint keeps a separate Master layout for title slides. That way, you can give your title slides a different layout than the other slides in your presentation.

There are two ways to call up the Title Master:

✔ Display the title slide and then Shift+click the Slide button.

✔ Choose the <u>V</u>iew⇨<u>M</u>aster⇨<u>T</u>itle Master command.

Figure 9-2 shows a Title Master. As you can see, it contains the same layout elements as the Slide Master, except that the "Object Area for AutoLayouts" is replaced with "Subtitle Area for AutoLayouts."

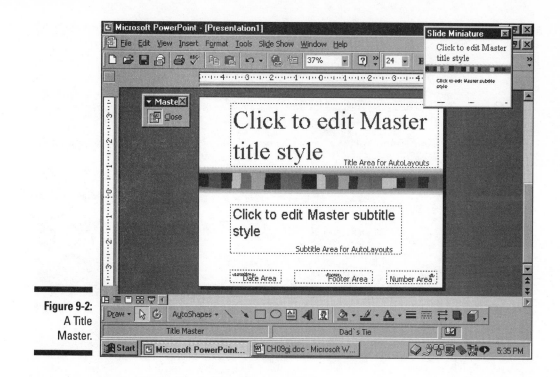

Figure 9-2:
A Title
Master.

Changing the Handout and Notes Masters

Like the Slide Master, the Handout and Notes Masters contain formatting information that's automatically applied to your presentation. This section tells you how you can modify these Masters.

Changing the Handout Master

Follow these simple steps to change the Handout Master:

1. **Choose the View⇨Master⇨Handout Master command or hold down the Shift key and click the Slide Sorter View button or the Outline View button.**

   The Handout Master rears its ugly head, as shown in Figure 9-3.

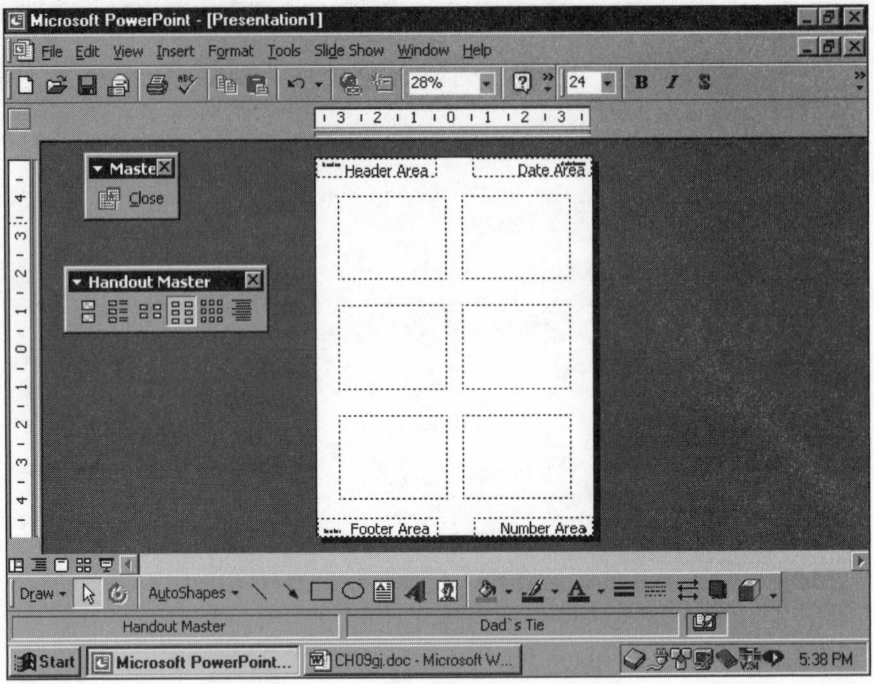

Figure 9-3:
A Handout
Master.

2. Mess around with it.

The Handout Master shows the arrangement of handouts for slides printed two, three, four, six and nine per page, plus the arrangement for printing outlines. You can switch among these different handout layouts by clicking the buttons on the floating Handout Master toolbar. Unfortunately, you cannot move, resize, or delete the slide and outline placeholders that appear in the Handout Master. But you can add or change elements that you want to appear on each handout page, such as your name and phone number, a page number, and maybe a good lawyer joke.

3. Go back.

Click the Close in the floating Master toolbar to return to Normal or Tri-pane view.

4. Print a handout to see whether your changes take effect.

Handout Master elements are invisible until you print them, so you should print at least one handout page to check your work.

When you print handout pages, the slides themselves are formatted according to the Slide Master. You cannot change the appearance of the slides from the Handout Master.

Changing the Notes Master

Notes pages consist of a reduced image of the slide, plus notes you type to go along with the slide. For more information about creating and using notes pages, refer to Chapter 5.

When printed, notes pages are formatted according to the Notes Master. To change the Notes Master, follow these steps:

1. **Choose the View⇨Master⇨Notes Master command.**

   The Notes Master comes to life.

2. **Indulge yourself.**

   The Notes Master contains two main placeholders: one for your notes text and the other for the slide. You can move or change the size of either of these objects, and you can change the format of the text in the notes placeholder. You also can add or change elements that you want to appear on each handout page. Also notice the convenient placement of the header, footer, date, and page number blocks.

3. **Click Close in the Master toolbar to return to Notes Page view.**

   Admire your handiwork. Unlike you do when using the Outline Master and Handout Master, you don't have to print anything to check the results of changes you make to the Notes Master. You can see them clearly when you switch to Notes Page view (or in the Slide Miniature if you squint).

At the least, add page numbers to your speaker notes. If you drop a stack of notes pages without page numbers, you will be up a creek without a paddle!

If public speaking gives you severe stomach cramps, add the text *Just picture them naked* to the Notes Master. It works every time for me.

Using Masters

You don't have to do anything special to apply the formats from a Master to your slide; all slides automatically pick up the Master format unless you specify otherwise. So this section really should be titled "Not Using Masters" because it talks about how to *not* use the formats provided by Masters.

Overriding the Master text style

To override the text style specified by a Slide Master or Notes Master, simply format the text however you want while you're working in Tri-pane, Slide, Outline, or Notes Page view. The formatting changes you make apply only to the selected text. The Slide Master and Notes Master aren't affected.

The only way to change one of the Masters is to do it directly by switching to the appropriate Master view. Thus, any formatting changes you make while in Slide view affect only that slide.

If you change the slide text style and then decide that you liked it better the way it was, you can quickly reapply the text style from the Slide Master by switching to Slide view and using the Format➪Slide Layout command. A Slide Layout dialog box appears; click the Reapply button to restore text formatting to the format specified in the Slide Master.

If you change the notes text style and want to revert to the text style specified in the Notes Master, switch to Notes Pages view and use the Format➪ Notes Layout command. When the Notes Layout dialog box appears, check the Reapply Master check box and click OK.

If you are using older versions of PowerPoint, I have two words for you: Be Ware. The Ctrl+spacebar key combination clears all text attributes, including those specified in the Slide Master or Notes Master. This key combination can wreak havoc on your formatting efforts. Suppose that the Slide Master specifies shadowed text. If you italicize a word and then decide to remove the italics by pressing Ctrl+spacebar, the shadow is removed as well. PowerPoint 2000 users can sleep at night knowing that this "feature" was fixed.

Changing the background for just one slide

Both Slide Masters and Notes Masters enable you to add background objects that appear on every slide or notes page in your presentation. You can, however, hide the background objects for selected slides or notes pages. You can also change the background color or effect used for an individual slide or notes page. These steps show you how:

1. **Display the slide or notes page you want to show with a plain background.**

2. **Summon either the Background or Notes Background dialog box.**

   To change the background for a slide, use the Format➪Background command. The Background dialog box appears, as shown in Figure 9-4. For notes, use Format➪Notes Background. (The Notes Background dialog box looks much like the Background dialog box; the only difference is their titles.)

You have to use View➪Notes Page to navigate to the Notes Page view in order to use this feature for changing the background on an individual Notes Page. All other views (Normal, Slide, and Slide Sorter) provide only the (Slide) Background dialog box.

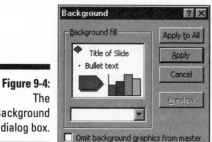

Figure 9-4:
The
Background
dialog box.

3. **Check the Omit Background Graphics from Master check box.**

   Check this box if you want to hide the Master background objects.

4. **Change the Background Fill if you want.**

   You can change to a different background color, or you can add an effect such as a pattern fill or a texture. These details are covered in Chapter 10.

5. **Click the Apply button or press Enter.**

   If you checked the Omit background graphics from master check box (Step 3), the background objects from the Slide Master or Notes Master vanish from the active slide or page, respectively. If you changed the background color or effect, you see that change, too. Don't be afraid to try the Preview feature.

Hiding background objects or changing the background color or effect applies only to the current slide or notes page. Other slides or notes pages are unaffected. In Slide Sorter view, all selected slides are affected.

If you want to remove some but not all the background objects from a single slide, try this trick:

1. **Follow the preceding Steps 1 through 5 to hide background objects for the slide.**

2. **Call up the Slide Master (View⇨Master⇨Slide Master).**

3. **Hold down the Shift key and click each object that you want to appear.**

4. **Press Ctrl+C to copy these objects to the Clipboard.**

5. **Return to Slide view.**

6. **Press Ctrl+V to paste the objects from the Clipboard.**

7. **Choose the Draw⇨Order⇨Send to Back command if the background objects obscure other slide objects or text. (The Draw menu is found on the Drawing toolbar.)**

Using Headers and Footers

Headers and footers provide a convenient way to place repeating text at the top or bottom of each slide, handout, or notes page. You can add the time and date, slide number or page number, or any other information that you want to appear on each slide or page, such as your name or the title of your presentation.

The PowerPoint Slide and Title Masters include three placeholders for such information:

- ✔ The *date area* can be used to display a date and time.
- ✔ The *number area* can be used to display the slide number.
- ✔ The *footer area* can be used to display any text that you want to see on each slide.

In addition, Handout and Notes Masters include a fourth placeholder, the *header area,* which provides an additional area for text that you want to see on each page.

Although the date, number, and footer areas normally appear at the bottom of the slide in the Slide and Title Masters, you can move them to the top by switching to Slide or Title Master view and then dragging the placeholders to the top of the slide.

Adding a date, number, or footer to slides

To add a date, a slide number, or a footer to your slides, follow these steps:

1. **Choose the <u>V</u>iew⇨<u>H</u>eader and Footer command.**

   The Header and Footer dialog box appears, as shown in Figure 9-5. (If necessary, click the Slide tab so that you see the slide footer options as shown in the figure.)

2. **To display the date, check the <u>D</u>ate and Time check box. Then select the date format you want in the list box beneath the <u>U</u>pdate Automatically option button.**

   Alternatively, you can type any text you wish in the Fixed text box. The text you type appears in the Date Area of the Slide or Title Master.

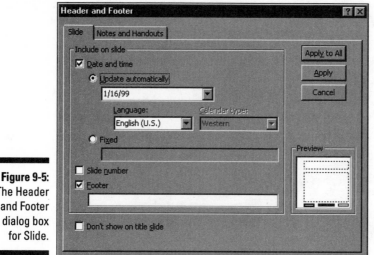

Figure 9-5:
The Header
and Footer
dialog box
for Slide.

If you're the sort of bloke who begins a presentation with "G'day mates!" then you might also enjoy the new PowerPoint 2000 Language option for dates. Different English speaking cultures use different conventions for displaying dates. Play with it and see. If your audience doesn't use the Western world's calendar, check out the Calendar.

3. **To display slide numbers, check the Slide Number check box.**

4. **To display a footer on each slide, check the Footer check box and then type the text that you want to appear on each slide in the Footer text box.**

   For example, you might type your name, your company name, a subliminal message, or the name of your presentation.

5. **If you want the date, number, and footer to appear on every slide except the title slide, check the Don't Show on Title Slide check box.**

6. **Click Apply to All.**

If you are going to be giving a presentation on a certain date in the future (for example, at a sales conference or a trade show), type the date that you will be giving the presentation directly into the Fixed text box. You can use the same technique to post-date presentations you never really gave but need to supply to your legal counsel to back up your alibi.

If you want to change the footer areas for just one slide, click Apply instead of Apply to All. This option comes in handy for those occasional slides that contain a graphic or a block of text that crowds up against the footer areas. You can easily suppress the footer information for that slide to make room for the large graphic or text.

Adding a header or footer to Notes or Handout pages

To add header and footer information to Notes or Handouts pages, follow the steps described in the preceding section, "Adding a date, number, or footer to slides," except click the Notes and Handouts tab when the Header and Footer dialog box appears. Clicking this tab displays the dialog box shown in Figure 9-6.

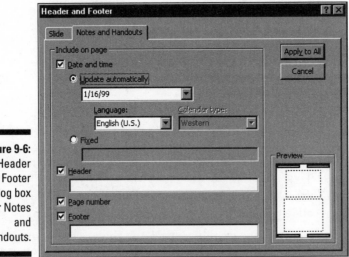

Figure 9-6:
The Header and Footer dialog box for Notes and Handouts.

This dialog box is similar to the Header and Footer dialog box for Slide, except that it gives you an additional option to add a header that appears at the top of each page. After you indicate how you want to print the date, header, number, and footer areas, click the Apply to All button.

Editing the header and footer placeholders directly

If you wish, you can edit the text that appears in the header and footer place-holders directly. First, display the appropriate Master — Slide, Title, Handout, or Notes. Then click on the date, number, footer, or header placeholder and start typing.

You may notice that the placeholders include special codes for the options you indicated in the Header and Footer dialog box. For example, the Date placeholder may contain the text *<date,time>* if you indicated that the date should be displayed. You can type text before or after these codes, but you should leave the codes themselves alone.

Thank Heavens for Templates

If you had to create Slide Masters from scratch every time you built a new presentation, you probably would put PowerPoint back in its box and use it as a bookend. Creating a Slide Master is easy. Creating one that looks good is a different story. Making a good-looking Master is tough even for the artistically inclined. For right-brain, nonartistic types like me, it's next to impossible.

Thank heavens for templates. A *template* is simply a PowerPoint presentation file with predefined formatting settings. When you create a presentation, PowerPoint gives you the option of stealing Masters from an existing template presentation. Any PowerPoint presentation can serve as a template, including presentations you create yourself. But PowerPoint comes with more than 100 template presentations designed by professional artists who understand color combinations and balance and all that artsy stuff. Have a croissant and celebrate.

Because the templates that come with PowerPoint look good, any presentation you create by using one of them will look good, too. It's as simple as that. The template also supplies the color scheme for your presentation. You can override it, of course, but you do so at your own risk. The color police are everywhere, you know. You don't want to be taken in for Felony Color Clash.

Templates use the special file extension POT, but you can also use ordinary PowerPoint presentation files (PPT) as templates. You can therefore use any of your own presentations as a template. If you make extensive changes to a presentation's Masters, you can use that presentation as a template for other presentations you create. Or you can save the presentation as a template by using the POT file extension.

Because a template is a presentation, you can open it and change it if you want.

Applying a different template

You're halfway through creating a new presentation when you realize that you can't stand the look of the slides. Oops — you picked the wrong template when you started the new presentation! Don't panic. PowerPoint enables you to assign a new presentation template at any time. These steps show you how:

1. **Choose the F̲ormat⇨Apply Design Template command.**

   The Apply Design Template dialog box appears, as shown in Figure 9-7.

2. **Rummage around for a template you like better.**

   If none of these templates floats your boat, then snoop over in the mysterious 1033 folder and dig around in the Presentations collection. (Why do they call it 1033? Who knows? Not me. Forget about it, be glad you found it, and move on.) To get to the 1033 folder, click the Up One Level icon (shown in the margin) on the Apply Design Template dialog box. You are in a folder called Templates. Templates has two subfolders: Presentation Designs (where you were before) and the 1033 folder. Choose 1033 and check out the choices.

   If you updated PowerPoint 97 to the PowerPoint 2000 version and had a few favorite templates that no longer appear on your list, fear not. In addition to the templates in your Presentation Designs folder, you see another folder on this list called Office 97 Templates. Follow it to a folder called Templates. In it, you find two other folders where your old favorites can be found. They are called Presentation Designs and Presentations (now called 1033 in PowerPoint 2000). Relax and enjoy.

   The differences in the two groups of templates are:

   - **1033 (or Presentations):** Contains templates that include suggested content. These templates are used by the AutoContent Wizard to create skeleton presentations when you tell the Wizard the type of presentation that you want to create.

   - **Presentation Designs:** Contains designer templates. These templates do not contain sample content, but they look marvelous.

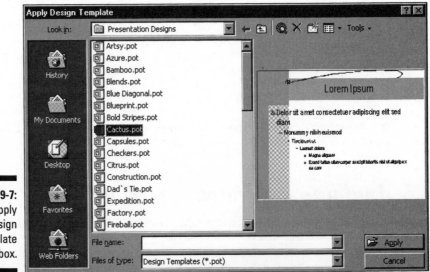

Figure 9-7:
The Apply
Design
Template
dialog box.

When you click a presentation name, PowerPoint displays a preview of the template's appearance in the Apply Design Template dialog box.

3. **Click the Apply button or double-click the template filename to apply the template.**

   Make sure that you like the new template better than the first one!

You may still want to make minor adjustments to the Slide Master to make the slides look just right.

When you apply a new template, PowerPoint copies the Masters and the color scheme into your presentation. As a result, any changes you made to the presentation's Masters or color scheme are lost. Too bad. If you added background objects to the Slide Master, you have to add them again.

You don't have to worry about the new template undoing any formatting changes that you have made to individual slides. PowerPoint remembers these deviations from the Master format when it applies a new template.

Another way to bring up the Apply Design Template dialog box is to double-click the name of the template in the status bar at the bottom of the PowerPoint window.

Creating a new template

If none of the templates that come with PowerPoint appeals to you, you can easily create your own. All you have to do is create a presentation with the Masters and the color scheme set up just the way you want and then save it as a template. Here are a few points to remember about templates:

✔ The design templates that come with PowerPoint have no slides in them. To create a template without any slides, choose the New button, and then click the Cancel button when the Add New Slide dialog box appears. Then choose the View⇨Masters command to switch to the Slide, Title, Notes, or Handout Master.

✔ If you want to make minor modifications to one of the supplied templates, open the template by using the File⇨Open command and then immediately save it under a new name by using the File⇨Save As command. Then change the Masters and the color scheme. Don't forget to save the file again when you're finished!

✔ Your templates are easily accessible if you store them in the \Microsoft Office\Templates\Presentation Designs folder along with the templates supplied with PowerPoint.

✔ You can also create your own presentation templates complete with skeleton slides. Just create the template as a normal presentation and add however many slides you want to include. Then save the presentation as a template in the folder \Microsoft Office\Templates\ Presentations.

✔ When you are ready to save your template, use the Save as type: command. Set your type to Design Template (*.pot).

Creating a new default template

When you create a new presentation using the File⇨New command, PowerPoint asks whether you want to base the presentation on an existing template or to create a blank presentation. This question is a little misleading because it suggests that the blank presentation doesn't use a template. It does — it uses a default template named BLANK PRESENTATION.POT to obtain bare-bones Masters and a black-on-white color scheme.

If you want to create your own default template, all you have to do is save your template file by using the filename BLANK PRESENTATION.POT in the \Microsoft Office\Templates folder. Then, whenever you create a blank presentation, the Masters and the color scheme are copied from your new default template rather than from the bland default template that comes with PowerPoint.

Make a copy of the original BLANK PRESENTATION.POT file before you overwrite it with your own changes. You may someday want to revert to the PowerPoint standard default template. To make a copy of the default template, open it and choose the File⇨Save As command to save it with a new name (for example, OLD BLANK PRESENTATION.POT).

These steps show you how to create a new default template:

1. **Open the default template.**

   It's named BLANK PRESENTATION.POT and lives in the \Microsoft Office\Templates folder.

2. **Make any changes you want.**

   For example, add your name to the Slide Master and add the page number and date to the Notes Master, Title Master, and Handout Master.

3. **Save your changes.**

Chapter 10

When I Am Old, I Shall Make My Slides Purple

· ·

In This Chapter

▶ Using color schemes

▶ Changing the colors in a color scheme

▶ Creating new colors

▶ Shading the slide background

▶ Coloring objects and text

▶ Copying colors from other objects

· ·

*W*elcome to the Wonderful World of Color. Here is your opportunity to unleash the repressed artist hidden deep within you. Take up your palette, grasp your brush firmly, and prepare to attack the empty canvas of your barren slides.

PowerPoint 2000 enables you to use more than 16 million colors, but you shouldn't feel obligated to use them all right away. Pace yourself. Now would be a good time to grow a goatee or to cut off your ear. (Just kidding.)

Using Color Schemes

The PowerPoint templates come with built-in color schemes, which are co-ordinated sets of colors chosen by color professionals. Microsoft paid these people enormous sums of money to debate the merits of using mauve text on a teal background. You can use these professionally designed color schemes, or you can create your own if you think that you have a better eye than the Microsoft-hired color guns.

As far as I'm concerned, the PowerPoint color schemes are the best thing to come along since Peanut M&Ms. Without color schemes, people like me are free to pick and choose from among the 16 million or so colors that PowerPoint lets you incorporate into your slides. The resulting slides can easily appear next to Cher and Roseanne in *People* magazine's annual "Worst Dressed of the Year" issue.

Each color scheme has eight colors, with each color designated for a particular use, as shown in this list:

- **Background color:** Used for the slide background.
- **Text-and-lines color:** Used for any text or drawn lines that appear on the slide, with the exception of the title text (described in this list). It is usually a color that contrasts with the background color. If the background color is dark, the text-and-lines color is generally light, and vice versa.
- **Shadows color:** Used to produce shadow effects for objects drawn on the slide. It is usually a darker version of the background color.
- **Title text color:** Used for the slide's title text. Like the text-and-lines color, the title text color contrasts with the background color so that the text is readable. The title text usually complements the text-and-lines color to provide an evenly balanced effect. (That sounds like something an artist would say, doesn't it?)
- **Fills color:** When you create an object, such as a rectangle or an ellipse, this color is the default fill color to color the object.
- **Accent colors:** The last three colors in the color scheme. They are used for odds and ends that you add to your slide. They may be used to color the bars in a bar chart, for example, or the slices in a pie chart. Two of these accent colors are also used to indicate hyperlinks.

Each slide in your presentation can have its own color scheme. The Slide Master also has a color scheme, used for all slides that don't specify their own deviant color scheme. To ensure that your slides have a uniform look, simply allow them to pick up the color scheme from the Slide Master. If you want one slide to stand out from the other slides in your presentation, assign it a different color scheme.

PowerPoint picks up the initial color scheme for a presentation from the template on which the presentation is based as a part of the template's Slide Master. But each template also includes several alternate color schemes, which are designed to complement the main color scheme for the template. You can change the Master scheme later, but if you apply a new template, the new template's scheme overrides any change you made to the original template's color scheme.

Metaphor alert!

If you want, you can think of the color scheme as a magic artist's palette. The artist squeezes out eight little dabs of paint to use for various elements of a painting: one for the sky, another for the mountains, and still another for the trees. Then the artist paints the picture. So far, nothing special. But here's what makes this palette magic: If the artist sets it down and picks up a different palette (with eight different little dabs of color squeezed out), the entire painting is instantly transformed to the new colors, as though the artist used the second palette all along.

This magic palette enables the artist to make subtle changes to the painting's appearance with little effort. The artist can change the painting from midday to dusk, for example, simply by switching to a palette that has a darker blue for the sky color. Or the artist can change the scene from spring to fall by switching to a palette that has yellow or orange paint rather than green paint for the trees. Or maybe switch to a winter scene by changing the mountain color to white.

PowerPoint color schemes work just like this magic palette. The color scheme gives you eight colors to work with, with each color assigned to a different slide element. If you change the color scheme, the entire presentation changes as well.

If you find a template you like but aren't happy with any of its color schemes, you can create your own. The easiest way is to choose a scheme that's close to the colors you want and then modify the scheme's colors. I present the procedure to do so later in this chapter.

You can override the Master color scheme for an individual slide. You also can change the color for any object to any color in the scheme, or to any other color known to science. You can find step-by-step instructions later in this chapter.

Don't get all in a tizzy about color schemes if you plan to print overhead slides on a black-and-white laser printer. The slides look dazzling on-screen, but all those stunning colors are printed in boring shades of gray.

Using a different color scheme

If you don't like your presentation's color scheme, change it! Here's a simple way:

1. **Switch to Slide view so that you can see what you're doing.**

   Shift+click the Slide View button or use the View➪Master➪Slide Master command to do so.

2. **Choose the Format➪Slide Color Scheme command.**

   The Color Scheme dialog box appears, as shown in Figure 10-1.

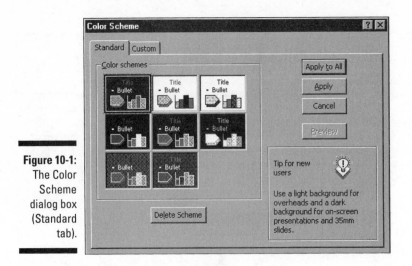

Figure 10-1:
The Color
Scheme
dialog box
(Standard
tab).

3. **Click the color scheme you want to use.**

   The color schemes that appear in the Color Scheme dialog box vary depending on the template that's being used, but most templates have at least three alternate color schemes to choose from.

4. **Click Apply to All.**

   The color scheme is applied to all slides in the presentation. In addition, the color scheme for the Slide and Title Masters is changed so that any new slides added to the presentation assume the new color scheme.

   You're done!

Overriding the color scheme

If you want a few slides to use a different color scheme from the rest of the presentation, you can override the color scheme for just those slides. Follow the steps outlined in the preceding section, with one important exception: Click Apply rather than Apply to All. With this choice, the color scheme you select is applied only to the current slide, not to the entire presentation.

You may want to use this technique to color-code your slides so that your audience has an immediate visual clue to your slide's contents. If a market-analysis presentation frequently shifts back and forth between current data and last year's data, for example, consider using a different color scheme for the slides that depict last year's data. That way, the audience is less likely to become confused.

You can override a slide's color scheme from Slide Sorter view also. This feature is handy if you want to change the color scheme for a single or several consecutive slides at one time. Click the slide you want to change. Then choose the Format➪Slide Color Scheme command, pick a new color scheme, and then click the Apply button. If you want to change several slides in a row, click the first slide you want to change, hold down the Shift key, and click the last slide you want to change in that series. Changing the Color Scheme affects each slide on either end and all the slides in between.

Be careful if you are familiar with older versions of PowerPoint. You can no longer use the previous technique to select individual slides without picking up all the slides in between!

When you change the color scheme for the entire presentation by clicking Apply to All, any slides to which you have applied a custom color scheme are changed as well. For example, suppose you create a presentation using a color scheme that has a deep blue background, and you highlight certain slides by applying an alternate (light blue) color scheme for those slides. You then decide that you'd rather use a maroon background for the bulk of the slides, so you call up the Format➪Slide Color Scheme command, select the new color scheme, and click Apply to All. After you do so, you discover that all slides are changed to the maroon background — even the ones that you had highlighted with the light blue color scheme.

Changing colors in a color scheme

To change one or more of the colors in the current color scheme, follow these steps:

1. **Select the slide whose color scheme you want to change.**

   If you are going to change the color scheme for all slides, you can skip this step. But if you want to change the applied color scheme for just one slide, switch to Slide view and display the slide whose color scheme you want to change.

   To change the color scheme for several slides, switch to Slide Sorter view and hold down the Shift key while you click the slides you want to change.

2. **Choose the Format➪Slide Color Scheme command.**

   The Color Scheme dialog box appears. Refer to Figure 10-1, if you have forgotten what it looks like.

3. **Click the Custom tab to display the color scheme's colors.**

   As you can see in Figure 10-2, choosing the Custom tab displays the eight colors that make up the color scheme.

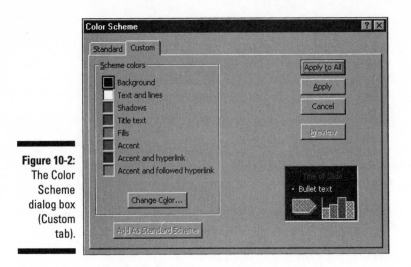

4. Click the color box you want to change.

To change the background color, for example, click the Background color box.

5. Click the Change Color button.

A dialog box similar to the one in Figure 10-3 appears. As you can see, PowerPoint displays what looks like a tie-dyed version of Chinese checkers.

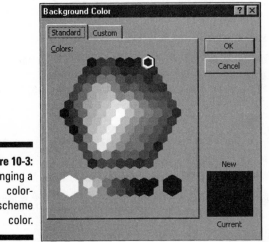

6. **Click the color you want and click OK.**

   If you want white or black or a shade of gray, click one of the color hexagons at the bottom of the dialog box. Otherwise, click one of the colored hexagons. After you click OK, you zip back to the Color Scheme dialog box (refer to Figure 10-2).

7. **Choose Apply or Apply to All.**

   To apply the change to just the slide or slides you chose, click Apply. To apply the change to all the slides in the presentation, click Apply to All.

Be warned that after you deviate from the preselected color scheme combinations, you better have some color sense. If you can't tell chartreuse from lime, you better leave this stuff to the pros.

The color choice dialog box in Figure 10-3 shows 127 popular colors, plus white, black, and shades of gray. If you want to use a color that doesn't appear in the dialog box, click the Custom tab. This step draws forth the custom color controls, shown in Figure 10-4. From this dialog box, you can construct any of the 16 million colors that are theoretically possible with PowerPoint. You need a Ph.D. in physics to figure out how to adjust the Huey, Dewey, and Louie controls, though. Mess around with this stuff if you want, but you're on your own.

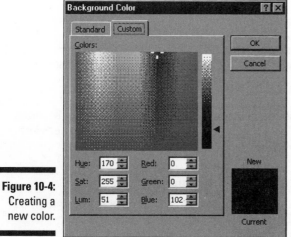

Figure 10-4:
Creating a
new color.

Shading the slide background

You may have noticed that the slide background used in many of the PowerPoint templates is not a solid color. Instead, the color is gradually shaded from top to bottom. This shading creates an interesting visual effect. For example, look at the slide in Figure 10-5. This slide was based on the templates supplied with PowerPoint, but I modified the color scheme and the background shading to achieve the effect that I wanted.

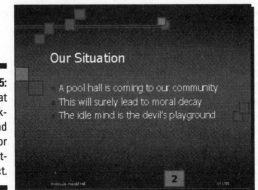

Figure 10-5: A slide that uses background shading for an interesting effect.

Shading for the slide background works much like the color scheme. If you apply it to all slides, the Slide Master is affected as well so that any new slides pick up the new shading. Alternatively, you can apply shading to an individual slide. These steps show you how to shade the slide background:

1. **Choose the slide you want to shade.**

   This step isn't necessary if you want to apply the shading to all slides in the presentation. To shade several slides, switch to Slide Sorter view and hold down the Shift key while you click the slides you want to shade.

2. **Summon the Format➪Background command.**

   The Background dialog box appears. This dialog box includes a drop-down list under the Background fill, as shown in Figure 10-6.

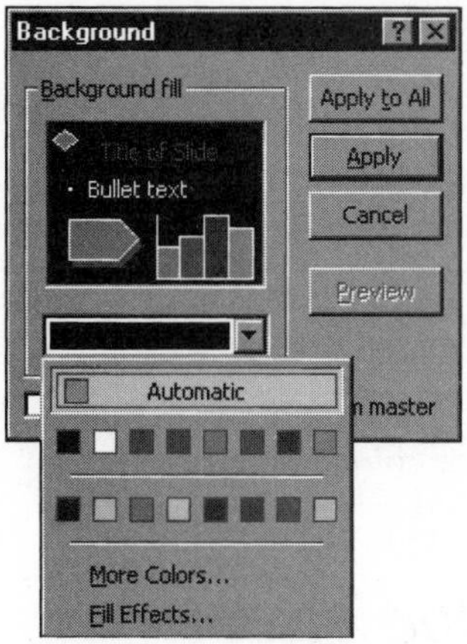

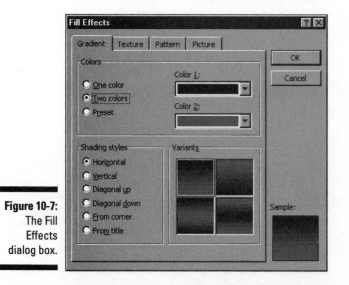

Figure 10-6:
The
Background
dialog box
with
Background
fill drop-
down list
activated.

3. Select Fill Effects from the drop-down list.

The Fill Effects dialog box appears, as shown in Figure 10-7.

Figure 10-7:
The Fill
Effects
dialog box.

4. On the Gradient tab page, choose the shade style you want.

Start by selecting a one-color shade, in which a single color fades to white or black, or a two-color shade, in which one color fades into another. Then select the Shade Style — Horizontal, Vertical, Diagonal up, and so on. Finally, select one of the variants in the Variants area.

Alternatively, you can select one of several preset shadings by picking the Preset option. The preset shading options include Early Sunset, Nightfall, Rainbow, and several other interesting effects.

5. **Click OK to return to the Background dialog box and then click Apply or Apply to all.**

   Clicking the Apply button applies the shading to just the slide or slides you chose (in Step 1). Clicking Apply to all applies the shading to all slides.

   You're done! Admire your work. Play with it some more if you don't like it.

When you apply a template, any background shading specified for the template's Masters is applied along with the color scheme.

Using other background effects

Besides gradient fills, the Format⇨Background command provides several other types of interesting background effects. All these effects — Texture, Pattern, and Picture — are accessed via the tabs in the Fill Effects dialog box, which was shown back in Figure 10-7.

If you select the Texture tab, the dialog box shown in Figure 10-8 appears. Here you can choose one of several textures to give your presentation that polished Formica look.

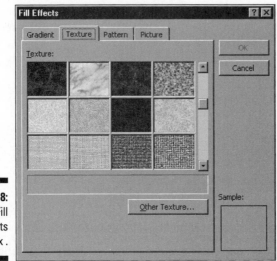

Figure 10-8:
The Fill
Effects
dialog box .

If you select the Pattern tab, you see the dialog box shown in Figure 10-9. Here you can choose from any of 48 different patterns using your choice of foreground and background colors.

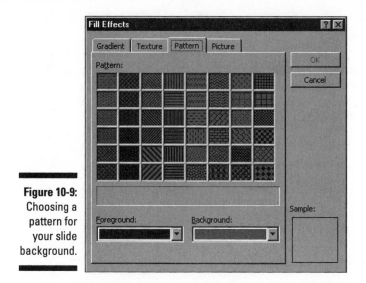

Figure 10-9:
Choosing a
pattern for
your slide
background.

If you click the Picture tab and then click the Select Picture button, the dialog box shown in Figure 10-10 appears. This dialog box allows you to select a picture to be used as a background for your slides. You may have to do some searching to find the image you want.

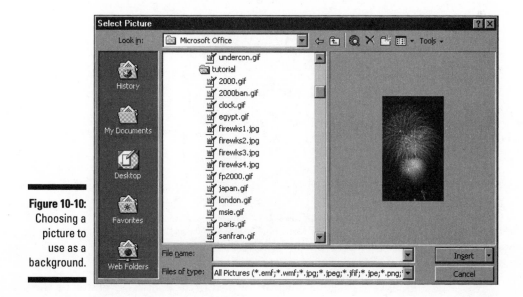

Figure 10-10:
Choosing a
picture to
use as a
background.

Coloring Text and Objects

Normally, the color scheme you choose for a slide determines the color of the various objects on the slide. If the text color is yellow, for example, all text on the slide is yellow (except the title text, which is controlled by the color scheme's Title Text color). Similarly, if the fill color is orange, any filled objects on the slide are orange.

If you change the colors in the color scheme, all the objects on the slide that follow the scheme are affected. But what if you want to change the color of just one object without changing the scheme or affecting other similar objects on the slide? No problemo. PowerPoint enables you to override the scheme color for any object on a slide. The following sections explain how.

Applying color to text

To change the color of a text object, follow these steps:

1. **Highlight the text whose color you want to change.**

2. **Summon the Format⇨Font command.**

   The Font dialog box appears. Click the Color control, and a cute little Color menu appears (see Figure 10-11).

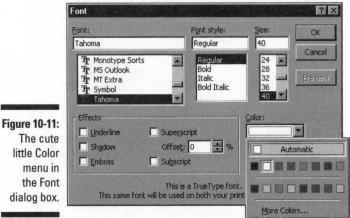

Figure 10-11: The cute little Color menu in the Font dialog box.

Alternatively, click the down arrow next to the Font Color button on the Drawing toolbar. The same cute little Color menu appears directly under the button.

3. **Click the color you like from the cute little Color menu.**

   The eight colors in the top row of the Color menu are the colors from the slide's color scheme. The next row shows colors that mysteriously seem to coordinate with any clip art or other colorful elements in your presentation. Choose one of these colors if you want a warm fuzzy feeling that the colors coordinate. If you're bold and trust your color sense, continue to Step 4.

4. **Click <u>M</u>ore Colors and choose a color you like.**

   The same dialog box you used to handpick colors for the color scheme appears (refer to Figure 10-3). You can choose one of the many sensible colors displayed therein, or you can toss caution to the wind, put on your painting clothes, and click the Custom tab to build your own color by setting the Huey, Louie, and Dewey buttons (refer to Figure 10-4).

5. **OK yourself back home.**

   You may have to click OK several times to fully unwind yourself.

Good news! If you use the More Colors option to assign a color, PowerPoint automatically adds to the Color menu the color you choose. You can distinguish your colors from the color scheme colors because your custom colors are always in the bottom line of eight complementary colors.

Changing an objects fill or line color

When you draw an object such as a rectangle or an ellipse, PowerPoint fills in the object with the color scheme's fill color and draws the object's outline using the color scheme's line color. You can change either of these colors by using the Fill Color and Line Color buttons on the Drawing toolbar. Just follow these steps:

1. **Select the object whose fill color you want to change.**

2. **To change the object's fill color, click the down arrow next to the Fill Color button and choose a color from the menu that appears.**

3. **To change the object's line color, click the down arrow next to the Line Color button and choose a color from the menu that appears.**

   That's all!

To create a transparent object — that is, an object that has no fill color, click the Fill Color button and choose No Fill. To create an object that has no outline, click the Line Color button and choose No Line.

TIP

The Fill Color button includes a Fill Effects command that lets you apply gradient fills, patterns, textures, or pictures to any object. The selections for these features are the same as shown in Figures 10-7 through 10-10.

Creating a semi-transparent object

You can create a ghostly semi-transparent fill by following these steps:

1. **Choose the object that you want to give a ghostly appearance.**

2. **Choose the Format⇨Colors and Lines command.**

   The Format AutoShape dialog box appears, as shown in Figure 10-12.

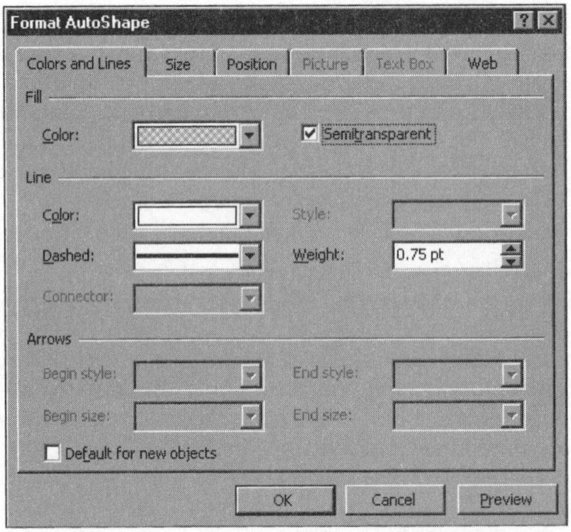

Figure 10-12:
The Format AutoShape dialog box.

3. **Click the Semitransparent check box.**

4. **Click OK.**

Note that this dialog box also lets you control the fill options for the object, plus it lets you set the line style for the border that's drawn around the object (if any).

Copying color from an existing object

If you want to force one object to adopt the color of another object, you can use a fancy tool called the *Format Painter*. It sucks up the formatting of one object and then spits it out onto another object at your command. It's a bit messy, but it gets the job done. (You should see it eat.)

To use the Format Painter, follow these steps:

1. **Choose the object whose color you like.**

   You can select a bit of text or an entire object.

2. **Click the Format Painter button (shown in the margin) on the Standard toolbar.**

   This step sucks up the good color.

3. **Click the object whose color you don't like.**

   This step spits out the desirable color onto the object.

In addition to the fill color, the Format Painter also picks up other object attributes, such as shading, textures, optional trim package, and aluminum alloy hubcaps.

If you want to apply one object's format to several objects, select the object whose color you like and then double-click the Format Painter. Now you can click as many objects as you want to apply the first object's format to. When you're done, press the Esc key.

Chapter 11

Using Clip Art

● ●

In This Chapter

▶ Using free pictures

▶ Finding a picture you like

▶ Moving, sizing, and stretching pictures

▶ Adding a box, shaded background, or shadow to a picture

▶ Editing a clip art picture

▶ Inserting clips from the Internet

● ●

Face it: Most of us are not born with even an ounce of artistic ability. Some day, soon we hope, those genetic researchers combing through the billions and billions of genes strung out on those twisty DNA helixes will discover The Artist Gene. Then, in spite of protests from the DaVincis and Monets among us (who fear that their NEA grants will be threatened), doctors will splice the little bugger into our own DNA strands so that we all can be artists. Of course, this procedure will not be without its side effects: Some will develop an insatiable craving for croissants, and others will inexplicably develop French accents and whack off their ears. But artists we shall be.

Until then, we have to rely on clip art.

Free Pictures!

Are you sitting down? Whether you buy PowerPoint 2000 by itself or get it as a part of Microsoft Office, you also get a collection of thousands of pictures, sound, and motion clips that you can pop directly into your presentations. The PowerPoint clip art pictures are managed by a program called the Clip Gallery. This nifty little program keeps track of clip art, sound, and motion files spread out all over your hard disk and spares you the unpleasant chore of rummaging through your directories to look for that picture of Elvis you know that you have somewhere. Clip Gallery also takes the guesswork out of using clip art: Rather than choose a filename like ELVISFAT.PCX and hope that it's the one you remembered, you can see the clip art before you add it to your presentation.

Clip Gallery organizes your clip art files into categories, such as Academic, Flags, and Gestures. This organization makes it easy to search through the clip art pictures, sound, or motion clips that come with PowerPoint 2000 and find just the right one. (Wouldn't it be great if the Metropolitan Museum of Art used similar categories?)

You also can add your own pictures to Clip Gallery. You may whip out a detailed replica of the Mona Lisa in Windows Paintbrush, for example, and then toss it into Clip Gallery. And now with all the motion and sound clip possibilities, you can add your own recordings using your Windows 95 or 98 sound recorder found in Accessories, or you can download and use video clips from any Web site with video clips.

Don't overdo the special effects. One surefire way to guarantee an amateurish look to your presentation is to load it down with three clip art pictures on every slide that all chime or go "zip" or "boing." Judicious use is much more effective.

The new version of Clip Gallery that comes with PowerPoint 2000 can handle digitized pictures, sounds, and motion clips as well as clip art. In fact, that's precisely why Microsoft has changed the name of this handy little program. It used to be called *Clip Art Gallery,* but for PowerPoint 97, and now again in 2000, Microsoft uses the name *Clip Gallery* to emphasize that the program handles more than just clip art files. However, in this chapter, I focus solely on clip art. In Chapter 16, I tackle sound and motion clips.

Dropping In Some Clip Art

These steps show you how to drop clip art into your presentation:

1. **Move to the slide on which you want to plaster the clip art.**

   If you want the same clip art picture to appear on every slide, move to Slide Master view by using the View⇨Master⇨Slide Master command (or Shift+click the Slide View button).

2. **Choose the Insert⇨Picture⇨Clip Art command.**

   Sorry, PowerPoint offers no shortcut key for this command. If you like the mouse, though, you can click the Insert Clip Art button instead (shown in the margin).

Where you place the cursor before you choose the Insert⇨Picture⇨ Clip Art command doesn't matter. PowerPoint sticks the clip art picture right smack dab in the middle of the slide anyway. The picture is probably way too big, so you have to move and shrink it.

3. Behold the Clip Gallery in all its splendor.

After a brief moment's hesitation, the Clip Gallery pops up. Figure 11-1 shows what the gallery looks like.

4. Choose the clip art picture you want.

To find the picture you want, first choose the clip art category that contains the picture (if you're not sure, make your best guess). When you first pop up the Clip Gallery, All Categories is the default; this category shows all the clip art pictures in your collection. To narrow your search, scroll through the Categories list until you find the category you want and then click it.

Next, find the specific picture you want. Clip Gallery can show anywhere from 6 to 60 some-odd pictures at once, depending on how big your window is. You can display other pictures from the same category by scrolling through the pictures. When the picture you want comes into view, click it. Notice that when you click it, a cute little floating toolbar that looks like a comic-strip character balloon appears to give you some choices. (See how user-friendly Bill's software is!) You can choose to Insert Clip, Preview Clip, Add Clip to Favorites or Other Category, or Find Similar Clips.

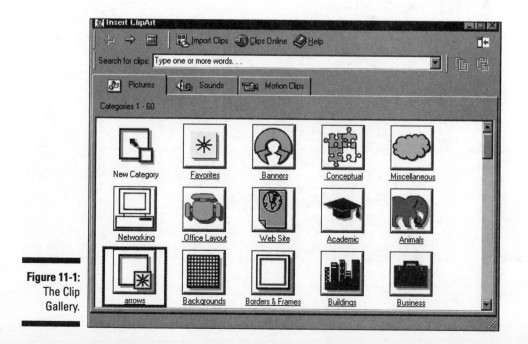

Figure 11-1:
The Clip
Gallery.

You may have noticed, if you were familiar with PowerPoint 97 or an earlier version, that the Clip Art dialog box has gotten cuter and more Web-friendly. In fact, Microsoft, in its endeavor to be totally Internet savvy and compatible, has added Web-page-looking stuff in all of its new software applications. If you're running Windows 98 as your operating system, you may have noticed that you get to make your desktop look like a Web page, and so on. The same is true here, with a clip art dialog box that features back, forward, and home commands, as well as an opportunity for you to put favorite clips into a favorite file.

5. **Click the Insert Clip button to insert the picture.**

   Now, minimize or close the Clip Gallery, and you see that your clip is on top of your slide, ready to be formatted, as shown in Figure 11-2.

You may have noticed after you inserted clip art that the Clip Gallery dialog box just sits there. The double-click feature of Office 97 Clip Gallery is gone. This new stay-there-until-you-move-it feature is supposed to be handier if you are adding more than one clip at a time. It's not a glitch. Just minimize it, and you are ready to go.

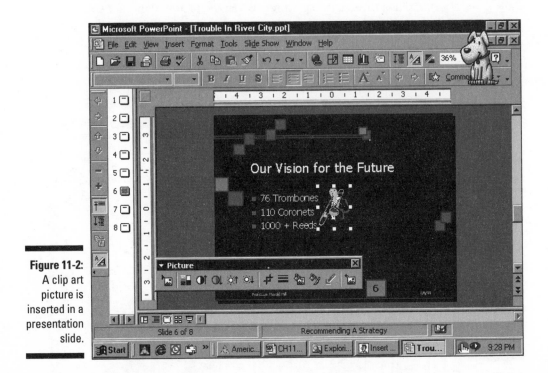

Figure 11-2: A clip art picture is inserted in a presentation slide.

You can see that PowerPoint sticks the picture right in the middle of the slide, which is probably not where you want it. And it may be too big or too small. You have to wrestle with the picture to get it just the way you want it. See the section "Moving, Sizing, and Stretching Clip Art" later in this chapter for instructions for forcing the picture into compliance.

If you can't find the clip art picture you're looking for, use the Search for clips text box in the Clip Gallery dialog box. This step enables you to search for clip art based on a keyword. For example, you can look for all pictures that have the word *band* in their description. Press Enter, and your clip art appears.

Another way to search, new in PowerPoint 2000, is to click your mouse on any clip and then click the Find Similar Clips button. You then see an interesting dialog box that lets you select the clips you would like to search for based on Artistic Style, Color & Shape, or keywords. The underlined keywords are hyperlinked searches for the specific underlined category. Note another cool way the Web technology comes into play.

Notice the tabs across the Clip Gallery dialog box. These tabs let you insert different types of clips besides pictures, such as sounds and motion clips. In PowerPoint 97, a distinction was made between pictures and clip art. This time around, in PowerPoint 2000, Bill has decided that they are related enough to be combined. If you want a photograph that's included in PowerPoint 2000, click the category Photographs. What, you ask, is the difference between clip art and pictures? That's a good question. The terms seem almost interchangeable. In Clip Gallery terminology, clip art refers to line drawings, whereas picture refers to digitized photographs, in which the image is made up of thousands of tiny dots. Microsoft thought that it was a distinction that no longer was needed with the added emphasis on sound, motion clips, and high-tech stuff like that.

The procedure for inserting a picture, sound, or video is the same as for inserting clip art, except that you must select the appropriate tab in the Clip Gallery dialog box to display the pictures, sounds, or videos that are available.

Moving, Sizing, and Stretching Clip Art

Because PowerPoint inserts clip art right in the middle of the slide, you undoubtedly want to move the clip art to a more convenient location. You probably also want to change its size if it is too big or too small.

Follow these steps to force your inserted clip art into full compliance:

1. **Click the picture and drag it wherever you want.**

   You don't have to worry about clicking exactly the edge of the picture or one of its lines; just click anywhere in the picture and drag it around.

2. **Notice the eight handles. Drag one of them to resize the picture.**

   Flip back to Figure 11-2 and notice the eight handles that surround the clip art. You can click and drag any of these handles to adjust the size of the picture. When you click one of the corner handles, the proportion of the picture stays the same as you change its size. When you drag one of the edge handles (top, bottom, left, or right) to change the size of the picture in just one dimension, you distort the picture's outlook as you go.

When you resize a picture, the picture changes its position on the slide. As a result, you can count on moving it after you resize it. If you hold down the Ctrl key while dragging a handle, however, the picture becomes anchored at its center point as you resize it. Therefore, its position is unchanged, and you probably don't have to move it.

Stretching a clip art picture by dragging one of the edge handles can dramatically change the picture's appearance. To illustrate, Figure 11-3 shows how the same clip art picture can resemble both Arnold Schwarzenegger *and* Danny DeVito. I just stretched one copy of the picture vertically to make it tall and stretched the other copy horizontally to make it, er, stout.

Figure 11-3: Twins.

Boxing, Shading, and Shadowing a Picture

PowerPoint enables you to draw attention to a clip art picture by drawing a box around it, shading its background, or adding a shadow. Figure 11-4 shows what these embellishments can look like.

Our Vision for the Future

- 76 Trombones
- 110 Coronets
- 1000 + Reeds

Figure 11-4:
Boxing in a
picture.

The following steps show you how to use these features:

1. **Click the picture you want to encase.**

   The Picture toolbar appears when you select the picture.

2. **Click the Format Picture button (shown in the margin) in the Picture toolbar.**

   This summons the Format Picture dialog box shown in Figure 11-5.

   Did you notice that one of the tabs for the Format picture dialog box is different than it used to be in PowerPoint 97? Very good. Web has been added as a tab, allowing you to make special picture formatting choices for Web pages. More about this later in Chapter 20.

3. **Use the Format Picture dialog box controls to draw a box around the picture or to shade its background.**

   Choose a fill color from the Fill Color drop-down list box to give the picture a background color. Then choose a color from the Line Color drop-down list box to draw a line around the picture. You also can choose the line style and set up dashed lines. Click OK to draw the box.

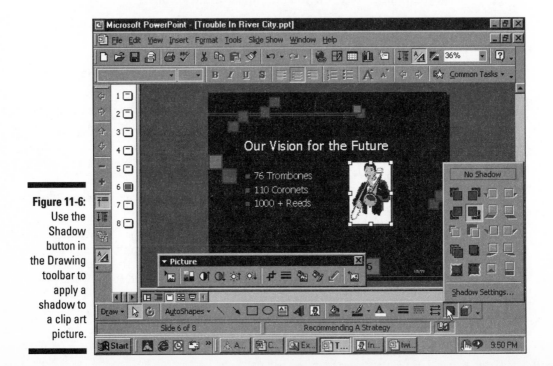

Figure 11-5:
The Format
Picture
dialog box.

4. **To add a shadow, click the Shadow button in the Drawing toolbar and select a shadow style.**

   Clicking the Shadow button brings up a menu of shadow styles, as shown in Figure 11-6. Pick the style you want by clicking the style in this menu.

Figure 11-6:
Use the
Shadow
button in
the Drawing
toolbar to
apply a
shadow to
a clip art
picture.

TIP

If you apply a shadow to a picture to which you have not applied a fill color, the shadow will be applied to the picture itself, as shown in the woman on the right in Figure 11-7. In this slide, both clip art pictures have a shadow. The one on the left also has a fill color and border, but the one on the right does not.

The Shadows Know

Figure 11-7:
The
Shadows
know.

TIP

You can also apply a shadow by choosing Shadow Settings from the Shadow menu that appears when you click the Shadow button. This brings up a Shadow toolbar that lets you control the size, position, and color of the shadow.

Editing a Clip Art Picture

Sometimes one of the clip art pictures supplied with PowerPoint is close but not exactly what you want. In that case, you can insert the picture and then edit it to make whatever changes are needed. For example, Figure 11-8 shows two versions of the same clip art picture. The original picture is on the left, and the one on the right has been edited by a misguided team of earthquake retrofitters.

You can't directly edit a clip art picture. Instead, you must first convert the picture to an equivalent bunch of PowerPoint shape objects. Then you can individually select and edit the objects using the shape-editing tools described in Chapter 12.

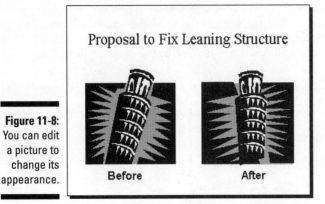

These steps tell how to edit a clip art picture:

1. **To display the shortcut menu, right-click the picture you want to edit and then choose the Grouping⇨Ungroup command.**

   PowerPoint displays the warning message shown in Figure 11-9, indicating that you are about to convert a clip art picture to a PowerPoint drawing so that you can edit it. If you do indeed want to convert the picture to PowerPoint shape objects that you can edit, click Yes.

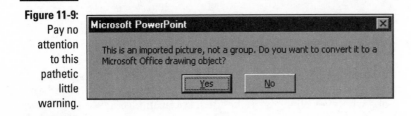

2. **Now edit the picture.**

   The clip art picture is converted to an equivalent group of PowerPoint shape objects, so you can use the PowerPoint shape-editing tools to change their appearance. You can drag any of the control handles to reshape an object, or you can change colors or add new stuff to the picture. See Chapter 12 for the details on editing PowerPoint shape objects.

Don't read this groupie stuff

✔ What is all this talk of *grouping* and *ungrouping?* These common drawing terms are explained in more detail in Chapter 12. For now, consider how you can draw a simple picture of a face. You may start with a circle for the head and then add ellipses for the eyes, nose, and mouth. By the time you finish, you have five ellipses objects.

✔ The only problem is, suppose that you want to move the face you just drew to the other side of the slide. If you just clicked and dragged it, odds are that you would move only the nose or one of the eyes. To move the whole thing, you have to select all five ellipses.

✔ Wouldn't it be great if you could treat all five ellipses as a single object? That's what *grouping* is all about. When you group objects, they are treated as if they were a single object. When you click any one of the grouped objects, you click them all. Move one, and they all move. Delete one, and they all vanish.

✔ What happens if, after grouping the five face ellipses, you discover that you made the nose too big? You have to *ungroup* them so that they become five separate objects again. Then you can select and resize just the nose.

✔ Most complex drawings use grouping. PowerPoint 2000 clip art pictures are no exception. That's why you have to ungroup them before you can edit them. Clip art pictures have the added characteristic that when you ungroup a clip art picture, you sever its connection to the Clip Gallery. The picture is no longer a Clip Gallery object but is now merely a bunch of PowerPoint rectangles, ellipses, and free-form shapes.

✔ Oops, this is way too much stuff about grouping for the clip art chapter. Maybe you should skip ahead to Chapter 12 if you're really this interested.

After you have ungrouped and edited a picture, you may want to regroup it. You're much less likely to pull the nose off someone's face if the face is a group rather than a bunch of ungrouped ellipse objects.

When you convert a picture to PowerPoint objects, you're actually placing a copy of the Clip Gallery picture in your presentation. Any changes that you make to the picture are reflected only in your presentation; the original version of the clip art picture is unaffected.

Colorizing a Clip Art Picture

After inserting a clip art picture into your presentation, you may find that the colors used in the clip art clash with the colors you've chosen for the presentation's color scheme. Never fear! PowerPoint allows you to selectively change the colors used in a clip art picture. Just follow these steps:

1. **Select the picture you want to colorize and then click the Recolor Picture button (shown in the margin) from the Picture toolbar.**

   The Recolor Picture dialog box appears, as shown in Figure 11-10.

Figure 11-10:
For color
that's out of
this world!

2. **In the list of Original colors, click the original color you want to change.**

   For example, to change the color of the man's shirt, click the green that matches his shirt.

3. **From the drop-down list adjacent to the original color you chose, select a new color to replace the chosen color.**

   The drop-down list displays a standard color menu, with the colors from the color scheme and an Other Color command that brings up a dialog box that allows you to choose a custom color.

   If you want to change the fill color but leave the line color unchanged, click the Fills option button.

4. **Repeat Steps 2 and 3 for any other colors you want to change.**

5. **Click OK when you're done.**

Getting Clip Art from the Internet

As if the 4,000 or so pictures that come on the PowerPoint 2000 CD aren't enough, Microsoft also maintains a clip library on the Internet that you can access from Clip Gallery. If you have access to the Internet, click the Clips Online button on the Clip Gallery dialog box (it's on the top of the dialog box and looks like the earth with clips sort of going into orbit). This button connects you to the Internet, fires up Internet Explorer, the Microsoft software for accessing the World Wide Web, and displays the Microsoft clip art page, called Clip Gallery Live (see Figure 11-11).

Clip Gallery Live lets you browse through clip art pictures by category, or you can search for key words such as *Chicken* or *Athlete.*

To download a clip art picture from the Internet, click the filename that appears beneath the picture that you want to download. The picture will be copied to your computer and added to Clip Gallery.

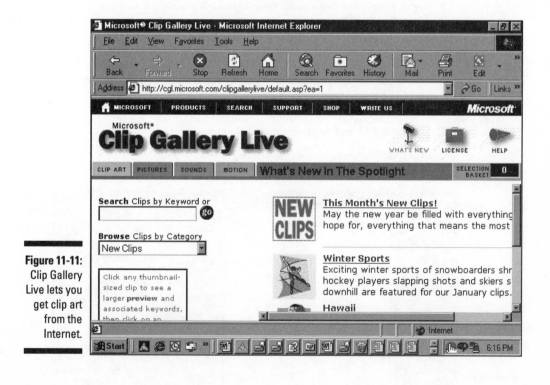

Figure 11-11: Clip Gallery Live lets you get clip art from the Internet.

Inserting Pictures without Using Clip Gallery

PowerPoint also enables you to insert pictures directly into your document without using Clip Gallery. Use this technique to insert pictures that aren't a part of the clip art collection that comes with PowerPoint. These steps show you how:

1. **Move to the slide on which you want to splash the clip art.**

   If you want the clip art to show up on every slide, conjure up Slide Master view with the View⇨Master⇨Slide Master command (or Shift+click the Slide View button).

2. **Choose the Insert⇨Picture⇨From File command.**

   Greet the Insert Picture dialog box, shown in Figure 11-12, with a smile.

3. **Dig through the bottom of your disk drive until you find the file you want.**

   It's easy to find files with the new Web-like dialog box features.

   The picture you want can be anywhere. Fortunately, the Insert Picture dialog box has all the controls you need to search high and low until you find the file. Just click the icons at the left-hand side of the box or click the Look In text box, and you are halfway there.

4. **Click the file and then click Insert.**

   You're done!

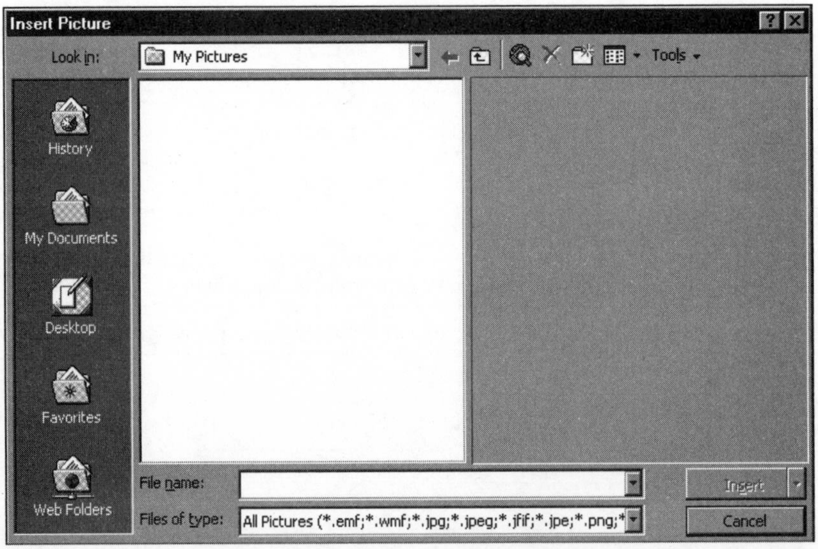

Figure 11-12: The Insert Picture dialog box.

You also can paste a picture directly into PowerPoint by way of the Clipboard. Anything you can copy to the Clipboard you can paste into PowerPoint. For example, you can doodle a sketch in Paintbrush, copy it, and then zap over to PowerPoint and paste it. Voilà — instant picture!

If you want to narrow your search to files of a particular type, use the Files of Type drop-down list box. PowerPoint comes with *filters* that can convert as many as 20 different types of picture files to PowerPoint. Table 11-1 lists the formats you're most likely to use.

If the file type you want doesn't show up in the Files of Type drop-down list box, you may not have installed all the graphics filters when you installed PowerPoint 2000. Run the PowerPoint Setup program and see whether the graphics filter you want is available. Better yet, bribe your local computer guru to do this for you. This is definitely Guru Stuff.

Table 11-1	Formats for Picture Files
Format	*What It Is*
BMP	Garden variety Windows bitmap file, used by Paintbrush and many other programs
CDR	CorelDRAW!, a popular, upper-crust drawing program
CGM	Computer Graphics Metafiles
DIB	Device Independent Bitmap files, a special format used by some Windows programs
DRW	Micrografx Designer or Micrografx Draw, two popular ooh-aah drawing programs
DXF	AutoCAD, a popular drafting program
EMF	Yet another type of Windows MetaFile format
EPS	Encapsulated PostScript, a format used by some high-end drawing programs
GIF	Graphics Interchange Format, commonly found on CompuServeGL HP Graphics Language files
HGL	Hewlett Packard Graphics Language files
JPG	JPEG files, a popular format for exchanging images on the Internet
PCD	Kodak's Photo CD format
PCT	Macintosh PICT files

(continued)

Table 11-1 *(continued)*

Format	What It Is
PCX	A variant type of bitmap file, also used by Paintbrush and other programs
PLT	Another type of Hewlett Packard Graphics Language file
PNG	Portable Network Graphics files
RLE	Another type of Windows bitmap
TGA	Targa files
TIF	Tagged Image Format file; another bitmap file format, used by highbrow drawing programs, scanners, and fax programs
WMF	Windows MetaFile, a format that many programs recognize
WPG	DrawPerfect, WordPerfect's artistic sibling

If you insert a picture by using the Insert⇨Picture⇨From command and then double-click the picture, PowerPoint throws you into the program that was used to create the file, where you can edit it any way you want. You also can ungroup the picture by using the Draw⇨Ungroup command to convert the picture to PowerPoint objects, which you can edit directly in PowerPoint.

Chapter 12

Drawing on Your Slides

● ●

In This Chapter

▶ Using the PowerPoint drawing tools

▶ Drawing lines, rectangles, and circles

▶ Using predefined AutoShapes

▶ Drawing fancier shapes such as polygons or curved lines

▶ Changing colors and line types

▶ Creating 3-D objects

▶ Flipping and rotating objects

▶ Understanding layers and groups

▶ Lining things up and spacing them out

● ●

C him-chiminey, chim-chiminey, chim-chim cheroo, I draws what I likes and I likes what I drew. . . .

Art time! Everybody get your crayons and glue and don an old paint shirt. You're going to cut out some simple shapes and paste them on your PowerPoint slides so that people will either think that you are a wonderful artist or scoff at you for not using clip art.

This chapter covers the drawing features of PowerPoint. One of the best things about PowerPoint 2000 is the cool drawing tools. Previous to PowerPoint 97, versions of the program let you create rudimentary drawings, but if you wanted to create fancy drawings, you had to use a separate drawing program. But since PowerPoint 97, the drawing tools that are available in PowerPoint are sufficient for all but the most sophisticated aspiring artists among us.

Some General Drawing Tips

Before getting into the specifics of using each PowerPoint drawing tool, this section describes a handful of general tips for drawing pictures.

Zoom in

When you work with the PowerPoint drawing tools, you may want to increase the zoom factor so that you can draw more accurately. I often work at 200, 300, or even 400 percent when I'm drawing. To change the zoom factor, click the down arrow next to the Zoom Control button (near the right side of the Standard toolbar) and choose a zoom factor from the list. Or you can click the zoom factor, type a new zoom percentage, and press Enter.

Before you change the zoom factor to edit an object, choose the object that you want to edit. That way, PowerPoint zooms in on that area of the slide. If you don't choose an object before you zoom in, you may need to scroll around to find the right location.

Display the ruler

If you want to be precise about lining up objects on the slide, consider activating the ruler. If you can't see the ruler on-screen already, choose View⇨Ruler to display it. Figure 12-1 shows how PowerPoint looks when you've activated the ruler.

When you work with drawing objects, PowerPoint formats the ruler so that zero is at the middle of the slide. When you edit a text object, the ruler changes to a text ruler that measures from the margins and indicates tab positions.

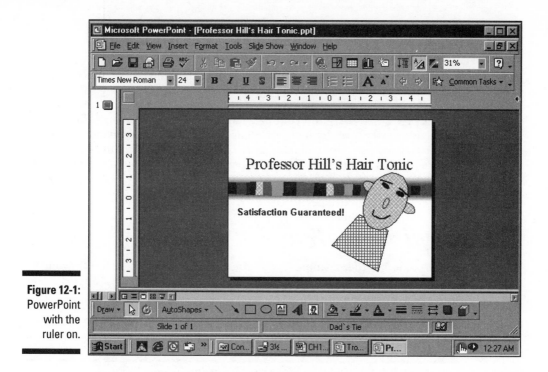

Figure 12-1:
PowerPoint
with the
ruler on.

Stick to the color scheme

You can assign individual colors to each object that you draw, but the point of the PowerPoint color schemes is to talk you out of doing that. If possible, let solid objects default to the color scheme's fill color. The beauty of doing this is that if you change the color scheme later on, the fill color for objects changes to reflect the new fill color. But after you change the fill color, the object ignores any change to the slide's color scheme.

If you must assign a separate color to an object, choose one of the eight colors that are a part of the color scheme. (If you decide to arbitrarily choose one of PowerPoint's 64 million colors for an object, a good lawyer may be able to get you off by using the "irresistible urge" defense.)

Save frequently

Drawing is tedious work. You don't want to spend two hours working on a particularly important drawing only to lose it all just because a comet strikes your building or an errant Scud lands in your backyard. You can prevent catastrophic loss from incidents such as these by pressing Ctrl+S, or clicking the Save button with your mouse, frequently as you work. And always wear protective eyewear.

Don't forget Ctrl+Z

Ctrl+Z is the most important key in any Windows 98 program, and PowerPoint is no exception. Always remember that you're never more than one keystroke away from erasing a boo-boo. If you do something silly — like forgetting to group a complex picture before trying to move it — you can always press Ctrl+Z to undo your last action. Ctrl+Z is my favorite and most frequently used PowerPoint key combination. (For left-handed mouse users, Alt+Backspace does the same thing.) And for those not ready to climb on a chair shrieking at the first sign of a mouse, try the handy Undo button on the Formatting toolbar.

The Drawing Toolbar

PowerPoint provides a whole row of drawing tools, located on the Drawing toolbar. If the Drawing toolbar has disappeared, you can make it appear again by choosing View⇨Toolbars and checking the Drawing check box.

Table 12-1 shows you what each drawing tool does.

Table 12-1	Basic Drawing Tools	
Drawing Tool	**What It's Called**	**What It Does**
Draw ▾	Draw menu	Displays a menu of drawing commands.
▸	Select Objects button	Not really a drawing tool, but rather the generic mouse pointer used to choose objects.
↻	Free Rotate button	When you click here, the Rotate button leaps from the water to make its escape into the open sea while Michael Jackson sings an inspiring song.

Drawing Tool	*What It's Called*	*What It Does*
AutoShapes ▾	AutoShapes button	Pops up the AutoShapes menu, which contains a bevy of shapes that you can draw, including fancy lines, arrows, crosses, flowchart symbols, stars, and more!
	Line button	Draws a line.
	Arrow button	Draws an arrow.
	Rectangle button	Draws a rectangle. To make a perfect square, hold down the Shift key while you draw.
	Oval button	Draws circles and ovals. To create a perfect circle, hold down the Shift key while you draw.
	Text box button	Adds a text object.
	Insert WordArt button	Summons forth WordArt, which lets you create all sorts of fancy text effects.
	Insert Clip Art button	Summons the Clip Gallery dialog box.
	Fill Color button	Sets the color used to fill solid objects such as circles and ellipses as well as AutoShapes.
	Line Color button	Sets the color used to draw lines, including lines around rectangles, ellipses, and AutoShapes.
	Font Color button	Sets the color used for text.

Originally, in Office 97, Microsoft couldn't decide whether the newfangled Drawing toolbar should contain buttons or menus, so it threw in some of both. The Draw and AutoShapes buttons are actually menus that behave just like menus on a normal menu bar: Click them to reveal a menu of choices or use the Alt key shortcuts to activate them (Alt+R activates the Draw menu, and Alt+U activates the AutoShapes menu).

Drawing Simple Text Objects

To draw an object on a slide, you just click the button that represents the object that you want to draw and then use the mouse to draw the object on the slide. Well, it's not always as simple as that. You find detailed instructions for drawing with the more important tools in the following sections. But first, I want to give you some pointers to keep in mind:

- Before you draw an object, move to the slide on which you want to draw the object. If you want the object to appear on every slide in the presentation, display the Slide Master by choosing View⇨Master⇨Slide Master or Shift+clicking the Slide View button on the status bar.

- PowerPoint has two types of objects: shapes, such as circles, rectangles, and crosses; and lines and arcs. PowerPoint enables you to add text to any shape object, but you can't add text to a line or arc object.

- Made a mistake? You can delete the object that you just drew by pressing the Delete key; then try drawing the object again. Or you can change its size or stretch it by clicking it and dragging its love handles.

- Table 12-2 summarizes some handy shortcuts that you can use while drawing. The last shortcut needs a bit of explanation. If you click a drawing tool button once (such as the rectangle or ellipse button), the mouse cursor reverts to an arrow after you draw an object. To draw another object, you must click a drawing tool button again. If you know in advance that you want to draw more than one object of the same type, double-click the drawing tool button. Then you can keep drawing objects of the selected type till who laid the rails. To stop drawing, click the Selection tool button (the arrow at the top of the Drawing toolbar).

- I have no idea what the expression "till who laid the rails" means. One of the residents of River City (the mayor, I believe) used it in *The Music Man,* and I've liked it ever since.

Table 12-2	Drawing Shortcuts
Shortcut	*What It Does*
Shift	Hold down the Shift key to force lines to be horizontal or vertical, to force arcs and ellipses to be true circles, to force rectangles to be squares, or to draw other regular shapes.
Ctrl	Hold down the Ctrl key to draw objects from the center rather than from end to end.
Ctrl+Shift	Hold down these two keys to draw from the center and to enforce squareness or circleness.
Double-click	Double-click any drawing button on the Drawing toolbar if you want to draw several objects of the same type.

Drawing straight lines

You use the Line button to draw straight lines on your slides. Here's the procedure:

1. **Click the Line button (shown in the margin).**

2. **Point to where you want the line to start.**

3. **Click and drag the mouse cursor to where you want the line to end.**

4. **Release the mouse button when you reach your destination.**

Previous versions of PowerPoint (prior to PowerPoint 97) also included an Arc button that you could use to draw curved lines. Since PowerPoint 97, the Arc button has been removed. In its place, Microsoft added a curved line as an AutoShapes type. Thus, you must use the AutoShapes tool to draw a curved line. See the section "Using AutoShapes" later in this chapter for details.

You can use the Format➪Colors and Lines command to change the line color and other features (thickness, dashes, and arrowheads) for a line or arc object. Or you can click the Line Style button (in the margin) or Line Color button on the Drawing toolbar (see Table 12-1) to change these attributes.

After you have drawn a line, you can adjust it by clicking it and then dragging the handles that appear on each end of the line.

Remember that you can force a line to be perfectly horizontal or vertical by holding down the Shift key while you draw.

Drawing rectangles, squares, ovals, and circles

To draw a rectangle, follow these steps:

1. **Click the Rectangle button (shown in the margin).**

2. **Point to where you want one corner of the rectangle to be positioned.**

3. **Click the mouse button and drag to where you want the opposite corner of the rectangle to be positioned.**

4. **Release the mouse button.**

The steps for drawing an oval are the same as the steps for drawing a rectangle except that you click the Oval button (shown in the margin) rather than the Rectangle button. To draw a square or perfectly round circle, hold down the Shift key while you draw.

You can use the Format➪Colors and Lines command to change the fill color or the line style for a rectangle or oval object. You also can use the Line Style button or the Fill Color button on the Drawing toolbar.

To apply a shadow, use the Shadow button. See the section "Applying a Shadow" later in this chapter for more information.

You can adjust the size or shape of a rectangle or circle by clicking it and dragging any of its love handles.

Using AutoShapes

Rectangles and circles aren't the only two shapes PowerPoint can draw automatically. When you click the AutoShapes button on the Drawing toolbar, a whole menu of AutoShapes appears. These AutoShapes make it easy to draw common shapes such as pentagons, stars, and flowchart symbols.

The AutoShapes menu organizes AutoShapes into the following categories:

✔ **Lines:** Straight lines, curved lines, lines with arrowheads, scribbly lines, and freeform shapes that can become polygons if you wish. The freeform AutoShape is useful enough to merit its own section, "Drawing a Polygon or Freeform shape," which immediately follows this section.

✔ **Connectors:** Lines with various shapes and arrowheads with connecting dots on the ends.

✔ **Basic Shapes:** Squares, rectangles, triangles, crosses, happy faces, lightning bolts, and more.

✔ **Block Arrows:** Fat arrows pointing in various directions.

✔ **Flowchart:** Various flowcharting symbols.

✔ **Stars and Banner:** Shapes that add sparkle to your presentations.

✔ **Callouts:** Text boxes and speech bubbles like those used in comic strips.

✔ **Action Buttons:** Buttons that you can add to your slides and click during a slide show to go directly to another slide or to run a macro.

✔ **More AutoShapes:** In fact, 55 more. Some of these will work great for your Web page presentation, and there is even one that looks like Santa's chimney.

These steps show you how to draw an AutoShape:

1. **Click the AutoShapes button on the Drawing toolbar.**

   The AutoShapes menu appears.

2. **Choose the AutoShape category you want.**

   A toolbar of AutoShapes appears. Figure 12-2 shows all the toolbars that you can access from the AutoShapes menu. Look this figure over to see what kind of AutoShapes are available. (Of course, when you actually use PowerPoint, only one of these toolbars is visible at a time.)

3. **Click the AutoShape that you want to draw.**

4. **Click the slide where you want the shape to appear and then drag the shape to the desired size.**

   When you release the mouse button, the AutoShape object takes on the current fill color and line style.

5. **Start typing if you want the shape to contain text.**

   Hold down the Shift key while drawing the AutoShape to create an undistorted shape.

To dismiss the AutoShapes toolbar, click its close button in the upper-right corner.

Some AutoShapes — especially the Stars and Banners — cry out for text. Figure 12-3 shows how you can use a star shape to add a jazzy burst to a slide.

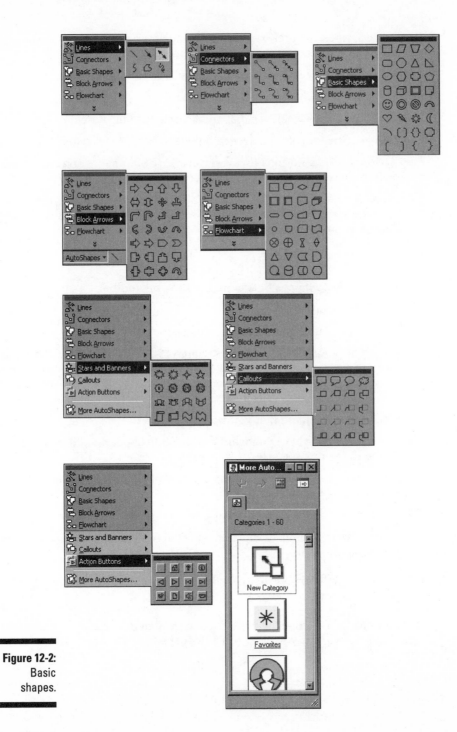

Figure 12-2:
Basic
shapes.

You can change an object's AutoShape at any time by selecting the object and then choosing the Draw➪Change AutoShape command.

Figure 12-3: Use a star shape to make your presentation look like a late-night television commercial.

Some AutoShape buttons have an extra handle that enables you to adjust some aspect of the object's shape. For example, the arrows have a handle that enables you to increase or decrease the size of the arrowhead. Figure 12-4 shows how you can use these extra handles to vary the shapes produced by several AutoShape buttons. For each of the six shapes, the first object shows how the AutoShape is initially drawn; the other two objects drawn with each AutoShape show how you can change the shape by dragging the extra handle.

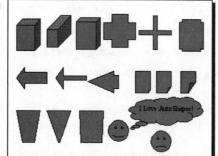

Figure 12-4: Interesting variations are possible by grabbing the extra handles on these AutoShapes.

Drawing a Polygon or Freeform Shape

Mr. Arnold, my seventh-grade math teacher, taught me that a *polygon* is a shape that has many sides and has nothing to do with having more than one spouse (one is certainly enough for most of us). Triangles, squares, and rectangles are polygons, but so are hexagons and pentagons, as are any unusual shapes whose sides all consist of straight lines. Politicians are continually inventing new polygons when they revise the boundaries of congressional districts.

One of the most useful AutoShapes is the Freeform tool. It's designed to create polygons, with a twist: Not all the sides have to be straight lines. The Freeform AutoShape tool lets you build a shape whose sides are a mixture of straight lines and freeform curves. Figure 12-5 shows three examples of shapes that I created with the Freeform AutoShape tool.

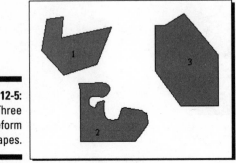

Figure 12-5:
Three
freeform
shapes.

Follow these steps to create a polygon or freeform shape:

1. **Click the AutoShapes button and then choose Lines.**

   The Lines toolbar appears.

    2. **Click the Freeform button (shown in the margin).**

3. **Click where you want to position the first corner of the object.**

4. **Click where you want to position the second corner of the object.**

5. **Keep clicking wherever you want to position a corner.**

6. **To finish the shape, click near the first corner, the one you created in Step 3.**

   You don't have to be exact; if you click anywhere near the first corner that you put down, PowerPoint assumes that the shape is finished.

You're finished! The object assumes the line and fill color from the slide's color scheme.

To draw a freeform side on the shape, hold down the mouse button when you click a corner and then draw the freeform shape with the mouse. When you get to the end of the freeform side, release the mouse button. Then you can click again to add more corners. Shape 2 in Figure 12-5 has one freeform side.

You can reshape a polygon or freeform shape by double-clicking it and then dragging any of the love handles that appear on the corners.

If you hold down the Shift key while you draw a polygon, the sides are constrained to 45-degree angles. Shape 3 in Figure 12-5 was drawn in this manner. How about a constitutional amendment requiring Congress to use the Shift key when it redraws congressional boundaries?

You also can use the Freeform AutoShape tool to draw a multisegmented line, called an *open shape.* To draw an open shape, you can follow the steps in this section, except that you skip Step 6. Instead, double-click or press the Esc key when the line is done.

Drawing a Curved Line or Shape

Another useful AutoShape tool is the Curve button, which lets you draw curved lines or shapes. Figure 12-6 shows several examples of curved lines and shapes drawn with the Curve AutoShape tool.

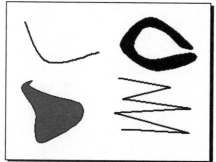

Figure 12-6:
Examples of curved lines and shapes.

Here is the procedure for drawing a curved line or shape:

1. **Click the AutoShapes button and then choose <u>L</u>ines.**

   The Lines toolbar appears.

2. **Click the Curve button (shown in the margin).**

3. **Click where you want the curved line or shape to begin.**

4. **Click where you want the first turn in the curve to appear.**

   The straight line turns to a curved line, bent around the point where you clicked. As you move the mouse, the bend of the curve changes.

5. **Click to add additional turns to the curve.**

   Each time you click, a new bend is added to the line. Keep clicking until the line is as twisty as you want.

6. **To finish a line, double-click where you want the end of the curved line to appear. To create a closed shape, double-click over the starting point, where you clicked in Step 3.**

Setting the Fill, Line, and Font Color

The three color controls that appear on the drawing toolbar let you set the fill color (that is, the color used to fill a solid object), the line color, and the color of an object's text. These buttons behave a little strangely, so they merit a bit of explanation.

Each of the color buttons actually consists of two parts: a button and an arrow. Click the button to assign the current fill, line, or text color to the selected object. Click the arrow to apply any color you want to the selected object.

When you click the arrow, a menu appears. For example, Figure 12-7 shows the Fill Color menu that appears when you click the arrow attached to the Fill Color button. As you can see, this menu includes a palette of colors that you can select. If you want to use a color that isn't visible on the menu, select More Fill Colors. This displays a dialog box that includes a color wheel from which you can select just about any color under the sun. Chapter 10 carefully explains this dialog box, so I won't review it here.

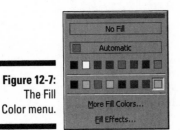

Figure 12-7:
The Fill
Color menu.

If you set the Fill Color, Line Color, or Font Color to Automatic, the fill color changes whenever you change the presentation's color scheme.

You can also apply a fill effect — such as gradient fill or a pattern — to an object by choosing the Fill Effects command from the Fill Color menu. This pops up the Fill Effects dialog box, which Chapter 10 describes in detail.

The Line Color and Font Color menus have similar commands. In addition, the Line Color menu includes a Patterned Lines command that lets you pick a pattern to apply to lines.

Setting the Line Style

Three buttons in the Drawing toolbar let you change the style of line objects:

✔ **Line Style:** The thickness of the lines that outline the object.

✔ **Dash Style:** The dashing pattern used for the lines that outline the object. The default uses a solid line, but different patterns are available to create dashed lines.

✔ **Arrow Style:** Lines can have an arrowhead at either or both ends. Arrowheads are used mostly on line and arc objects.

To change any of these object attributes, simply select the object or objects that you want to change and then click the appropriate button to change the style. A menu of style options appears.

The Line Style menu includes a More Lines command that summons the dialog box shown in Figure 12-8. From this dialog box, you can control all aspects of a line's style: its color, width, dash pattern, and end style (various arrowheads can be applied). The Arrow Style command includes a More Arrows command that summons the same dialog box.

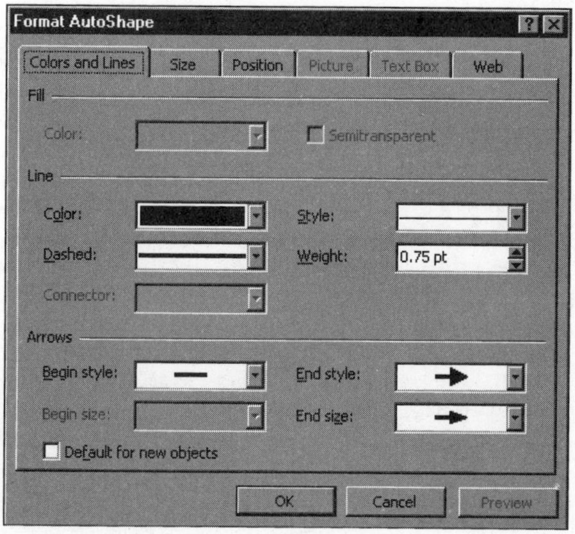

Figure 12-8:
Setting the
line style.

Applying a Shadow

 To apply a shadow effect to an object, select the object and click the Shadow button. The Shadow menu shown in Figure 12-9 appears, offering several shadow styles. Click the shadow style that you want the object to assume.

Figure 12-9:
The Shadow
menu.

If you select the Shadow Settings command from the Shadow menu, the Shadow Settings toolbar shown in Figure 12-10 appears. The buttons on this toolbar allow you to nudge the shadow into exactly the right position and change the shadow color to create a custom shadow effect.

Figure 12-10:
The Shadow
Settings
toolbar.

Adding 3-D Effects

 The 3-D button is one of the coolest buttons on the Drawing toolbar. It lets you transform a dull and lifeless flat object into an exciting, breathtaking three-dimensional object. Figure 12-11 shows how you can use the 3-D button to transform several shapes into 3-D objects. In each case, the object on the left is a simple AutoShape, and the three objects to the right of the simple AutoShape are three-dimensional versions of the same shape.

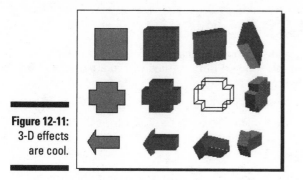

Figure 12-11:
3-D effects
are cool.

To apply a 3-D effect to a shape, select the shape and click the 3-D button.
The 3-D menu shown in Figure 12-12 appears. Click the effect that you want to
apply. Or click No 3-D if you want to remove 3-D effects.

Figure 12-12:
The 3-D
menu.

If you select 3-D Settings from the 3-D menu, the toolbar shown in Figure
12-13 appears. You can use the controls on this toolbar to tweak the 3-D settings of the object to obtain just the right effect. You can tilt the object in any
direction, set its depth, and apply lighting and surface textures.

Figure 12-13:
The 3-D
Settings
toolbar.

Flipping and Rotating Objects

To *flip* an object means to create a mirror image of it. To *rotate* an object means to turn it about its center. PowerPoint enables you to flip objects horizontally or vertically, rotate objects in 90-degree increments, or freely rotate an object to any angle.

Flipping an object

PowerPoint enables you to flip an object vertically or horizontally to create a mirror image of the object. To flip an object, follow these steps:

1. **Choose the object that you want to flip.**

2. **Click the Draw button to reveal the Draw menu, choose Rotate or Flip, and then choose Flip Horizontal or Flip Vertical.**

Rotating an object 90 degrees

You can rotate an object in 90-degree increments by following these steps:

1. **Choose the object that you want to rotate.**

2. **Click the Draw button to reveal the Draw menu, choose Rotate or Flip, and then choose Rotate Left or Rotate Right.**

3. **To rotate the object 180 degrees, click the appropriate Rotate button again.**

Using the Free Rotate button

Rotating an object in 90-degree increments is useful sometimes, but if you want to give just a bit of slant to an object, 90-degree rotation won't do. That's when the Free Rotate button comes in handy. It enables you to rotate an object to any arbitrary angle just by dragging it with the mouse.

The following steps show you how to use the Free Rotate button:

1. **Choose the object that you want to rotate.**

2. **Click the Free Rotate button on the Drawing toolbar (shown in the margin).**

3. Drag one of the corner rotation handles around the object.

As you drag, an outline of the object rotates around. When you get the object's outline to the angle you want, release the mouse button, and the object is redrawn at the new angle.

To restrict the rotation angle to 15-degree increments, hold the Shift key while dragging around the corner handle.

When you hold down the Ctrl key while dragging a corner handle, the object rotates about the opposite corner handle rather than the center. This feature is very strange, but it's occasionally useful.

Remember how all the bad guys' hideouts were slanted in the old _Batman_ TV show? Wasn't that cool?

Drawing a Complicated Picture

When you add more than one object to a slide, several problems come up. What happens when the objects overlap? How do you line up objects so that they don't look like they were thrown at the slide from a moving car? And how do you keep together objects that belong together?

This section shows you how to use PowerPoint features to handle overlapped objects, align objects, and group objects. If you're interested in a description of how to use these PowerPoint features together to draw a picture, check out the sidebar titled "Don't let me tell you how I drew that funny face!" in this chapter.

Changing layers

Whenever you have more than one object on a slide, the potential exists for objects to overlap one another. Like most drawing programs, PowerPoint handles this problem by layering objects like a stack of plates. The first object that you draw is at the bottom of the stack; the second object is on top of the first; the third is atop the second; and so on. If two objects overlap, the one that's at the highest layer wins; objects below it are partially covered.

So far, so good — but what if you don't remember to draw the objects in the correct order? What if you draw a shape that you want to tuck behind a shape that you've already drawn, or what if you want to bring an existing shape to the top of the pecking order? No problem. PowerPoint enables you to change the stack order by moving objects toward the front or back so that they overlap just the way you want.

Don't let me tell you how I drew that funny face!

In case you're interested, you can follow the bouncing ball to see how I created the face in Figure 12-1. By studying this creature, you can get an idea of how you use layers, groups, and alignment to create complicated pictures, as shown in these steps:

1. I drew this basic shape by using the Oval button. Then I filled it with gray.

    (In this color scheme, the fill color for this slide wasn't gray, so I used the Fill Color button to do this step.)

2. To draw the eyes, I started by using the Oval button to draw an oval for the left eye, which I filled with black.

    Next, I pressed Ctrl+D to make a duplicate of the oval. Then I dragged the duplicate eye to the right side of the face. Finally, I used the Line button to draw the two lines that make the eyebrows and the line that represents the mouth.

3. I drew the nose and ears by using the Oval tool.

    The only trick with the ears was using the Send to Back command to send the ears behind the face where they belonged.

4. To add the body, I used the Freeform AutoShape tool. Then I double-clicked the image to produce the Format Object dialog box. I selected Color, Fill Effects, and Pattern. I selected this lovely checkered shirt and sent the little guy on his way.

Oh, I almost forgot. The last step is to choose all the objects that make up the face (by dragging and clicking a dotted-line square around the entire picture) and group them using the Draw➪Group command. That way, I don't have to worry about accidentally dismembering the face.

The Draw menu on the Drawing toolbar provides four commands for changing the stacking order, all grouped under the Order command:

- **Draw➪Order➪Bring to Front:** Brings the chosen object to the top of the stack.
- **Draw➪Order➪Send to Back:** Sends the chosen object to the back of the stack.
- **Draw➪Order➪Bring Forward:** Brings the chosen object one step closer to the front of the stack.
- **Draw➪Order➪Send Backward:** Sends the object one rung down the ladder.

Layering problems are most obvious when objects have a fill color. If an object has no fill color, objects behind it are allowed to show through. In this case, the layering doesn't matter much.

To bring an object to the top of another, you may have to use the Bring Forward command several times. The reason is that even though the two objects appear to be adjacent, other objects may occupy the layers between them.

Line 'em up

Nothing looks more amateurish than objects dropped randomly on a slide with no apparent concern for how they line up with one another. The Draw menu on the Drawing toolbar provides several alignment commands. To use them, first select the objects that you want to align. Then click the Draw button, click Align or Distribute, and then choose one of the following commands from the menu that appears:

- ✔ Align Left
- ✔ Align Center
- ✔ Align Right
- ✔ Align Top
- ✔ Align Middle
- ✔ Align Bottom

The first three of these commands align items horizontally; the last three align items vertically.

You can also distribute several items so that they are spaced evenly. Select the items that you want to distribute, click the Draw button, choose Align or Distribute, and then choose Distribute Horizontally or Distribute Vertically.

If you want objects to automatically adhere to an invisible grid when you draw them or move them about, click the Draw button, click Snap, and then choose To Grid. To turn the snap-to-grid feature off, choose the Draw⇨Snap⇨To Grid command again.

Using the guides

If you activate the PowerPoint guides, two lines — one horizontal, the other vertical — appear on-screen. These lines do not show up in printed output, but any object that comes within a pixel's breath of one of these guidelines snaps to it. Guides are a great way to line up objects in a neat row.

To display the guides, use the View⇨Guides command (use the same command again to hide them). The guides initially pop up like crosshairs centered on the slide, but you can move them to any location that you want simply by dragging them with the mouse.

The keyboard shortcut to display or hide the guides is Ctrl+G.

Group therapy

A *group* is a collection of objects that PowerPoint treats as though it were one object. Using groups properly is one key to putting simple shapes together to make complex pictures without becoming so frustrated that you have to join a therapy group. ("Hello, my name is Doug, and PowerPoint drives me crazy.")

To create a group, follow these steps:

1. **Choose all objects that you want to include in the group.**

   You can do this by holding down the Shift key and clicking each of the items, or by holding down the mouse button and dragging the resulting rectangle around all the items.

2. **Click Draw in the Drawing toolbar and then select the Group command.**

To take a group apart so that PowerPoint treats the objects as individuals again, follow these steps:

1. **Select the object group that you want to break up.**

2. **Choose the Draw⇨Ungroup command.**

If you create a group and then ungroup it so that you can work on its elements individually, you can easily regroup the objects. These steps show you how:

1. **Select at least one object that was in the original group.**

2. **Choose the Draw⇨Regroup command.**

   PowerPoint remembers which objects were in the group and automatically includes them.

PowerPoint enables you to create groups of groups. This capability is useful for complex pictures because it enables you to work on one part of the picture, group it, and then work on the next part of the picture without worrying about accidentally disturbing the part that you've already grouped. After you have several such groups, select them and group them. You can create groups of groups of groups and so on, ad nauseam.

Part III
Neat Things You Can Add to Your Slides

The 5th Wave   By Rich Tennant

Gesundheit.

In this part . . .

Y ou'll hear nothing but yawns from the back row if your presentation consists of slide after slide of text and bulleted lists. Mercifully, PowerPoint 2000 is well equipped to add all sorts of embellishments to your slide — drawings, graphs, organizational charts, equations, animation, and more. You can even make your presentations belch on command.

Not that any of this is easy. That's why I devote an entire part to wrestling with these ornaments.

Chapter 13

Charts

● ●

In This Chapter

▶ Adding charts and graphs to PowerPoint

▶ Moving and resizing a chart

▶ Embellishing a chart with titles, legends, and other stuff

▶ Importing chart data from a spreadsheet

● ●

*O*ne of the best ways to prove a point is with numbers, and one of the best ways to present numbers is in a chart. With PowerPoint 2000, adding a chart to your presentation is easy. And getting the chart to look the way you want is usually easy, too. It takes a little bit of pointing and clicking, but it works.

PowerPoint charts are drawn by the Microsoft charting program, Microsoft Graph. Microsoft Graph, which was big news in PowerPoint 97, remains the usable and handy-dandy helper it always was. In fact, Microsoft Graph works so well with PowerPoint that you probably wouldn't know that it was a separate program if I hadn't just told you. If you are someone who runs screaming from the room at the first sight of a few numbers, you are going to love adding a chart — you may even get home tonight before the 6 o'clock news!

Adding Charts and Graphs to PowerPoint Slides

If you've never attempted to add a chart to a slide before, it can be a little confusing. Microsoft Graph takes a series of numbers and renders it as a chart. You can supply the numbers yourself, or you can copy them from an Excel or Lotus 1-2-3 worksheet. Microsoft Graph can create all kinds of different charts that range from simple bar charts and pie charts to exotic doughnut charts and radar charts. Very cool, but a little confusing to the uninitiated.

This list shows some of the jargon that you have to contend with when you're working with charts:

- **Graph or chart:** Same thing. These terms are used interchangeably. A graph or chart is nothing more than a bunch of numbers turned into a picture. After all, a picture is worth a thousand numbers.

- **Graph object:** A chart inserted on a slide. Microsoft Graph draws the chart, so whenever you try to modify the chart's appearance, PowerPoint summons Microsoft Graph.

- **Chart type:** Microsoft Graph supports several chart types: bar charts, column charts, pie charts, line charts, scatter charts, area charts, radar charts, Dunkin' Donut charts, and others. Graph can even create cone charts that look like one of the Spice Girls' costumes! Let's just call this chart "Chart-Spice." Different types of charts are better suited to displaying different types of data.

- **3-D chart:** Some chart types have a 3-D effect that gives them a jazzier look. Nothing special here; the effect is mostly cosmetic.

- **Datasheet:** Supplies the underlying data for a chart. After all, a chart is nothing more than a bunch of numbers made into a picture. The numbers come from the datasheet, which works just like a spreadsheet program. So if you know how to use Excel or Lotus 1-2-3, finding out how to use the datasheet should take you about 30 seconds. The datasheet is part of the Graph object, but it doesn't appear on the slide. Instead, the datasheet appears only when you edit the Graph object.

- **Series:** A collection of related numbers. For example, a chart of quarterly sales by region may have a series for each region. Each series has four sales totals, one for each quarter. Each series is usually represented by a row on the datasheet, but you can change the datasheet so that each column represents a series. Most chart types can plot more than one series. Pie charts can chart only one series at a time, however.

- **Axes:** The lines on the edges of a chart. The *X-axis* is the line along the bottom of the chart; the *Y-axis* is the line along the left edge of the chart. The X-axis usually indicates categories. Actual data values are plotted along the Y-axis. Microsoft Graph automatically provides labels for the X and Y axes, but you can change them.

- **Legend:** A box used to identify the various series plotted on the chart. Microsoft Graph can create a legend automatically if you want one.

You know how even though Microsoft Graph looks like it is part of PowerPoint it is really a separate program, not part of the PowerPoint program? The Microsoft Graph that comes with PowerPoint 2000 is the same as the chart creating functions in Microsoft Excel. So if you know how to use Excel to create charts, you can pretty much skip this chapter: You already know everything you need to know.

When you create or edit a chart, Microsoft Graph comes to life. But rather than pop up in its own dialog box, Microsoft Graph sort of takes over the PowerPoint window and replaces the PowerPoint menus and toolbars with its own. So don't panic if the room seems to spin and your toolbar changes.

Microsoft Graph has its own Help system. To see Help information for Microsoft Graph, first call up Microsoft Graph by inserting a chart object or double-clicking an existing chart object. Then press F1 or click the Help button to summon the Assistant, or choose <u>H</u>elp⇨<u>C</u>ontents and Index to access Graph help directly.

Creating a Chart

To add a chart to your presentation, you have two options:

- ✔ Create a new slide by using an AutoLayout that includes a chart object.
- ✔ Add a chart object to an existing slide.

Using an AutoLayout is the easier way to create a new slide because the AutoLayout positions other elements on the slide for you. If you add a chart to an existing slide, you probably have to adjust the size and position of existing objects to make room for the chart object.

Inserting a new slide with a chart

These steps show you how to insert a new slide that contains a chart:

1. Move to the slide that you want the new slide to follow.

2. Click the New Slide button on the Common Tasks toolbar to summon the New Slide dialog box, shown in Figure 13-1.

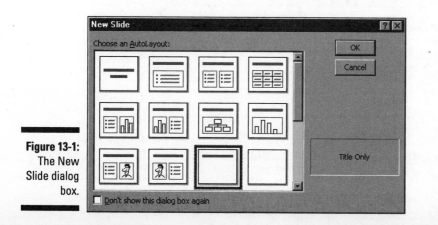

Figure 13-1:
The New
Slide dialog
box.

3. Choose the slide type that you want to add and click OK.

Several slide types include chart objects. Choose the one that you want and then click OK. PowerPoint adds a new slide of the chosen type. As you can see in Figure 13-2, the chart object is simply a placeholder; you have to use Microsoft Graph to complete the chart.

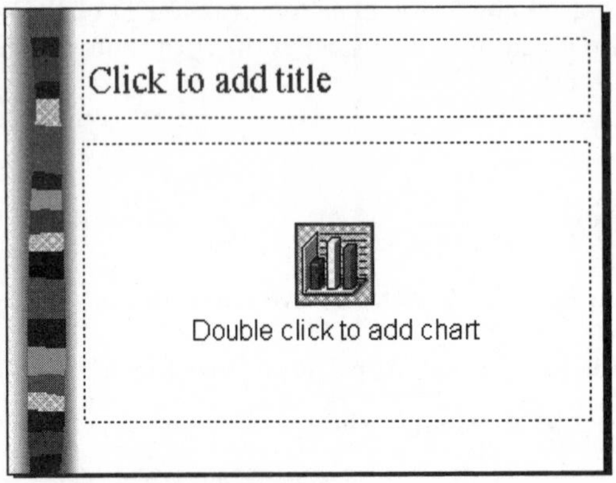

Figure 13-2:
A new slide with a virgin chart object.

Click to add title

Double click to add chart

4. Double-click the chart object to conjure up Microsoft Graph.

PowerPoint awakens Microsoft Graph from its slumber, and the two programs spend a few moments exchanging news from home. Then Microsoft Graph takes over, creating a sample chart with make-believe data, as shown in Figure 13-3. Notice that your regular toolbar setup goes away to make room for the Graph toolbar buttons. Again, click the down arrows to find the buttons you remember from PowerPoint 97. But this Graph toolbar feature only pops up when you use Microsoft Graph. You can't call it up from the toolbar menu just for kicks.

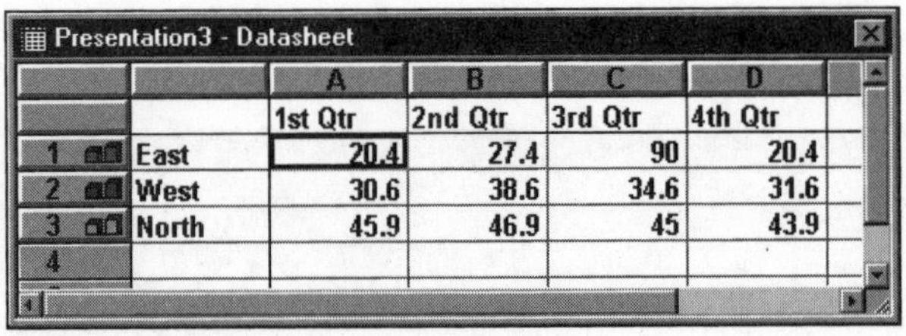

Figure 13-3:
Microsoft Graph takes over.

		A	B	C	D
		1st Qtr	2nd Qtr	3rd Qtr	4th Qtr
1	East	20.4	27.4	90	20.4
2	West	30.6	38.6	34.6	31.6
3	North	45.9	46.9	45	43.9
4					

Presentation3 - Datasheet

5. Change the sample data to something more realistic.

The *datasheet,* visible in Figure 13-3, supplies the data on which the chart is based. The datasheet is in a separate window and is not a part of the slide. The datasheet works just like a spreadsheet program. For more information about using it, see the section "Working with the Datasheet" later in this chapter.

6. **Return to the slide.**

   Click anywhere on the slide outside the chart or the datasheet to leave Microsoft Graph and return to the slide. You can then see the chart with the new numbers, as shown in Figure 13-4.

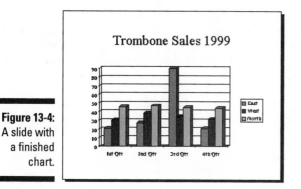

Figure 13-4:
A slide with
a finished
chart.

Inserting a chart in an existing slide

Remember that this method is the more difficult of the two methods of adding charts to your slides. Use the preceding method unless you have already created your slide.

Follow these steps to add a chart to an existing slide:

1. **Move to the slide on which you want to place the chart.**

2. **Choose Insert⇨Chart.**

   Or click the Insert Chart button (shown in the margin).

3. **Type your data in the datasheet.**

   Replace the sample data with your numbers.

4. **Click outside the chart to return to the slide.**

5. **Rearrange everything.**

   The chart undoubtedly falls on top of something else already on the slide. You probably need to resize and move the chart object and perhaps other objects on the slide to make room for the chart. Or you may want to delete any unnecessary text or clip art objects from the slide. See the next section, "Moving and Resizing a Chart," to find out how to move your chart around.

Moving and Resizing a Chart

You can move or resize charts the same way you do any other PowerPoint object. To move a chart, just click the mouse anywhere in the chart and drag it to its new location. To resize a chart, click the object and then drag one of the eight love handles that appear.

If you drag one of the edge love handles (top, bottom, left, or right), the proportions of the chart are distorted. Depending on the chart type, this procedure may emphasize or de-emphasize differences between values plotted on the chart.

Holding down the Ctrl key while resizing an object keeps the object centered over its original position. This rule also holds true for charts.

Working with the Datasheet

The datasheet contains the numbers plotted in your Microsoft Graph chart. The datasheet works like a simple spreadsheet program, with values stored in cells that are arranged in rows and columns. Like a spreadsheet, each column is assigned a letter, and each row is assigned a number. You can identify each cell in the datasheet, therefore, by combining the column letter and row number, as in A1 or B17. (Bingo!)

Ordinarily, each series of numbers is represented by a row in the spreadsheet. You can change this orientation so that each series is represented by a column by clicking the By Column button on the toolbar (shown in the margin) or by choosing Data⇨Series in Columns. The Data menu is a function of Microsoft Graph, and like the toolbar, when your datasheet is complete it vanishes.

The first row and column in the datasheet are used for headings and are not assigned a letter or number.

If you want to chart a large number of data values, you may want to increase the size of the datasheet window. Unfortunately, someone forgot to put the maximize button on the datasheet window, but you can still increase the size of the datasheet window by dragging any of its corners.

You can choose an entire column by clicking its column letter, or you can choose an entire row by clicking its row number. You also can choose the entire datasheet by clicking the blank box in the upper-left corner of the datasheet.

You can change the font used in the datasheet by choosing Format⇨Font. You also can change the numeric format by choosing Format⇨Number. Changing the font and number format for the datasheet affects not only the way the datasheet is displayed, but also the format of data value labels included in the chart.

Although the datasheet resembles a spreadsheet, you cannot use formulas or functions in a datasheet. If you want to use formulas or functions to calculate the values to be plotted, use a spreadsheet program, such as Excel, to create the spreadsheet and then import it into Microsoft Graph. (Or create the chart in Excel rather than in PowerPoint. Then import the Excel chart into the PowerPoint presentation by choosing Insert⇨Object or copy the chart into PowerPoint by way of the Clipboard.)

To get rid of the datasheet, click the View Datasheet button on the toolbar (shown in the margin). To summon the datasheet back, click the View Datasheet button again.

Changing the Chart Type

Microsoft Graph enables you to create 14 basic types of charts. Each type conveys information with a different emphasis. Sales data plotted in a column chart may emphasize the relative performance of different regions, for example, and the same data plotted as a line chart may emphasize the increase or decrease in sales over time. The type of chart that's best for your data depends on the nature of the data and which aspects of it you want to emphasize.

Fortunately, PowerPoint doesn't force you to decide the final chart type up front. You can easily change the chart type at any time without changing the chart data. These steps show you how:

1. **Double-click the chart to activate Microsoft Graph.**

2. **Choose Chart⇨Chart Type.**

   Microsoft Graph displays the Chart Type dialog box, shown in Figures 13-5 and 13-6. From this dialog box, you can choose the chart type that you want to use. The chart types are arranged in two groups: two-dimensional and three-dimensional. Figure 13-5 shows the standard chart types, which are shown on the Standard Types tab, and Figure 13-6 shows the additional chart types, which can be found on the Custom Types tab. (To show the custom types, click the Custom Types tab at the top of the dialog box.)

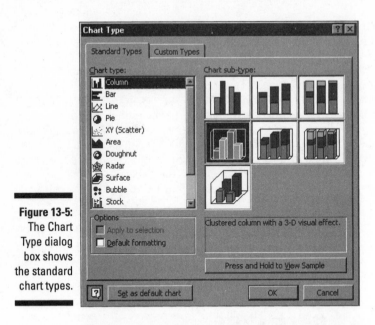

Figure 13-5:
The Chart
Type dialog
box shows
the standard
chart types.

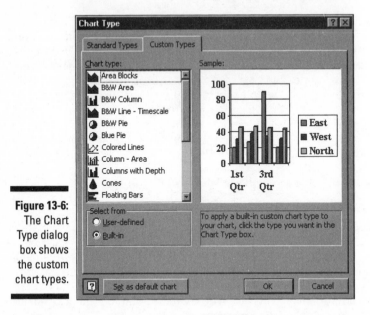

Figure 13-6:
The Chart
Type dialog
box shows
the custom
chart types.

3. **Click the chart type that you want.**

4. **To use a variant of the chart type, click the chart sub-type that you want to use.**

   For example, the Column chart type has seven sub-types that enable you to use flat columns or three-dimensional columns and to change how the columns are positioned relative to one another.

5. **Click OK, and you're done.**

Another way to summon the Chart Types dialog box is to double-click the chart object and then right-click the chart. When the quick menu appears, choose Chart Type. Make sure your arrow is on a series value when you double-click (one of those bars in the graph), or it won't work. The Chart area is very sensitive to random clicking, so be careful and proceed with patience.

You can change the chart type another way by using the Chart Type button on the Microsoft Graph toolbar. When you click the down arrow next to the button, a palette of chart types appears, as shown in Figure 13-7. The Chart Type button provides an assortment of 18 popular types of charts. If you want to use a chart type that isn't listed under the button, you have to use the Chart⇨Chart Type command.

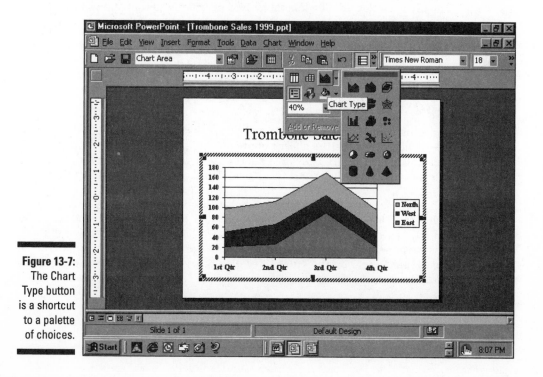

Figure 13-7:
The Chart Type button is a shortcut to a palette of choices.

If you choose one of the 3-D chart types, you can adjust the angle from which you view the chart by choosing Chart⇨3-D View. Experiment with this one; it's kind of fun.

Unlike chart types, the characters in most modern novels come in only two-dimensional varieties.

Embellishing a Chart

Microsoft Graph enables you to embellish a chart in many ways: You can add titles, labels, legends, and who knows what else. You add these embellishments by choosing Chart⇨Chart Options, which summons a Chart Options dialog box that has several tabs from which you can control the appearance of the chart.

To add a chart embellishment, choose Chart⇨Chart Options, click the tab that relates to the embellishment that you want to add, fiddle with the settings, and click OK. The following sections describe each of the Chart Options tabs in turn.

The Chart Options dialog box includes a preview area that shows how any changes affect the appearance of the chart. So feel free to experiment with different settings; you can always click Cancel to dismiss the Chart Options dialog box without applying any changes that you may have made.

Chart titles

Microsoft Graph enables you to add two types of titles to your chart: a *chart title,* which describes the chart's contents, and *axis titles,* which explain the meaning of each chart axis. Most charts use two axes: the *value axis* and the *category axis.* Some 3-D chart types use a third axis called the *series axis.*

To add these titles, choose Chart⇨Chart Options and click the Titles tab to reveal the Titles settings, shown in Figure 13-8. (Usually, the Titles tab is already selected, so you don't have to click it.) Then type the titles that you want to appear on your chart and click OK. The number and type of text boxes that appear on the Titles tab dialog box varies based on the type of chart you have selected.

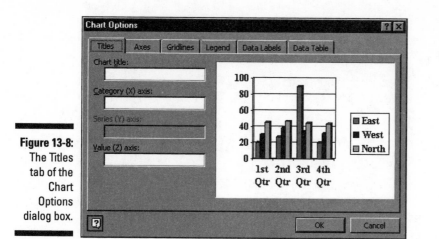

Figure 13-8:
The Titles
tab of the
Chart
Options
dialog box.

After you add a title to a chart, you can move the title to a new position by dragging it around. And you can change the title's font by selecting the title text and choosing Format⇨Font.

In most cases, the slide title serves as a chart title for a chart included on a PowerPoint slide. If that's the case, you don't need to use a chart title.

The Value axis title is sometimes handy for pointing out that sales are in thousands or millions or that the number of hamburgers served is in the billions. The Category axis title is a good place to add a note, such as Sales by Quarter.

To remove a title, click it and press the Delete key. Or call up the Chart Options dialog box, click the Titles tab, and delete the titles that you want to remove.

Axes

Sometimes an ax is what you'd like to use to fix your computer. But in this case, *axes* refers to the X and Y axis on which chart data is plotted. The *x-axis* is the horizontal axis of the chart, and the *y-axis* is the vertical axis. For 3-D charts, a third axis — Z — is also used.

The Axes tab of the Chart Options dialog box, shown in Figure 13-9, lets you show or hide the labels used for each chart axis.

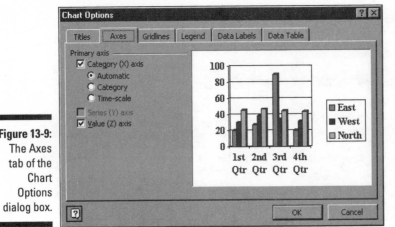

Figure 13-9:
The Axes
tab of the
Chart
Options
dialog box.

Gridlines

Gridlines are light lines drawn behind a chart to make it easier to judge the position of each dot, bar, or line plotted by the chart. You can turn gridlines on or off via the Gridlines tab of the Chart Options dialog box, pictured in Figure 13-10.

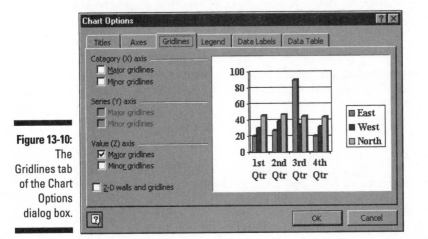

Figure 13-10:
The
Gridlines tab
of the Chart
Options
dialog box.

Legends

A *legend* explains the color scheme used in the chart. If you want a legend to appear in your chart, click the Legend tab of the Chart Options dialog box, shown in Figure 13-11. Indicate where you want the legend to be placed (Bottom, Corner, Top, Right, or Left) and then click OK.

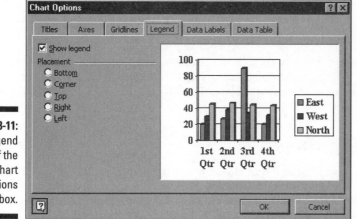

Figure 13-11:
The Legend
tab of the
Chart
Options
dialog box.

Microsoft Graph enables you to create a legend, but you're on your own if you need a myth or fable.

Labels

A *label* is the text that's attached to each data point plotted on the chart. You can tell Microsoft Graph to use the actual data value for the label, or you can use the category heading for the label. This setting is controlled by the Data Labels tab of the Chart Options dialog box, shown in Figure 13-12.

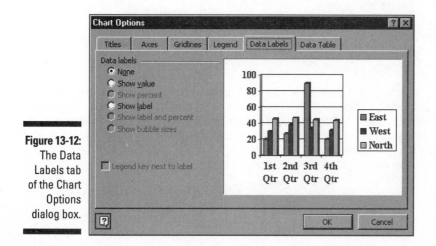

Figure 13-12:
The Data
Labels tab
of the Chart
Options
dialog box.

For most slide types, data labels add unnecessary clutter without adding much useful information. Use labels only if you think that you must back up your chart with exact numbers.

Some chart types — such as pie charts — enable you to display a percentage rather than an exact value as the label. This type of label is very helpful because percentages are often difficult to judge from an unlabeled pie chart.

Data tables

A *data table* is a table that shows the data used to create a chart. To add a data table to your chart, summon the Chart Options dialog box and click the Data Table tab, shown in Figure 13-13. Check the Show Data Table check box and then click OK.

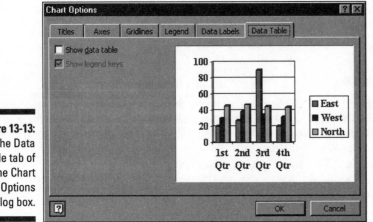

Figure 13-13: The Data Table tab of the Chart Options dialog box.

To include the best looking tables in your slides, I suggest that you forget about the Show data table function and go directly to Chapter 15. Do not pass Go. Do not collect $200. Microsoft finally gave PowerPoint a table editor that is as good as the one in Word. Check it out. It's one of the biggest improvements in PowerPoint 2000.

Chapter 14

Organizational Charts (Or, Who's in Charge Here?)

● ●

In This Chapter

▶ Creating an organizational chart

▶ Adding boxes

▶ Reorganizing your chart

▶ Adding fancy stuff

● ●

*O*rganizational charts — you know, those box-and-line charts that show who reports to whom, where the buck stops, and who got the lateral arabesque — are an essential part of many presentations. You can draw organizational charts by using the PowerPoint 2000 standard rectangle- and line-drawing tools, but that process is tedious at best. If Jones gets booted over to advertising, redrawing the chart can take hours.

Mercifully, Microsoft has a program designed just for creating organizational charts. It calls it — hold on to your hat — Microsoft Organization Chart. It's not as tightly integrated with PowerPoint as Microsoft Graph is, but it gets the job done. (Because Microsoft Organization Chart is a bit of a mouthful, I call the program OrgChart from now on.)

Keep in mind that organizational charts are useful for more than showing employee relationships. You also can use them to show any kind of hierarchical structure. For example, back when I wrote computer programs for a living, I used organizational charts to plan the structure of my computer programs. They're also great for recording family genealogies, although they don't have any way to indicate that Aunt Milly hasn't spoken to Aunt Beatrice in 30 years.

Creating an Organizational Chart

You can add an organizational chart to a presentation in two ways:

- ✔ Create a new slide by using an AutoLayout that includes an organizational chart.
- ✔ Add an organizational chart to an existing slide.

The easier of the two methods is to create a new slide by using an AutoLayout. That way, the organizational chart is already positioned in the correct location on the slide. If you add an organizational chart to an existing slide, PowerPoint usually plops it down right on top of something else important, so you have to move things around to make room for the chart.

If you create an organizational chart with more than four or five boxes, it probably won't fit within the OrgChart window. To see the whole chart, maximize OrgChart by clicking the maximize button in the upper-right corner of the window.

OrgChart terms you can skip

OrgChart thrusts a bunch of specialized terminology in your face. This list explains some of the more important terms:

- ✔ **Manager:** A box that has subordinate boxes reporting to it.

- ✔ **Subordinate:** A box beneath a manager box that reports to that manager in a line relationship.

- ✔ **Co-worker:** Two or more boxes that report to the same manager.

- ✔ **Assistant:** A box that has a staff relationship to another box rather than a line relationship. Assistant boxes are drawn differently to indicate their different relationship to the chart.

- ✔ **Co-managers:** Two or more boxes that share subordinates. Don't you feel sorry for those subordinates?

- ✔ **Group:** All the boxes that report to a particular manager.

- ✔ **Group style:** The way a group of boxes are drawn to show their relationships. OrgChart has several group style options you can choose. You can freely mix group styles within the same chart.

- ✔ **Branch:** A box and all the boxes that report directly and indirectly to it.

- ✔ **Connecting line:** A line that shows a relationship between two boxes.

Inserting a new slide with an organizational chart

Follow these steps to add a new slide with an organizational chart:

1. **Move to the slide that you want the new slide to follow.**

2. **Click the New Slide button on the Common Tasks toolbar.**

   The New Slide dialog box, shown in Figure 14-1, shows its familiar face.

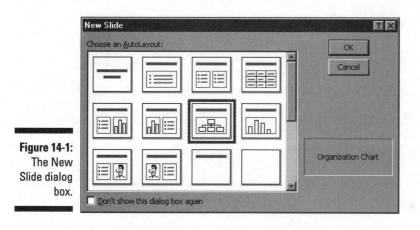

Figure 14-1:
The New
Slide dialog
box.

3. **Pick the OrgChart slide type and click OK.**

   PowerPoint adds a new slide with a placeholder for an organizational chart (see Figure 14-2).

4. **Double-click where it says** Double click to add org chart.

   PowerPoint launches Microsoft Organization Chart, which pops up in its own window and enables you to create the chart. OrgChart starts off with a simple four-box chart, as shown in Figure 14-3.

5. **Draw the organizational chart.**

   Click the boxes that are already on the sample chart and type the names for your chart boxes. OrgChart enables you to type a name, title, and one or two comment lines for each box.

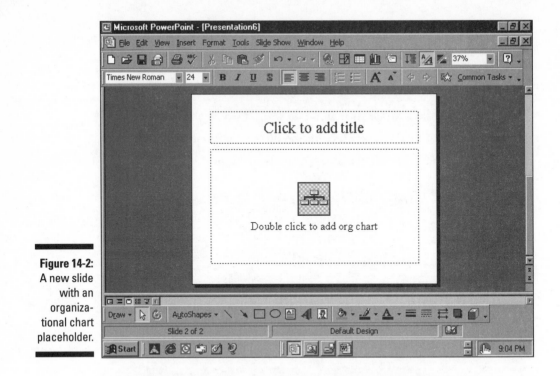

Figure 14-2:
A new slide with an organizational chart placeholder.

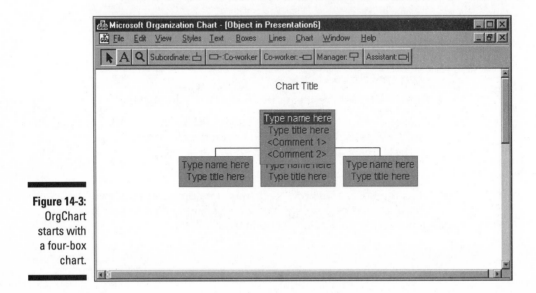

Figure 14-3:
OrgChart starts with a four-box chart.

Subordinate: 占

If you want to add boxes, click the Subordinate button (shown in the margin) and then click the box you want the new box to be subordinate to. (For more information about adding boxes to a chart, see the steps listed later in this chapter, under the heading "Adding Boxes to a Chart.")

Figure 14-4 shows the OrgChart window after I finished creating a simple chart with seven boxes. For the first four boxes (Doc, Sneezy, Grumpy, and Bashful), I just replaced the text *Type name here* with the names I wanted to use. I added the other three boxes by using the Subordinate button.

6. **Use the File⇨Exit and Return command to return to PowerPoint.**

Back in PowerPoint, you can see your organizational chart in all its glory. Figure 14-5 shows how a finished organizational chart looks on the slide.

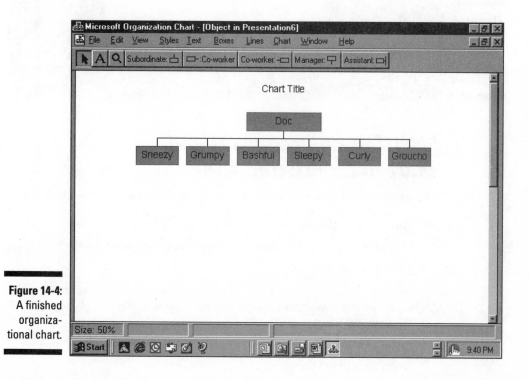

Figure 14-4:
A finished organizational chart.

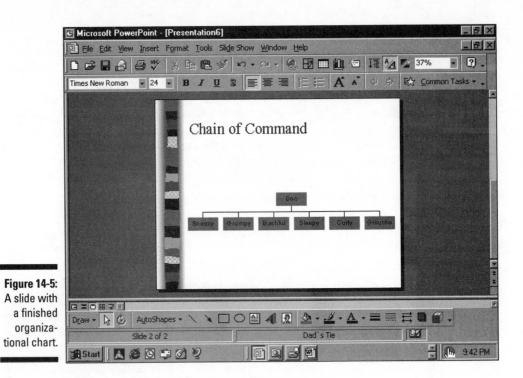

Figure 14-5:
A slide with a finished organizational chart.

Inserting an organizational chart in an existing slide

These steps show you how to add an organizational chart to an existing slide:

1. **Move to the slide on which you want the chart placed.**

2. **Choose the Insert⇨Picture⇨Organization Chart command.**

3. **Draw the chart.**

   Replace the text *Type here* with your own text and add new boxes by clicking the Subordinate button and then clicking the slide that you want the new box to be subordinate to.

4. **Invoke the File⇨Exit and Return command to return to PowerPoint.**

5. **Rearrange everything.**

   If the chart landed on top of something important, rearrange the objects on the slide so that everything is visible. Drag them, resize them, or delete them if you must.

Adding Boxes to a Chart

To add a new box to an organizational chart, you use one of the five box buttons listed in Table 14-1.

Table 14-1	The OrgChart Box Buttons
Box Button	**What It Does**
Subordinate:	Inserts a new box subordinate to the box you click.
:Co-worker	Inserts a co-worker to the left of the box you click. The new box is subordinate to the same box as the existing box you click.
Co-worker:	Inserts a co-worker to the right of the box you click. The new box is subordinate to the same box as the existing box you click.
Manager:	Inserts a manager box above the box you click.
Assistant:	Inserts an assistant box for the box you click.

Follow these general steps for adding a new box:

1. **Click the appropriate Box button for the type of box that you want to add.**

2. **Click the existing box that you want the new box related to.**

3. **Type the name and, if you want, the title and comments for the new box.**

   Press the Tab or Enter key to move from line to line within the box. Press the Esc key or click anywhere outside the box when you're finished.

To add several boxes, hold down the Shift key when you click the Box button. Then you can create several boxes without having to reset the Box button each time.

OrgChart automatically adjusts the size of the box based on the amount of text that you type in the box. To keep the boxes small, type as little text as you can.

To insert a new manager box between an existing box and its subordinates, first select the boxes that you want to be subordinate to the new manager box. Then hold down the Ctrl key and click the Manager button.

Rearranging the Chart

Some companies continually rearrange their organizational charts. If you're the lucky winner of this thankless chore, you better study this section closely.

Selecting boxes

The easiest way to select a box is to click it with the mouse. To select several boxes, hold down the Shift key while clicking. Or if you're a keyboard junkie, you can use the shortcuts summarized in Table 14-2.

Table 14-2	Keyboard Shortcuts for Selecting Boxes
Keyboard Action	*What It Does*
Ctrl+G	Selects all the current box's co-workers (the boxes in the same group).
Ctrl+B	Selects an entire branch, beginning with the current box.
Ctrl+A	Selects all boxes in the chart.
Ctrl+ ←	Selects the box to the left of the current box.
Ctrl+ →	Selects the box to the right of the current box.
Ctrl+ ↑	Selects the current box's manager.
Ctrl+ ↓	Selects the first box that reports to the current box.

Deleting chart boxes

To delete a box from an organizational chart, click the box to select it and press the Delete key. OrgChart automatically adjusts the chart to compensate for the lost box.

When you delete a box from an organizational chart, you should observe a moment of somber silence — or throw a party. It all depends on whose name was on the box, I suppose.

Moving a box

To move a box to a different position on the chart, drag the box with the mouse until it lands right on top of the box that you want it to be subordinate to. OrgChart automatically rearranges the chart to accommodate the new arrangement. Dragging boxes can be a handy way to reorganize a chart that has gotten a little out of hand.

Suppose that you want to recast the organizational chart shown in Figure 14-5 to introduce a new layer of management. Figure 14-6 shows the result. To create this chart, I dragged Sneezy and Bashful on top of Grumpy. Then I dragged Curly and Groucho on top of Sleepy.

Moving a box precisely on top of another box is a bit tricky. OrgChart clues you that you've made it by changing the color of the box. Release the mouse button as soon as you see the color change. If you move a box in a way that OrgChart thinks is crazy, a dialog box with an exclamation point explains how to easily correct your blunder.

If you move a box by dragging it, any subordinate boxes are moved also. To move a box without moving its subordinates, select the box, press Ctrl+X to cut it to the Clipboard, select the box that you want to move the cut box to, and press Ctrl+V to insert the box.

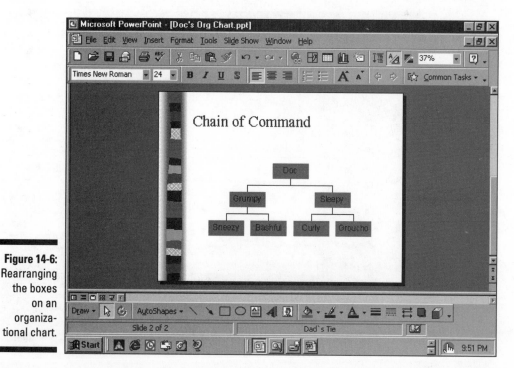

Figure 14-6:
Rearranging the boxes on an organizational chart.

Using group styles

OrgChart enables you to arrange groups of boxes in several different ways. Suppose that you decide that the six boxes subordinate to Doc in Figure 14-5 cause the chart to be too wide. You can easily rearrange those six boxes so that they are shown as in Figure 14-7. All you have to do is apply a different *group style*.

Follow these steps to apply a group style:

1. **Select all the boxes that you want rearranged.**

   Hold down the Shift key while you click the boxes.

2. **Choose the Styles menu command.**

   The Groups menu appears, as shown in Figure 14-8.

3. **Click the group style that you want.**

   OrgChart applies the style to the boxes that you selected and adjusts the chart as necessary.

Made an oops? Don't forget about the Undo command (Ctrl+Z or Alt+Backspace).

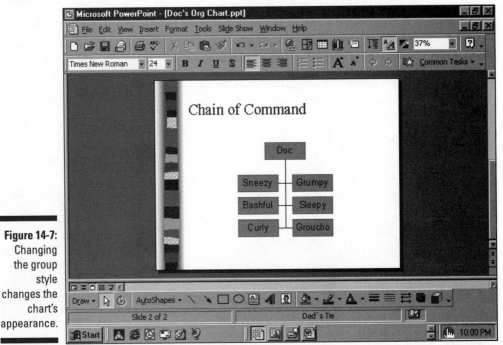

Figure 14-7: Changing the group style changes the chart's appearance.

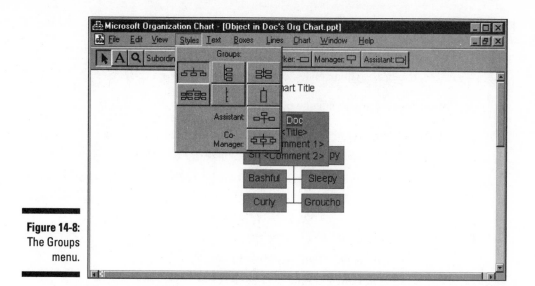

Figure 14-8:
The Groups
menu.

You can mix and match group styles any which way you please to create some bizarre-looking charts. Figure 14-9 shows an organizational chart in which Grumpy reports to Doc as a subordinate and has an assistant named Morticia and two subordinate workers named Hawkeye and Fonzie. Groucho and Sleepy are co-managers over Curly, Bashful, and Sneezy.

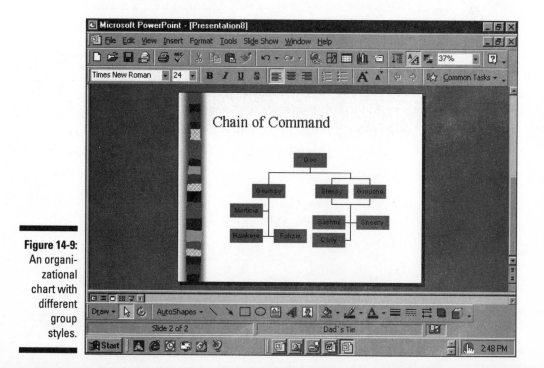

Figure 14-9:
An organi-
zational
chart with
different
group
styles.

Formatting Chart Boxes

OrgChart enables you to apply fancy formatting options to the text in chart boxes, the boxes themselves, or the lines that connect the boxes.

Follow these steps to spruce up your boxes:

1. **Select the box or boxes whose format you want to change.**

2. **Use the following commands to format the box text:**

   • Text⇨Font: Changes the font and font characteristics for the box text.

   • Text⇨Color: Changes the text color.

   • Text⇨Left: Left-justifies the text.

   • Text⇨Right: Right-justifies the text.

   • Text⇨Center: Centers the text.

3. **Use the following commands to format the boxes:**

   • Boxes⇨Color: Sets the box color.

   • Boxes⇨Shadow: Creates a shadow effect for the box.

   • Boxes⇨Border Style: Sets the box border style.

   • Boxes⇨Border Color: Sets the color for the box border.

   • Boxes⇨Border Line Style: Sets the line style for the box border.

To add emphasis to the lines that connect the boxes, follow these steps:

1. **Select the line segments that you want to emphasize.**

2. **Use the following commands to change the line segments:**

   • Lines⇨Thickness: Sets the thickness of the lines.

   • Lines⇨Style: Enables you to create dashed or solid lines.

   • Lines⇨Color: Sets the line color.

Unfortunately, because OrgChart doesn't implement the expected keyboard shortcuts for text formatting, you can't italicize text by pressing Ctrl+I or bold it by pressing Ctrl+B.

Chapter 15

Equations, WordArt, and Other Ornaments

*G*raphs and organizational charts aren't the only ornaments that you can add to your presentations. For the math nuts out there, PowerPoint 2000 comes with an Equation Editor that helps you create Einsteinian equations that make even the most resolute audience members hide under their chairs. For the typographers out there who would give their pica sticks to skew some text, there's WordArt. For all those Word for Windows and Excel zealots, PowerPoint includes OLE 2 links to both those programs so that you can stick a table or worksheet right in the middle of a slide. All these features are very useful — well, if you happen to need them. Otherwise, they just take up disk space.

Using Equation Editor

Stephen Hawking has said that his editor told him that every mathematical equation that he included in his book, *A Brief History of Time,* would cut the book's sales in half. So he included just one: the classic $E=mc^2$. See how easy that equation was to type? The only trick was remembering how to format the little 2 as a superscript.

My editors promised me that every equation that I included in this book would double its sales, but I didn't believe them, not even for a nanosecond. Just in case, Figure 15-1 shows some examples of the equations that you can create by using the PowerPoint handy-dandy Equation Editor program. You

$$\mu_{Y-X} = \bar{Y}_X \pm t_a s_{Y-X} \sqrt{\frac{1}{n} + \frac{(X-Y)^2}{\sum X^2 - nX^2}}$$

$$I = \frac{\sum (\frac{p_n}{p_o} \times 100)\upsilon}{\sum \upsilon}$$

$$t = \frac{\bar{X}_A - \bar{X}_B}{\sqrt{\frac{(n_A - 1)s_A^2 + ((n_B - 1)s_B^2}{n_A + n_B - 2}} \sqrt{\frac{1}{n_A} + \frac{1}{n_B}}}$$

$$f(x) = y = \sqrt[3]{\frac{x-1}{x^2+1}}$$

$$\sigma_p = \sqrt{\frac{\pi(1-n)}{n}} \sqrt{\frac{N-n}{N-1}}$$

$$\sqrt{(x-h-c)^2 + (y-k)^2} = \left| h + \frac{c}{e^2} - xe \right|$$

$$t = \frac{b}{\frac{s_{X-Y}}{\sqrt{\sum X_2 - n\bar{X}^2}}}$$

$$d_1^* = -z_{a/2} \sqrt{P_c(1-P_c)\left(\frac{1}{nA} + \frac{1}{nB}\right)}$$

Figure 15-1:
Eight equations that will probably not affect the sales of this book one way or another.

wouldn't even consider using ordinary text to try to create these equations, but they took me only a few minutes to create with Equation Editor. Aren't they cool? Tell all your friends about the cool equations that you saw in this book so that they'll all rush out and buy copies for themselves.

Equation Editor is a special version of a gee-whiz math program called MathType, from Design Science. Equation Editor isn't always installed when you install PowerPoint or Office. In Office 2000, many application features are not installed until you need them. This is the case with Equation Editor. The first time you try to use Microsoft Equation, you need to agree to installation. You need your CD-ROM for this. Choose Insert⇨Object⇨Microsoft Equation 3.0. Bill's genie notices that you don't have what you want and gives it to you.

Equation Editor also comes with Microsoft Word for Windows and Microsoft Office. If you have Word or Office and already know how to use its Equation Editor, you're in luck; they're identical.

You don't have to know anything about math to use Equation Editor. I don't have a clue what any of the equations in Figure 15-1 do, but they sure look great, don't they?

Don't forget to tell your friends how great the equations in Figure 15-1 are. They alone are worth the price of the book.

Equation Editor has its own complete Help system. After you're in Equation Editor, press F1 or use the Help command to call up complete information about using it.

Adding an equation to a slide

To add an equation to a slide, follow these steps:

1. **Choose Insert⇔Object.**

   Alternatively, create a new slide by using one of the AutoLayouts that includes an Object placeholder and then double-click the Object place-holder. Either way, the Insert Object dialog box appears, as shown in Figure 15-2.

2. **Choose Microsoft Equation 3.0 from the Object Type list box and then click OK.**

   You need to do this not only the first time you install Microsoft Equation, but every time you want to add an equation to a slide, too.

   This step summons Equation Editor, which appears in its own window, as shown in Figure 15-3.

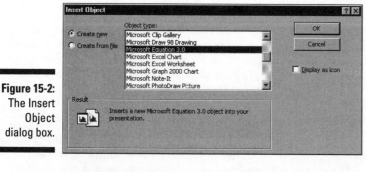

Figure 15-2: The Insert Object dialog box.

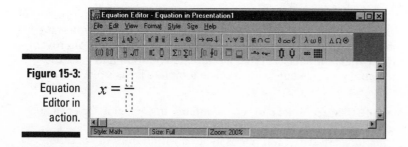

Figure 15-3: Equation Editor in action.

3. **Start typing your equation.**

   The variables and basic operators, such as plus and minus signs, are easy enough. But how do you get those fancy symbols, such as square root and summation? The answer lies in the Equation toolbar, dangling up by the top of the Equation Editor window.

4. **To add a symbol that's not on the keyboard, use one of the buttons in the top row of the Equation toolbar.**

   Each button yields a menu of symbols, most of which only Robert Oppenheimer — the father of the atomic bomb — could understand. To insert a symbol, first place the insertion point where you want the symbol to be inserted. Then click the toolbar button for the type of symbol you want to insert to display a menu of symbols and then click the symbol you want to insert. You may have to hunt around a bit to find the symbol you're looking for, but most common math symbols are included somewhere in the top row of toolbar buttons.

   The real magic of Equation Editor lies in the bottom row on the toolbar, which enables you to build the parts of the equation that have elements stacked on top of one another, such as fractions, superscripts, and roots.

5. **To add a stacked symbol, use one of the buttons in the bottom row of the Equation toolbar.**

   Each button in the bottom row of the toolbar is attached to a menu of templates, which you use to create stacked symbols. Most templates include a symbol and one or more slots, in which you type text or insert other symbols. Back in Figure 15-3, for example, I used a template to create a fraction. You can see that the fraction template consists of a horizontal stroke with slots for the numerator above and the denominator below.

   The beauty of templates such as the fraction template shown in Figure 15-3 is that as you continue to build the equation by adding additional elements, the template stretches as needed. For example, if you add additional elements to the numerator or the denominator slots in the fraction template, the length of the horizontal stroke between the slots is automatically adjusted.

   To insert a template, first position the insertion point where you want the template to be inserted. Then click the button on the bottom row of the toolbar that contains the type of template you want and click the specific template you want to insert. The template is inserted into the equation.

   To complete this fraction, I can type a number in each slot. Or I can add another symbol or template to make the equation more interesting. Most equations consist of templates nestled within the slots of other templates. The beauty of it is that Equation Editor adjusts the equation on the fly as you add text or other templates to fill a slot. If you type something like *ax2+bx+c* in the top slot, for example, Equation Editor stretches the fraction bar accordingly.

To move from one template slot to the next, press the Tab key.

6. **When you're done, choose File➪Exit and Return.**

Equation Editor bows out, and the equation is added to the slide. You can now drag the equation object to change its size or location.

Confused? I don't blame you. After you latch on to the idea behind templates and slots, you can slap together even the most complex equations in no time. But the learning curve here is steep. Stick with it.

Sometimes Equation Editor leaves behind droppings that obscure the clean appearance of the equation. When that happens, use View➪Redraw to clean up the equation.

Spend some time exploring the symbols and templates available on the toolbar. You have enough stuff here to create a presentation on how to build your own atomic bomb. (None of the equations in Figure 15-1 has anything to do with atomic bombs. Honest.)

Editing an equation

To edit an equation, follow these steps:

1. **Double-click the equation.**

This step summons Equation Editor.

2. **Make your changes.**

For example, suppose that you just doubled the mass of Jupiter by typing a *4* when you meant *2.* Just click the *4* to select the template that contains it and then type a *2* in its place.

3. **Choose File➪Exit and Return.**

All the standard Windows editing tricks work in Equation Editor, including the Ctrl+X, Ctrl+C, and Ctrl+V shortcuts for cutting, copying, and pasting text, respectively.

Equation Editor watches any text that you type in an equation and does its level best to figure out how the text should be formatted. If you type the letter *x,* for example, Equation Editor assumes that you intend for the *x* to be a variable, so the *x* is displayed in italics. If you type *cos,* Equation Editor assumes that you mean the cosine function, so the text is not italicized.

You can assign several different styles to text in an equation:

- **Math:** The normal equation style. When you use the Math style, Equation Editor examines text as you type it and formats it accordingly by using the remaining style types.

- **Text:** Text that is not a mathematical symbol, function, variable, or number.

- **Function:** A mathematical function such as *sin, cos,* and *log.*

- **Variable:** Letters that represent equation variables, such as *a, b,* or *x.* Normally formatted as italic.

- **Greek:** Letters from the Greek alphabet that use the Symbol font.

- **Symbol:** Mathematical symbols, such as +, =, and S. Based on the Symbol font.

- **Matrix-Vector:** Characters used in matrices or vectors.

You can change the text style by using the Style commands, but you should normally leave the style set to Math. That way, Equation Editor can decide how each element of your equation should be formatted.

On occasion, Equation Editor's automatic formatting doesn't work. Type the word *cosmic,* for example, and Equation Editor assumes that you want to calculate the cosine of the product of the variables *m, i,* and *c.* When that happens, highlight the text that was incorrectly formatted and choose Style⇨Text.

Equation Editor's default text sizes are designed for use with Word for Windows, not PowerPoint. They are much too small. If you plan to use Equation Editor exclusively with PowerPoint, choose Size⇨Define and double all the point sizes shown in the dialog box that's displayed. (You can always revert to the default sizes by choosing Size⇨Define and clicking the Defaults button.)

Don't use the spacebar to separate elements in an equation — let Equation Editor worry about how much space to leave between the variables and the plus signs. Use the spacebar only when you're typing two or more words of text formatted with the Text style.

The Enter key has an interesting behavior in Equation Editor: It adds a new equation slot, immediately beneath the current slot. This technique is sometimes a good way to create stacked items, but using the appropriate template instead is better.

Using WordArt

WordArt is a little program that takes a snippet of ordinary text and transforms it into something that looks like you paid an ad agency an arm and a leg to design. And the best part is that WordArt is free! Figure 15-4 is an example of what you can do with WordArt in about three minutes.

Once again, you're in luck if you already know how to use WordArt in Word for Windows. WordArt is the same in PowerPoint 2000 and Word for Windows.

Follow these steps to transform mundane text into something worth looking at:

1. **Choose Insert⇨Picture⇨WordArt.**

   The WordArt Gallery appears, as shown in Figure 15-5.

2. **Click the WordArt style that most closely resembles the WordArt that you want to create and then click OK.**

   The Edit WordArt Text dialog box appears, as shown in Figure 15-6.

3. **Type the text that you want to use for your WordArt in the Edit WordArt Text dialog box and then click OK.**

   The WordArt object appears along with the WordArt toolbar.

Figure 15-4:
You too can
do this with
WordArt.

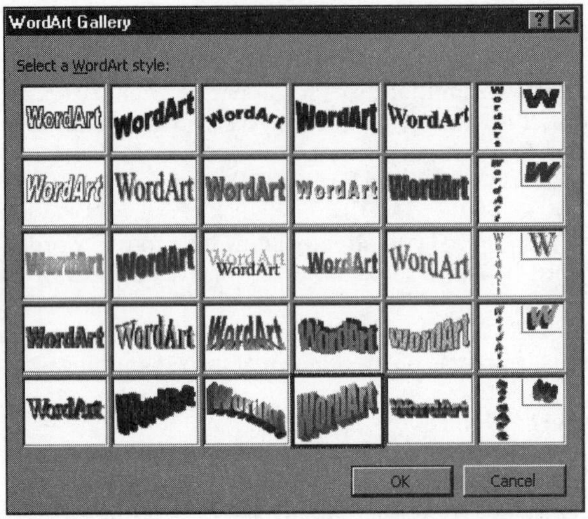

WordArt Gallery
Select a WordArt style:
OK
Cancel

Figure 15-5: The WordArt Gallery offers a choice of WordArt styles.

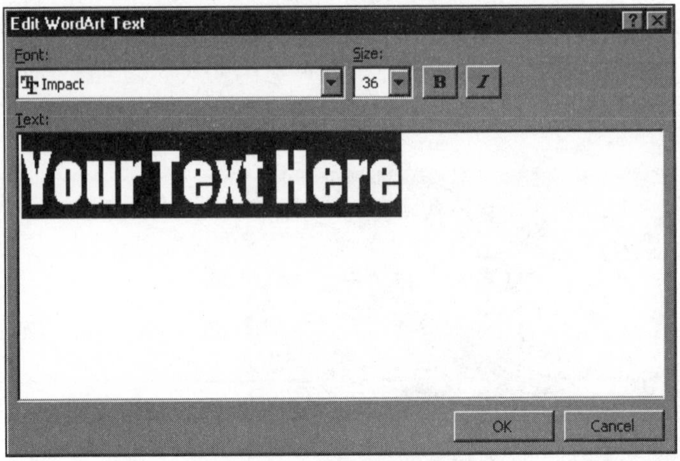

Edit WordArt Text
Font:
Impact
Size:
36
B
I
Text:
Your Text Here
OK
Cancel

Figure 15-6: The Edit WordArt Text dialog box.

4. **Fool around with other WordArt controls.**

   The various controls available on the WordArt toolbar are summarized in Table 15-1. Experiment as much as you want until you get the text to look just right.

5. **Click anywhere outside the WordArt frame to return to the slide.**

Table 15-1	WordArt Buttons	
Button	**Name**	**What It Does**
	Insert WordArt	Creates another WordArt object
Edit Text...	Edit Text	Opens the Edit WordArt Text dialog box so that you can change the text
	WordArt Gallery	Opens the WordArt Gallery so that you can quickly apply a different format
	Format WordArt	Calls up a dialog box that allows you to change the size and color of lines in the WordArt object and change other WordArt settings
	WordArt Shape	Enables you to change the shape of the WordArt text
	Free Rotate	Enables you to change the rotation angle of the WordArt object
	WordArt Same Letter Heights	Alternates between normal letters and same-height letters, in which upper- and lowercase letters are the same height
	WordArt Vertical Text	Alternates between horizontal and vertical text
	WordArt Alignment	Changes the alignment
	WordArt Character Spacing	Changes the space between letters

Don't forget that, in the eyes of PowerPoint, a WordArt object is not text. You can't edit it just by clicking it and typing. Instead, you have to double-click it to conjure up WordArt and then edit the text from within WordArt.

Adding Tables and Spreadsheets

If you want to create a slide that has columnar information, in PowerPoint 97 you had to struggle with trying to line up the text by using the crude tab stops in PowerPoint. In PowerPoint 2000 you can take advantage of the PowerPoint's native capability to embed a table you create directly in PowerPoint, and you can even use PowerPoint's drawing and erasing tools.

For more complex tables, or if old habits just die hard, you can still embed a Word table, Excel spreadsheet, or even an Access datasheet directly in a PowerPoint slide. When you insert another Microsoft Office product's table as an object in PowerPoint, all of their native features for creating and editing are available to you from within PowerPoint.

The PowerPoint 2000 Better Table Maker

It used to be that really the only way to get a really nice table was to go to Word or Excel and import (or to slip a twenty to the maître d'). Now, you can summon the table in PowerPoint and not bother to go to Word or Excel, depending on the complexity of your table. (If you prefer Word or Excel, that's okay, too — but remember, if you want a good table, you're gonna need some cash.)

One interesting and useful PowerPoint 2000 feature is the new Tables and Borders floating toolbar. This new toolbar lets you do almost anything you need to do to your table. Look at Table 15-2 to see what the interesting little buttons do. Activate the toolbar by choosing View⇨Toolbars⇨Tables and Borders, or by choosing the Tables and Borders button shown in the margin from the Standard toolbar.

Table 15-2	Tables and Borders Toolbar Buttons	
Button	*Name*	*What It Does*
	Draw Table	Creates a table by dragging a box where you want to put it. Use the same function to draw lines for rows and columns.
	Eraser	Removes lines and borders by dragging over the unwanted lines.
	Border Style	Choose the flavor of line you enjoy.
1 pt	Border Width	Determines border width — hey that was easy!
	Border Color	Never miss an opportunity to make your presentation special.

Button	Name	What It Does
	Outside Borders	Choose from 12 styles of cells and borders.
	Fill Color	Make your table stand out from the slide background. Includes gradients, textures, and patterns.
Table ▾	Table	Brings up a healthy drop-down menu of its own. See Figure 15-7. You can start a new table, completely rearrange/insert/delete the rows and columns, and maul your table beyond recognition with this toolset. Don't even mention the Borders and Fill option here. It brings up a dialog box which is completely redundant and also duplicates the functions already on the Tables and Borders toolbar. So there! I won't even mention it.
	Merge Cells	Removes cell dividers and combines the contents of multiple selected cells.
	Split Cell	Divides a cell into what PowerPoint thinks are logical breaking points. Get ready to edit. For fun try merging cells and splitting them. How often did it split the cells back to their original form? Do not mistake this for an Undo button.
	Align Top	Sets up the text near the top of the cell.
	Center Vertically	Vertically centers the text in the cell.
	Align Bottom	Plops the text close to the bottom of the barrel.

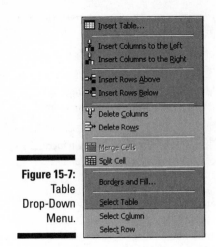

Figure 15-7:
Table
Drop-Down
Menu.

The following steps help you make a simple table:

1. Start your table by doing one of the following:

- At the Slide Layout stage of the New Slide or Slide Layout function, select the Table AutoLayout (see Figure 15-8).

- Select the Insert Table button from the Standard toolbar.

- Choose Insert⇨Picture⇨Microsoft Word Table.

  Why is this under the picture menu? Dunno. Don't lose any sleep over it. We all make mistakes.

- Select the Insert Table button from the Table pull down menu on the Tables and Borders toolbar.

If you choose the first, third, or fourth method, you see the Insert Table dialog box shown in Figure 15-9.

If you choose the second method, you see the graphical guide shown in Figure 15-10. Hold down the Shift key to get a table bigger than 4 x 5. The maximum number of rows and columns you can choose depends on your screen resolution settings and the exact location of the Insert Table button.

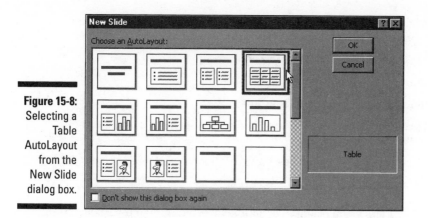

Figure 15-8:
Selecting a
Table
AutoLayout
from the
New Slide
dialog box.

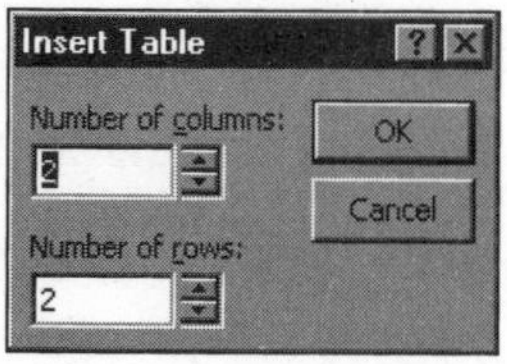

Figure 15-9:
How many
pecks of
pickled
peppers will
Peter Piper
pick?

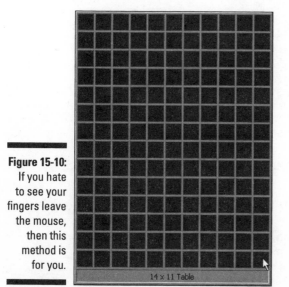

Figure 15-10:
If you hate
to see your
fingers leave
the mouse,
then this
method is
for you.

Each row or column counter maxes out at 25. PowerPoint 97 users used to max out at 30 columns and 7 rows.

2. **Pick the number of rows and columns.**

   Don't forget your row and column headings.

3. **Start typing in your information.**

4. **Format your table using the Tables and Borders toolbar and Fill dialog box.**

   This is the same dialog box you get when you choose Format⇨Table.

5. **Stop and smell the roses.**

Figure 15-11 shows an example of a table inserted into a PowerPoint slide. Notice the borders that mark the individual table cells. These borders were created by using Tables and Borders toolbar formatting commands, not the PowerPoint line-drawing button.

Don't try to cram more than four columns into a table. PowerPoint can handle it, but the mere humans in the room were not created by Bill Gates, and they have limits. Remember that folks have to be able to read the table from the back of the room.

Figure 15-11:
A table
inserted
into a
PowerPoint
slide.

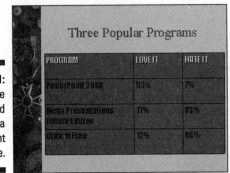

Three Popular Programs		
PROGRAM	LOVE IT	HATE IT
PowerPoint 2000	93%	7%
Mega Presentations Deluxe Edition	17%	83%
Draw 'N Flaw	12%	88%

Inserting a table from Microsoft Word

Not good enough for you, eh? Well, Word has lots of way cool table formatting functions that aren't available in PowerPoint. If you know how to do all that neat stuff — or if you're just trying to capture an existing table that you don't want to recreate (or if you "only work here" and are just following orders) — then follow these steps to insert a Word table:

1. **Open Microsoft Word and find the existing table you like so much.**

2. **Select the table.**

3. **Copy or cut the table.**

4. **Go back into PowerPoint.**

5. **Paste the table.**

   See the following Tip for a great way to do this.

6. **Size it to fit your needs.**

Save yourself some aggravation when you paste your table into PowerPoint. Instead of typing Ctrl+V or pressing the Paste button or choosing Edit⇨Paste stretch yourself and do something wacky. Choose Edit⇨Paste Special. Paste Special presents the dialog box shown in Figure 15-12. Choose Paste As Picture. Rather than inserting an editable table in your PowerPoint slide, you get a picture of the table. The picture is much easier to stretch and squeeze. You'll have far fewer problems with font size adjustments with this method.

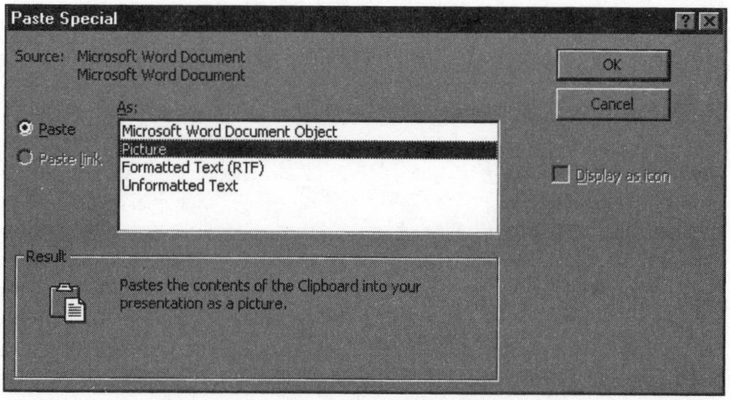

Figure 15-12: Isn't that special?

Paste Special		? X
Source: Microsoft Word Document		OK
Microsoft Word Document		Cancel
As:		
● Paste	Microsoft Word Document Object	
○ Paste link:	Picture	
	Formatted Text (RTF)	□ Display as icon
	Unformatted Text	
Result		
	Pastes the contents of the Clipboard into your presentation as a picture.	

Don't be confused by the Insert⇨Picture⇨Microsoft Word Table selection. It has nothing to do with tables that exist in Microsoft Word. It's a carry-over from older versions of PowerPoint. That function only performs the native PowerPoint table creation function. You do not get any of the Table AutoFormat toys available in Microsoft Word here, nor does it perform any kind of a table import operation.

Inserting an Excel worksheet

You can also insert an Excel worksheet into a PowerPoint presentation. This capability gives you access to the Excel advanced features for calculating values with sophisticated formulas and functions. You can import data that is 4,000 rows long by 4,000 columns wide if you have a lot more data to contend with than you ever thought possible, but no more than 255 data series will fit in a chart.

For these features to work, you must have Excel installed on your computer. There's no such thing as a free lunch.

Use this method to insert an Excel Worksheet:

- ✔ Choose Insert⇨Object and browse the Object Type list box for Excel Worksheet. (Notice in the Object Type text box that you can also insert an MS Excel Worksheet.)
- ✔ Select one of the ten Slide Layouts that include an Object. That gets you to the same dialog box as the one I mentioned in the previous bullet.

You must have Excel 5 or later for these feature options to work.

After you insert the worksheet, you can toil with it by using the Excel worksheet-editing tools. When you're done, click anywhere outside the worksheet to return to the slide.

You can always do the cut/copy and paste (or paste special) boogie discussed previously with Word tables. Whatever makes you happy.

Chapter 16

Lights! Camera! Action! (Adding Sound and Video)

. . . .

In This Chapter

▶ Adding burps, chortles, and gee-whizzes to your presentation

▶ Fiddling with video

. . . .

*O*ne of the cool things about PowerPoint 2000 is that it lets you create slides that contain not only text and pictures but sounds and even movies as well. You can add sound effects such as screeching brakes or breaking glass to liven up dull presentations. You can even add your own applause, making your presentation like a TV sitcom or game show. And you can insert a film clip from *The African Queen* or a picture of the space shuttle launching if you think that will help keep people awake. This chapter shows you how to add those special effects.

This chapter is short because you can't do as much with sound and video in PowerPoint as you can with, say, a professional multimedia-authoring program such as Multimedia Director. Still, PowerPoint allows you to paste sound and video elements into your slide show, giving you the power to craft some impressive high-tech presentations.

PowerPoint 2000 comes with a healthy collection of sound and video files. However, if you need more, you can find additional sounds and videos at the Microsoft Clip Gallery Live page on the World Wide Web. To access it, summon the Clip Gallery as described in this chapter and then click the Connect to Web button. If you have access to the Internet, PowerPoint 2000 automatically connects you to Clip Gallery Live, where you can download additional sounds and videos.

Adding Sound to a Slide

A sterile *beep* used to be the only sound you could get from your computer. Nowadays, you can make your computer talk almost as well as the computers in the *Star Trek* movies, or you can give your computer a sophomoric sense of audible distaste. At last, the computer can be as obnoxious as the user!

There's a catch. Your computer must be equipped with a *sound card* to play these types of sounds. Most PCs and all Macs have sound capability. If you don't have sound, you probably figured out that your computer is kinda old. However, you can buy and install a sound card for a reasonable price. These days, however, the price of complete systems are such that most people spend their time updating from one system to the next, rather than adding a variety of extras, but either way works.

Adding sound capability to a Windows computer used to be a major undertaking. Now, thanks to Windows 98, adding sound capability is almost a no-brainer. Windows 98 automatically configures the sound card, so you don't have to mess around with driver files and other messy details. Chances are, however, that you already have sound if you bought your computer any time from 1997 on. (Windows 95 has this capability, too.)

All about sound files

Computer sounds are stored in *sound files,* which come in two varieties:

  ✔ **WAV files:** Contain digitized recordings of real sounds, such as Darth Vader saying, "I find your lack of faith disturbing" or DeForest Kelly (that's Dr. McCoy, for you non-Trekkers) saying, "I'm a doctor, not a bricklayer." If you have Windows 98 installed as your operating system, you have access to many interesting sounds. Windows 98 comes with a variety of WAV files; for example: CHIMES.WAV, CHORD.WAV, DING.WAV, and TADA.WAV. Notice that these files all have names that end with WAV.

  Try searching for WAV files on your computer by selecting the Start menu and Find⇨Files or Folders. Then Type *.WAV in the Named text box and click Find Now. You will be amazed at the sound bytes you already have if you are running Windows 98.

  ✔ **MIDI files:** Contain music stored in a form that the sound card's synthesizer can play. Windows comes with lots of these, including a Looney Tunes MIDI File. All MIDI files have names that end in MID. Why not try the file search again and see whatcha have?

To insert a sound into a PowerPoint presentation, all you have to do is paste one of these sound files into a slide. Then when you run the presentation in Slide Show view, you can have the sounds play automatically during slide transitions, or you can play them manually by clicking the Sound button.

You're more likely to use WAV files than MIDI files in a PowerPoint presentation. MIDI files are great for playing music, but the WAV files enable you to add truly obnoxious sounds to a presentation.

Although you have a number of sound options in Windows 98, fortunately we have no national shortage of sound files. PowerPoint itself comes with a handful of useful sound files, including drumrolls, breaking glass, gunshots, and typewriter sounds. If you have access to the Web, you can check out the Microsoft Web site for loads of possibilities. Also, Windows 95 or greater has a sound recorder in its Accessories folder that enables you to experiment with your own sounds if you dare.

You can also download sound files from just about any online system (such as The Microsoft Network, CompuServe, and America Online), purchase them in collections from computer software stores, or beg, borrow, or steal them from your computer-geek friends. Most computer geeks will gladly offer you a disk full of *Star Trek* sounds in exchange for a large bag of Cheetos.

As I mentioned, if you have a microphone, you can plug into your sound card, and you can even record your own sounds. Move your computer into the living room some weekend and rent the following movies:

- *Star Wars*
- Any *Pink Panther* movie
- *The Great Muppet Caper*
- *Star Trek IV* and *Star Trek VI*
- *The African Queen*
- *2001: A Space Odyssey*
- *Annie Hall, Bananas,* or *Sleeper*

Have a ball, but remember not to violate any copyright laws with what you use. The copyright cops may be watching!

Sound files consume large amounts of disk space. A typical two-second sound clip can take up 25K of precious disk real estate. It doesn't seem like much space, but it adds up.

Inserting a sound in PowerPoint

To make your PowerPoint presentation as obnoxious as possible, follow these steps:

1. **Move to the slide to which you want to add the sound.**

2. **Choose the Insert⇨Movies and Sounds⇨Sound from Gallery command.**

   The Clip Gallery appears with the Sounds tab activated, as shown in Figure 16-1. Notice that although the Clip Gallery appears, only the Sounds tab is available.

3. **Select the sound file that you want to insert.**

   Scroll through the list of Clip Gallery sounds until you find the one you are looking for and then click it to select it. Don't be concerned if this looks like clip art categories; in PowerPoint 2000, this is the way the sound files are organized into categories, too. You can click Play Clip before you insert the sound if you want to make sure you like it first.

4. **Click the Insert button.**

5. **Make an important choice: Do you want to have the sound byte play as you move to the slide automatically, or would you prefer to click on the sound icon?**

   Figure 16-2 is an example of the dialog box that enables you to make this important choice.

   If you decide to click it yourself, the sound byte appears as a sound icon as seen in Figure 16-3. If it plays automatically, no sound icon appears.

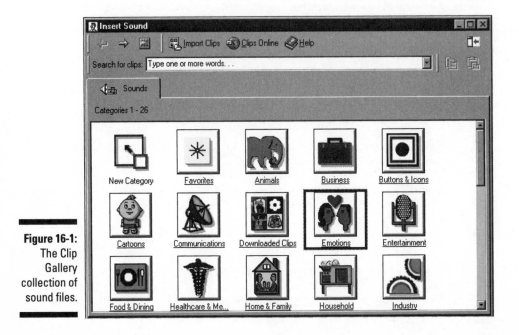

Figure 16-1:
The Clip
Gallery
collection of
sound files.

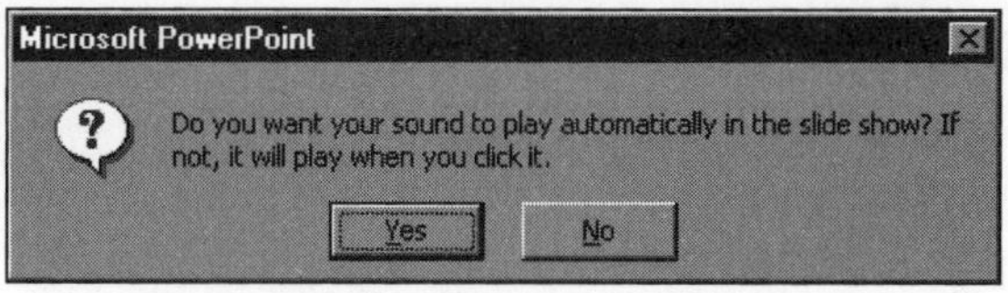

Figure 16-2:
Decisions,
decisions,
decisions!

Microsoft PowerPoint   [X]

(?) Do you want your sound to play automatically in the slide show? If
     not, it will play when you click it.

        [Yes]   [No]

If you want to insert a sound that has not been cataloged in the Clip Gallery, choose the Insert➪Movies and Sounds➪Sound from File command. Then rummage about your hard disk until you find the sound you want, click the sound to select it, and click OK.

Playing an embedded sound

To play an embedded sound while working in Slide view, double-click the sound icon.

To play the sound during a slide show, only a single click is needed.

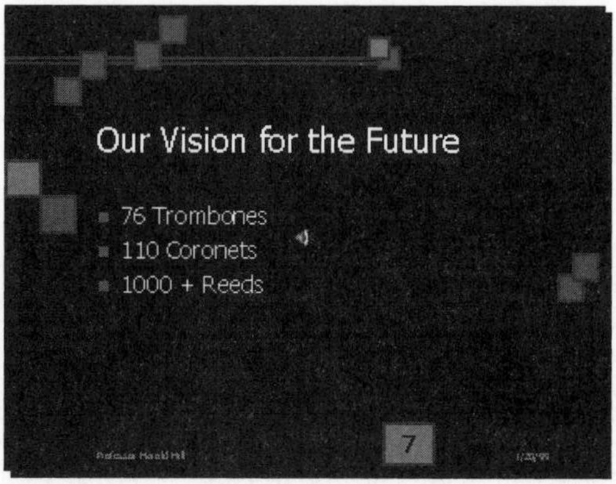

Our Vision for the Future

- 76 Trombones
- 110 Coronets
- 1000 + Reeds

7

Figure 16-3:
The sound is
inserted as
an icon.

Removing a sound

If you finally come to your senses and realize that sounds are a bit frivolous, you can easily remove them. To remove a sound, click it and press the Delete key.

Using transition sounds

You can also use sounds to embellish slide transitions. This embellishing is covered in Chapter 17.

Working with Video

Welcome to the MTV era of computing. If your computer has the chutzpah, you can add small video clips, called motion clips in Office 2000, to your presentations and play them at will. I'm not sure why you would want to, but hey, who needs a reason?

Adding a motion clip to a slide is similar to adding a sound clip. A crucial difference exists, however, between motion clips and sound bites: Video is meant to be *seen* (and sometimes *heard).* An inserted motion clip should be given ample space on your slide.

If you think sound files are big, wait till you see how big motion clips are. Ha! The whole multimedia revolution is really a conspiracy started by hard disk manufacturers.

Fortunately, Windows 95 or better handles most of the nasty setup and configuration details necessary to get videos to work. All you have to do is follow the steps outlined in the following sections, and you're on your way.

Adding a movie to a slide

These steps show you how to add a video clip to a slide:

1. **Find a good movie.**

   The hardest part about using video in a PowerPoint presentation is finding a video file that's worth showing. Many good sources offer video clips; the PowerPoint 2000 CD contains samples from several collections. Clip Gallery comes with 20 movies already cataloged. You can also find a wide variety of video clips available for download on the Web.

2. **Move to the slide on which you want to insert the movie.**

   Hopefully, you left a big blank space in the slide to put the movie in. If not, rearrange the existing slide objects to make room for the movie.

3. **Choose the Insert➪Movies and Sounds➪Movie from Gallery command.**

   The Clip Gallery appears with the Motion Clips tab selected, as shown in Figure 16-4.

4. **Select the movie that you want to insert.**

   You may need to scroll the list to find the movie you're looking for.

5. **Click Insert.**

   The movie is inserted on the slide, as shown in Figure 16-5.

6. **Resize the movie if you wish and drag it to a new location on the slide.**

That's all there is to it!

Playing a movie

To play a movie, double-click it while in Slide view. In Slide Show view, a single click is sufficient to play the movie.

Figure 16-4:
The Motion Clips tab of the Clip Gallery.

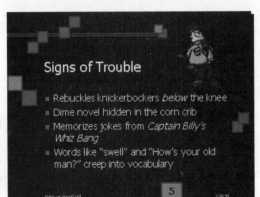

Figure 16-5:
A movie
right in a
slide.

Chapter 17

Transitions and Animation Effects

· ·

In This Chapter

▶ Using slide transitions

▶ Animating slide text

▶ Using simple animations

▶ Setting up self-running presentations

· ·

*I*f you plan to run your presentation on your computer's screen, you can use or abuse a bagful of exciting on-screen PowerPoint slide show tricks. Your audience probably won't be fooled into thinking that you hired Industrial Light and Magic — the folks behind the whiz-bang stuff in *Star Wars* — to create your special effects, but they'll be impressed all the same. Using special effects is just one more example of how PowerPoint 2000 makes even the dullest content look spectacular.

You set up most of these special effects from the PowerPoint Slide Sorter view. In fact, aside from providing an easy way to rearrange the order of your slides, creating special effects is Slide Sorter view's main purpose in life.

Using Slide Transitions

A transition is how PowerPoint gets from one slide to the next during an on-screen slide show. The normal way to segue from slide to slide is simply to cut to the new slide — effective, but boring. PowerPoint 2000 enables you to assign any of over 40 different special effects to each slide transition. For example, you can have the next slide scoot over the top of the current slide from any direction, or you can have the current slide scoot off the screen in any direction to reveal the next slide. And you can use various types of *dissolves,* from a simple dissolve to checkerboard or venetian-blind effects.

Keep these points in mind when using slide transitions:

- ✔ Transition effects look better on faster computers, which have more raw processing horsepower to implement the fancy pixel dexterity required to produce good-looking transitions.

- ✔ Some of the transition effects come in matched sets that apply the same effect from different directions. You can create a cohesive set of transitions by alternating among these related effects from slide to slide. For example, set up the first slide using Wipe Right, the second slide using Wipe Left, the third with Wipe Down, and so on.

- ✔ If you can't decide which transition effect to use, set all the slides to Random Transition by selecting all the slides and then choosing Random Transition from the toolbar. PowerPoint then picks a transition effect for each slide at random.

Slide transitions the easy way

Here's the easy way to assign transition effects:

1. **Switch to Slide Sorter view.**

    Click the Slide Sorter View button (shown in the margin) or choose the View⇨Slide Sorter command.

    Figure 17-1 shows how PowerPoint displays a presentation in Slide Sorter view. Notice that the Formatting toolbar is replaced by the Slide Sorter toolbar, which enables you to apply special effects quickly for on-screen presentations.

2. **Click the slide for which you want to create a transition — that is, the slide you want to transition to.**

3. **Choose the transition effect you want from the drop-down list box.**

    The Slide Sorter toolbar has two list boxes; the one on the left is for transition effects. In Figure 17-1, the transition is currently set to Wipe Right.

    When you assign a transition effect to a slide, a special icon appears beneath the slide to indicate that the slide has a transition effect.

4. **Do it to other slides.**

    The other slides will become jealous if you don't give them fancy transition effects, too. Repeat Steps 2 and 3 to give transition effects to other slides.

    You can set the transition for several slides at once by selecting each slide to which you want the effect applied before choosing the effect. To select several slides, hold down the Ctrl or Shift key while clicking each slide.

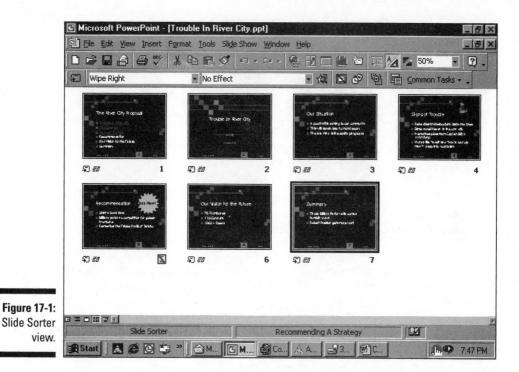

Figure 17-1:
Slide Sorter
view.

 To get an idea of what the transition looks like, click the Transition Effect button beneath the slide in Slide Sorter view. PowerPoint quickly replaces the slide with the preceding slide and then redisplays the slide using the transition effect you choose.

When you have applied all the transitions you want, switch to Slide Show view to make sure the transitions work as you expect.

Slide transitions the other way

You can also set slide transitions by using the menus. Here's how:

1. **Head for Slide Sorter view.**

   Use the View➪Slide Sorter command or click the Slide Sorter View button (shown in the margin).

2. **Select the slide to which you want to add an effect — that is, the slide you want to transition to.**

3. **Choose the Slide Show➪Slide Transition command.**

   Or, as a shortcut, click the Slide Transition button (shown in the margin) on the Slide Sorter toolbar. Either way, the Slide Transition dialog box, shown in Figure 17-2, appears.

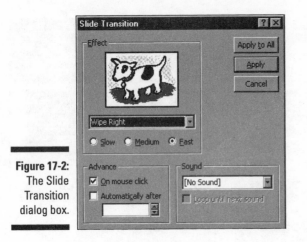

Figure 17-2:
The Slide
Transition
dialog box.

4. **Choose the transition effect that you want from the _E_ffect drop-down list box.**

5. **(Optional) Choose the speed of the transition.**

   Fast is almost always best, unless you're trying to fill time and you don't really have anything to say.

6. **Choose a sound to accompany the transition.**

   PowerPoint gives you 16 common sounds to choose from, including Applause, Broken Glass, Gunshot, Ricochet, and Slide Projector. (Note that you can't apply transition sounds from Slide Sorter view. Using sound is one of the advantages of applying transitions via the Sli_d_e Show⇨Slide _T_ransition command.)

7. **Click _A_pply or press Enter.**

   PowerPoint demonstrates the transition effect you pick in the picture near the middle-right of the Slide Transition dialog box. Each time you pick a different effect, the picture changes from a dog to a key (or vice versa) to show you how the transition looks.

The dog and key are arbitrary images Microsoft chose to represent slide transitions in the Slide Transition dialog box. I had an English professor in college who would have tried to attach some deep significance to these images, such as that the dog represents Microsoft Chairman Bill Gates' animalistic desire to dominate the entire software industry, all the while appearing to be cute and cuddly; and the key obviously represents the fact that Bill Gates feels that the new version of PowerPoint will finally unlock his plans for global domination. More likely, the Microsoft programmer who created this dialog box simply thought the dog and key were cute.

Although adding sounds to slide transitions is kind of fun, I suggest steering clear of the Loop Until Next Sound check box unless you have a deep desire to drive your audience criminally insane.

Animating Text

You can set up a text animation for any slide that contains text. When you animate slide text, the text is displayed on the screen one paragraph at a time. The animation effect you choose dictates the entrance made by each text paragraph. You can have paragraphs appear out of nowhere, drop from the top of the screen, march in from the left or right, or do a back somersault followed by two cartwheels and a double-twist flip (talc, please!).

Versions previous to PowerPoint 97 called text animations *build effects,* because they allowed you to "build" a slide paragraph by paragraph. Since PowerPoint 97, PowerPoint no longer uses the term *build effect,* but text animations do the same thing.

PowerPoint 2000 offers more than 50 animation effects to choose from. Like the transition effects, some of the text animations come in matched sets. For example: Fly from Left, Fly from Right, Fly from Top, and Fly from Bottom. Use these effects on consecutive slides to add some continuity to your presentation.

The text animation effect you choose for a slide is used for all text on that slide. However, if you pick Random Effect, PowerPoint uses a different effect for each paragraph. Your audience members will be on the edge of their seats, waiting to see the next animation effect.

Experts refer to text animations as *progressive disclosure*. These same people also refer to jumping jacks as *two-count side-step straddle hops*.

Text animation the easy way

Here's the easy way to assign a text animation:

1. **Switch to Slide Sorter view.**

   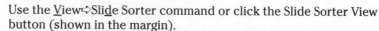

   Use the <u>V</u>iew⇨Sli<u>d</u>e Sorter command or click the Slide Sorter View button (shown in the margin).

2. **Click the slide to which you want to add an animation effect.**

3. **Choose the animation effect from the drop-down list box.**

The Slide Sorter toolbar has two list boxes (refer to Figure 17-1); the one on the right is for animation effects, the one on the left is for transition effects between slides.

When you use an animation effect on a slide, PowerPoint displays a special icon below the slide to help you remember that you've added the animation effect. To remove the animation effect from the slide, choose No Effect in the drop-down list box.

Text animation the other way

For complete control over text animation effects, you must follow these steps:

1. **Zip over to Slide view.**

Use the Viewⴖ➪Slide command or click the Slide View button (shown in the margin).

2. **Display the slide to which you want to add an effect.**

3. **Select the text object you want to animate.**

4. **Choose the Slide Show➪Custom Animation command.**

The Custom Animation dialog box appears, as shown in Figure 17-3. This dialog box has several tabs, but only the Effects tab applies to text animation.

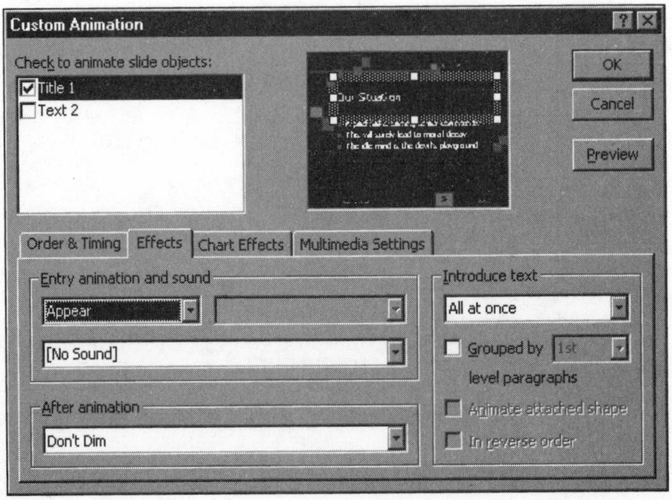

Figure 17-3:
Applying a custom animation.

5. Choose an animation effect and sound effect from the Entry animation and sound list boxes.

The first list box offers the same animation choices that are available from the Text Animation drop-down list in the Slide Show toolbar. The second list box offers several canned sound effects such as applause or broken glass.

6. Choose how you want text introduced in the Introduce text drop-down list.

The choices are All at Once, By Word, or By Letter. All at Once is usually best, but By Word or By Letter can be used for interesting effects. For example, the Typewriter preset animation uses By Letter so that it appears as if text is being typed on the slide.

7. Choose any other animation effects you want to apply.

The remaining settings on the Custom Animation dialog box let you group paragraphs if your slide has more than one bullet level, dim each paragraph after it is animated, and build the slide in reverse order.

8. Click OK or press Enter.

Click the Preview button in the Custom Animation dialog box to see a preview of the animation effects you have chosen. If you don't like the animation, change it before leaving the Custom Animation dialog box.

Note that you can change the animation applied to a slide by repeating the procedure.

Animating Other Slide Objects

You can use animation effects with any object on a slide, not just with text objects. For example, suppose you include a clip art picture of a race car. Rather than just have the car appear on the slide, you can apply an animation effect so that the car appears to drive onto the screen, complete with a race car sound effect. It isn't exactly Disney-quality animation, but it's kind of fun.

To animate an object, follow these steps:

1. In Slide View, click the object that you want to animate.

2. Choose the Slide Show⇨Custom Animation command.

Or, right-click the object and select the Custom Animation command from the shortcut menu that appears. Either way, the Custom Animation dialog box appears. (Refer to Figure 17-3.)

3. Choose an animation effect and sound effect from the Entry animation and sound list boxes.

You can click the Preview button in the Custom Animation dialog box to see a preview of how the animation effect will appear.

4. **Click OK.**

Using the Predefined Animation Effects

PowerPoint 2000 comes with an Animation Effects toolbar that includes several predefined animation effects. This toolbar saves you the trouble of wading through the Custom Animation dialog box to set the animation type and sound effects manually.

 To use the preset animation effects, click the Animation Effects button on the Standard toolbar. The Animation Effects toolbar appears, as shown in Figure 17-4. Then select the slide or object you want to animate and click the appropriate Animation buttons to apply a preset effect. Table 17-1 summarizes the buttons on the Animation Effects toolbar.

These predefined animations are also available from the Slide Show⇨ Preset Animation command.

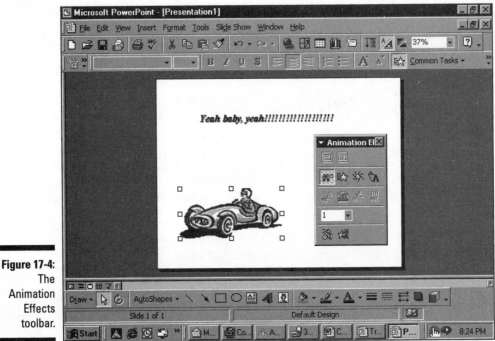

Figure 17-4:
The
Animation
Effects
toolbar.

Table 17-1	Buttons on the Animation Effects Toolbar	
Button	*Name*	*What It Does*
	Animate Title	Causes the slide title to drop in from above.
	Animate Text	Applies an animation effect to the slide text.
	Drive-In Effect	Applies the Fly From Right build effect and the Screeching Brakes sound to the selected object.
	Flying Effect	Applies the Fly From Left build effect and the Whoosh sound to the selected object.
	Camera Effect	Applies the Box Out build effect and the Camera sound to the selected object.
	Flash Once	Applies the Flash Once (Medium) build effect to the selected object, with no sound.
	Laser Text Effect	Applies the Fly From Top Right, By Letter build effect and the Laser sound effect to the selected object.
	Typing Text Effect	Applies the Wipe Down, By Letter build effect and the Typewriter sound effect to the selected object.
	Reverse Text Order Effect	Applies the Wipe Right effect to each bullet, and each bullet appears from bottom to top.
	Drop-In Text Effect	Applies a Fly From Top, By Word build effect with no sound.
1	Animation Order	Lets you control the order in which objects are animated.
	Custom Animation	Summons the Custom Animation dialog box.
	Animation Preview	Lets you preview the animation effect.

Setting Up a Presentation That Runs by Itself

You can use the PowerPoint slide transitions and animation effects to set up a slide show that runs completely by itself. Just follow these steps:

1. **Switch to Slide Sorter view.**

   Use the View➪Slide Sorter command or click the Slide Sorter View button (shown in the margin).

2. **Set the transitions and text animations however you wish.**

   Refer to the sections "Using Slide Transitions" and "Animating Text" for help with this step.

3. **Press Ctrl+A to select all slides in the presentation.**

4. **Click the Slide Transition button (shown in margin).**

   The Slide Transition dialog box appears (refer to Figure 17-2).

5. **Select the Automatically After check box and then select the number of seconds that you want to pause between each slide.**

6. **Click Apply.**

To run the slide show automatically, choose the Slide Show➪Set Up Show command to summon the Set Up Show dialog box, shown in Figure 17-5. Select the Browsed at a kiosk (full screen) option and then click OK. To view the show, choose the Slide Show➪View Show command.

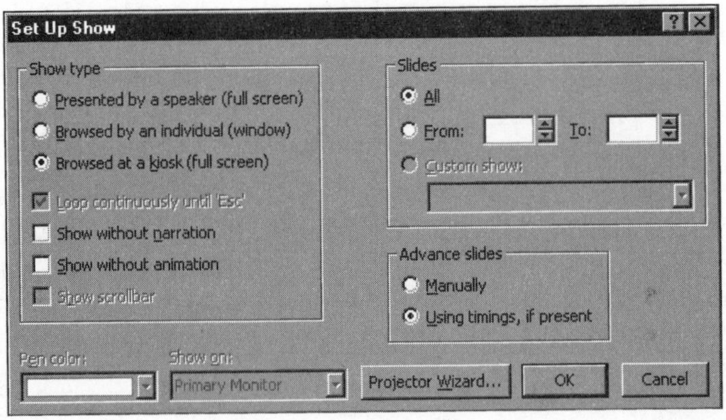

Figure 17-5:
The Set Up Show dialog box.

Part IV

Oh, What a Tangled Web We Weave

The 5th Wave   By Rich Tennant

BUNGCO
BUNGEE CABLE
COMPANY

"Come on, Walt — time to freshen the company Web page."

In this part . . .

Some of the hottest new features of PowerPoint 2000 are Web-compatibility features. Bill Gates is riding the wave of the future again, and the results include zupped-up online collaboration, cool stuff for your Intranet, and HTML formatting ability that makes PowerPoint fit the Internet like an expensive suit. If you, too, have been caught up in the hype of the Internet, and you sleep with your modem under your pillow, you'll appreciate the chapters in this part.

Chapter 18

Working with Hyperlinks and Action Buttons

*I*magine you, a community-minded businessperson, giving a presentation on how a marching band can cure your town's budding juvenile problem when the librarian — you know, the one named Marian — interrupts. She wants you to go back to that section about how pool halls are breeding grounds for all sorts of ills, something you finished several slides ago. How do you skip back to the section quickly?

Now imagine that you're giving a presentation before the executive committee of your company, and the vice president of finance raises a question about some information on a slide. You anticipated the question, and you know that another presentation has a slide that will put the matter to rest, but how do you get to that slide?

With hyperlinks and action buttons, that's how. And this chapter explains the way to use them.

Using Hyperlinks

In PowerPoint, a *hyperlink* is simply a bit of text or a graphic image that you can click when viewing a slide to summon another slide, another presentation, or perhaps some other type of document such as a Word document or an Excel worksheet. The hyperlink may also lead to a page on the Internet's World Wide Web.

For example, suppose that you have a slide that contains a chart of sales trends. You can place a hyperlink on the slide that, if clicked during a slide show, summons another slide presenting the same data in the form of a table. That slide can in turn contain a hyperlink that, when clicked, summons an Excel spreadsheet that contains the detailed data on which the chart is based.

Another common use for hyperlinks is to create a table of contents for your presentation. A slide — usually the first or second slide in the presentation — is created that contains links to other slides in the presentation. The table of contents slide may include a link to every slide in the presentation, but more likely it contains links to selected slides. For example, if a presentation contains several sections of slides, the table of contents slide may contain links to the first slide in each section.

Hyperlinks are not limited to slides in the current presentation. Hyperlinks can lead to other presentations. When you use this kind of hyperlink, a person viewing the slide show clicks the hyperlink, and PowerPoint automatically loads the indicated presentation. The hyperlink can lead to the first slide in the presentation, or it can lead to a specific slide within the presentation.

A common use for this type of hyperlink is to create a menu of presentations that can be viewed. For example, suppose that you have created the following four presentations:

✔ The Detrimental Effects of Pool

✔ Case Studies in Communities Destroyed by Pool Halls

✔ Marching Bands through the Ages

✔ Understanding the Think System

You can easily create a slide listing all four presentations and containing hyperlinks to them. The person viewing the slide show simply clicks on a hyperlink, and off he or she goes to the appropriate presentation.

Here are a few additional thoughts to ponder concerning hyperlinks:

✔ Hyperlinks aren't limited to PowerPoint presentations. In PowerPoint, you can create a hyperlink that leads to other types of Microsoft Office documents, such as Word documents or Excel spreadsheets. When the person viewing the slide show clicks one of these hyperlinks, PowerPoint automatically runs Word or Excel to open the document or worksheet.

✔ A hyperlink can also lead to a page on the Internet's World Wide Web. When the user clicks the hyperlink, PowerPoint runs Internet Explorer to connect to the Internet and display the Web page.

For more information about browsing the World Wide Web, see my book *Internet Explorer 5 For Windows For Dummies,* published by IDG Books Worldwide, Inc.

✔ Hyperlinks only work when the presentation is shown in Slide Show view. You can click on a hyperlink all you want while in Slide view, Outline view, or Slide Sorter view, and the only thing that happens is that your finger gets tired. Links are active only when viewing the slide show.

Creating a hyperlink to another slide

Adding a hyperlink to a presentation is easy. Just follow these steps:

1. **Select the text or graphic object that you want to make into a hyperlink.**

   The most common type of hyperlink is based on a word or two of text in a slide's body text area. For example, in Figure 18-1, I've selected some text ("Trouble in River City") that I want to make into a hyperlink.

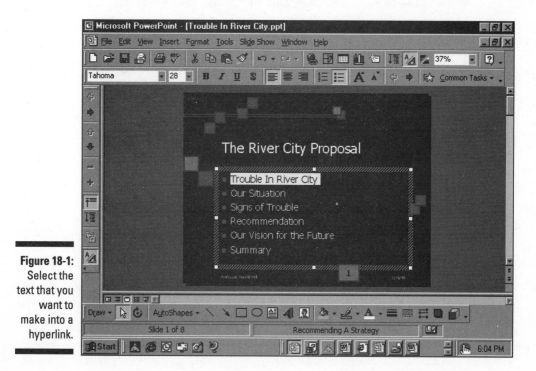

Figure 18-1: Select the text that you want to make into a hyperlink.

2. **Choose the Insert⇨Hyperlink command.**

   Alternatively, click the Insert Hyperlink button (shown in the margin) found on the standard toolbar or use the keyboard shortcut Ctrl+K. One way or the other, the Insert Hyperlink dialog box shown in Figure 18-2 is summoned.

   If you were an Office 97 user, you may be thinking, "Hmmmm!" And right you are. The new Insert Hyperlink Dialog box has some very cool goodies to make you more link-savvy and appear like a techie in all those IT meetings you have to go to. At the top of the dialog box, you see a text box called Text to Display. This is the text for which you are currently creating the link. Right next to it is a button called ScreenTip. Clicking Screen Tip allows you to link a pithy remark to your linked text or object. You can't view this without Internet Explorer 4.0 or later if you are saving this to view it as a Web page, so don't try it if you don't have it. You can view it in a regular presentation even without IE 4.0 or better; the difference is that you need IE 4.0 for Web interface.

3. **Choose a link by clicking one of the four icons on the left side of the Insert Hyperlink Dialog box.**

   They are:

   Existing File or Web Page: This means you can link to another file in another application, or to a Web page on the Internet.

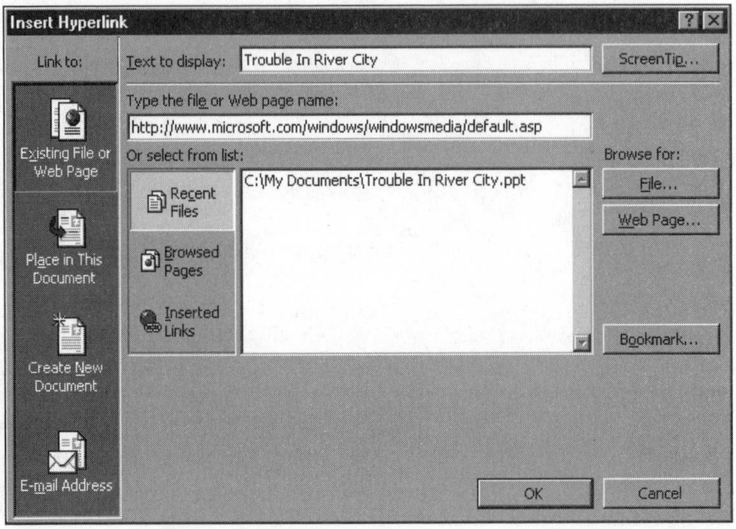

Figure 18-2:
The Insert
Hyperlink
dialog box.

Insert Hyperlink

| Link to: | Text to display: | Trouble In River City | ScreenTip... |

Type the file or Web page name:
http://www.microsoft.com/windows/windowsmedia/default.asp

Or select from list:

Existing File or Web Page

Place in This Document

Create New Document

E-mail Address

Recent Files

Browsed Pages

Inserted Links

C:\My Documents\Trouble In River City.ppt

Browse for:
File...
Web Page...
Bookmark...

OK   Cancel

Pla**ce in This Document:** This means you can link one part of your PowerPoint presentation to another part.

Create **N**ew **Document:** This is just what it says it is. You can, however, choose now or another time to edit the new document by clicking the appropriate button.

E-mail Address: Use this to link to an e-mail address. This feature is useful in an intranet or Internet setting because this link allows the reader to write e-mail to the e-mail address you link to.

If you click Existing File or Web Page, you can then select your link from the following:

- **Re**c**ent Files:** Enables you to view recently used files, which is a subdirectory in windows.

- **B**rowsed **Pages:** Allows you to choose any page you have browsed using your Web browser recently.

- **I**nserted **Links:** Choose from recent links.

You can then make up your mind whether you want to browse for a file, a Web file, or a bookmark, or if you want to turn off the computer and go for coffee. Don't ask me which one I suggest. Then after you have found it and clicked it, click OK. And you have lift off — er, I mean hyperlink.

Suppose you want to just link something to something else in the same presenation. Click Place in this Document, and the text box to the right displays the list of slides in your document. As you click each slide, you can see a slide preview.

4. **Click the slide that you want the hyperlink to lead to, and then click OK.**

   You return to Tri-pane or Normal view.

   The Insert Hyperlink dialog box vanishes, and the hyperlink is created.

If you create the hyperlink on text, the text changes color and is underlined, as shown in Figure 18-3. Graphic objects such as AutoShapes, WordArt, or clip art pictures are not highlighted in any way to indicate that they are hyperlinks. However, the mouse pointer always changes to a hand pointer whenever it passes over a hyperlink, providing a visual clue that the user has found a hyperlink.

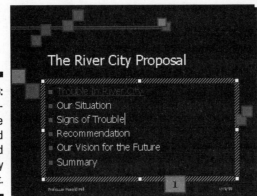

Figure 18-3:
Text hyper-
links are
colored and
underlined
so they
stand out.

The River City Proposal

- Trouble In River City
- Our Situation
- Signs of Trouble|
- Recommendation
- Our Vision for the Future
- Summary

1

Creating a hyperlink to another presentation

Creating a hyperlink that opens another presentation is much like the procedure described in the section "Creating a hyperlink to another slide" but with
a couple important differences. Here are the steps:

1. **Select the text or graphic object that you want to make into a hyperlink.**

2. **Choose the Insert⇨Hyperlink command or click the Insert Hyperlink button.**

   The Insert Hyperlink dialog box appears.

3. **Click Existing File or Web Page.**

   Type the filename in the text box labeled Type the File or Web Page
   Name; you can select from any of the file lists you see that were
   described previously, or you can click the button under Browse for: File.
   You see the Link to File dialog box, as shown in Figure 18-4.

4. **From the Link to File dialog box, select the file that you want to link to and then click OK.**

   You return to the Insert Hyperlink dialog box.

5. **Click OK.**

The presentation that you link to does not have to be in the same folder or
even on the same drive as the current presentation. In fact, you can link to a
presentation that resides on a network file server if you want.

```
Link to File                                                    ? X
 Look in:  [📁 Hill's Presentations]  ▼  ⇐ 🔳 🔍 ✕ 🗂 ▦ ▾ Tools ▾

          [📁]        📄 Doc's Org Chart.ppt
        History       📄 Trombone Sales 1999.ppt

          [📁]
      My Documents

          [📁]
        Desktop

          [📁]
       Favorites

          [📁]       File name:  [                    ] ▼    [📁 OK  ]
      Web Folders    Files of type:  [Office Files (*.htm; *.html; *.doc; *.xls; *.ppt; *.pps; *.o▼]  [ Cancel ]
```

Figure 18-4:
The Link to
File dialog
box.

You can also link to a specific slide within another presentation. Select the text or object in your presentation at which point you would like the hyperlink to appear and click Insert Hyperlink. Under Link to, click Existing File or Web Page and then, if you need to, click Browse for File. Click the file that includes the specific slide you want to hyperlink. Click Bookmark and click the slide you want. Click OK again to dismiss the Insert Hyperlink dialog box.

If you want to create a hyperlink to an existing Web page, just type the address of the Web page in your outline or on your slide, and a hyperlink automatically appears. You can select any page of a Web site as long as you know the URL for that specific page.

Removing a hyperlink

To remove a hyperlink, follow these steps:

1. **Select the hyperlink that you want to remove.**

   Select the entire text for the hyperlink.

2. **Choose the Insert⇨Hyperlink command.**

   Yes, I know that you want to remove a hyperlink, not insert one. Nevertheless, you must use the Insert⇨Hyperlink command to do so. You can also click the Insert Hyperlink button or press Ctrl+K. In any case, the Edit Hyperlink dialog box appears, as shown in Figure 18-5.

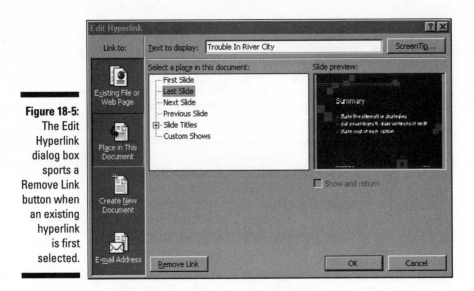

Figure 18-5:
The Edit
Hyperlink
dialog box
sports a
Remove Link
button when
an existing
hyperlink
is first
selected.

3. **Click the Remove Link button.**

   The Insert Link dialog box vanishes, and the link is removed.

You can also remove a hyperlink by right-clicking your mouse as you point your cursor to the hyperlinked text or graphic. You see a floating drop-down menu that allows you to click Hyperlink and Remove Hyperlink. This is also another quick way to get back to the Edit Hyperlink dialog box.

Using Action Buttons

An *action button* is a special type of AutoShape that places a button on the slide. When the user clicks the button during a slide show, PowerPoint takes whatever action you have designated for the button. The following sections describe how action buttons work and show you how to add them to your presentations.

Button actions

When you create a button, you assign a shape for the button (you have 12 shapes to choose from; the shapes are described a bit later in this section) and an action to be taken when the user clicks the button or merely points the mouse pointer at it. The action for a button can be any of the following:

✔ **Activate a hyperlink.** This is the most common button action. It causes a different slide in the current presentation, a different presentation altogether, a non-PowerPoint document, or even an Internet Web page to appear.

✔ **Run a program.** For example, you can set up a button that runs Microsoft Word or Excel.

✔ **Run a macro.** PowerPoint lets you create *macros,* which are programs written in a powerful programming language called Visual Basic for Applications. Chapter 24 explains macros.

✔ **Play a sound.** Adding sound is explained in Chapter 16.

Action buttons are usually set up as hyperlinks, so that when the user clicks the button, a different slide in the current presentation or a different presentation altogether is displayed. A well-planned arrangement of action buttons scattered throughout a presentation can make it easy for someone to view the presentation in any order he or she wants.

Button shapes

PowerPoint provides a selection of built-in shapes for action buttons. Table 18-1 lists the action button shapes that you can place in your presentation and indicates what type of hyperlink is associated with each type.

Table 18-1		Action Buttons
Button Image	**Name**	**What Button Does**
	Custom	No default action for this button type
	Home	Displays the first slide in the presentation
	Help	No default action for this button type
	Information	No default action for this button type
	Back or Previous	Displays the previous slide in the presentation
	Forward or Next	Displays the next slide in the presentation
	Beginning	Displays the first slide in the presentation
	End	Displays the last slide in the presentation
	Return	Displays the most recently viewed slide
	Document	No default action for this button type

(continued)

Table 18-1 (continued)

Button Image	Name	What Button Does
🔊	Sound	No default action for this button type
🎞	Movie	No default action for this button type

Creating a button

To add a button to a slide, follow these steps:

1. **Move to the slide on which you want to place a button.**

2. **Click the AutoShapes button in the drawing toolbar and then click Action Buttons.**

   The Action Buttons toolbox appears, as shown in Figure 18-6.

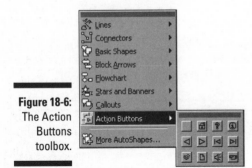

Figure 18-6:
The Action
Buttons
toolbox.

3. **Click the button for the action button shape that you want to create.**

4. **Draw the button on the slide.**

   Start by pointing to the spot where you want the upper-left corner of the button to appear. Then press and hold the left mouse button and drag the mouse to where you want the lower-right corner of the button to appear.

   When you release the mouse button, the Action Settings dialog box appears, as shown in Figure 18-7.

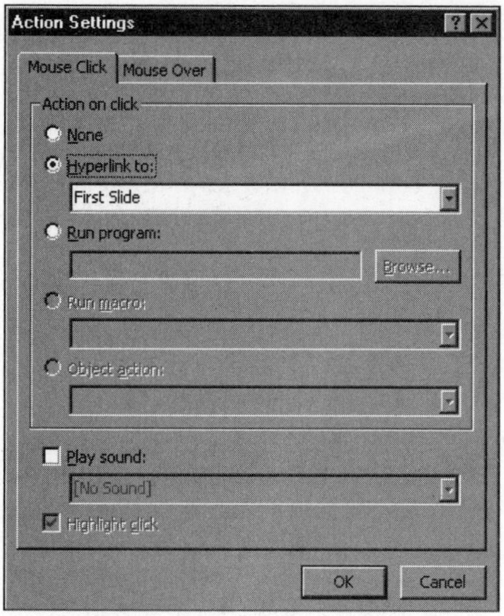

Figure 18-7:
The Action
Settings
dialog box.

5. If you want, change the action settings for the action button.

In most cases, the default setting for the action button that you chose is appropriate for what you want the button to do. For example, the action setting for a Forward or Next Button is Hyperlink to Next Slide. If you want the slide to hyperlink to some other location, change the Hyperlink to setting.

6. Click OK.

The Action Settings dialog box vanishes, and the button is created.

Here are some additional thoughts concerning action buttons:

✔ Like many other AutoShapes, the action button shapes have a fifth handle. *Handles,* by the way, are those little black squares that appear around the corners of objects when you click them. The fifth handle floats near the object; its exact position varies depending on the shape that you select. Dragging this handle changes the apparent depth of the button image.

✔ To move a button, just click it to select it. Then drag the button with the mouse to a new location.

✔ You can change the action setting for a button by right clicking the button and choosing the Action Settings command.

✔ Action buttons by default assume the fill color from the slide's color scheme. You can apply any fill color you want to the button, just like you can to any other drawing object. Refer to Chapter 12 for details.

Creating a navigation toolbar

Grouping action buttons into a navigation toolbar makes a slide show easy to navigate. You can add a set of navigation buttons to the bottom of your Slide Master. For this example, I use Beginning, Backward or Previous, Forward or Next, and Ending buttons, but you can include any buttons you want. To create a navigation toolbar that appears on every slide, follow these steps:

1. **Switch to Slide Master view.**

   Hold down the Shift key while you click the Slide View button or choose the View⇨Master⇨Slide Master command.

2. **Create the action button that you want to include.**

   Follow the procedure described in the section "Creating a button" to create each button. Make sure all the buttons are the same size and line them up to create a tight cluster of buttons.

3. **Return to Slide view.**

   Click the Slide View button or choose the View⇨Slide command.

The buttons that you created will appear on every slide in your presentation. For example, Figure 18-8 shows how a slide might appear with navigation buttons added to the Slide Master.

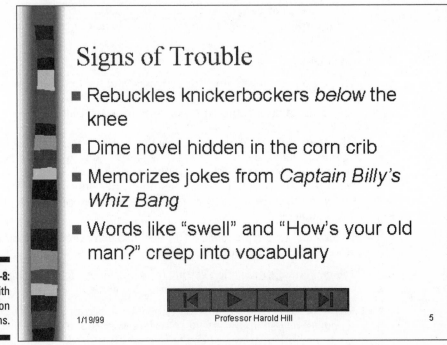

Figure 18-8:
A slide with navigation buttons.

Signs of Trouble

- Rebuckles knickerbockers *below* the knee
- Dime novel hidden in the corn crib
- Memorizes jokes from *Captain Billy's Whiz Bang*
- Words like "swell" and "How's your old man?" creep into vocabulary

1/19/99   Professor Harold Hill   5

Chapter 19

Surfing the Web with PowerPoint 2000

• •

• •

*O*ffice 2000 has one big, gigantic goal — to make everything in the entire Office suite work compatibly with the Internet. In keeping with the times, Office 2000 has been designed with the idea that users will use the Internet, so the software that users select must be Internet-compatible.

I know what you're thinking: You think you have to use special Internet software — such as Microsoft Internet Explorer or Netscape Navigator — to access the Internet. Isn't a browser program required to access the World Wide Web?

Until Microsoft released Office 97, it was. But since then, all the Office programs — including of course PowerPoint 2000 — let you access files on the Internet directly, without going through a Web browser. PowerPoint 2000 lets you open PowerPoint presentation files whether they reside on your computer or on the Internet.

The Internet features described in this chapter also apply to a type of network that has lately become cutting edge in companies around the world, called an *intranet*. An intranet is like a local version of the Internet. It looks, feels, and behaves just like the Internet but is local to a specific company and cannot be accessed by outside users. If your company has an intranet, you can use PowerPoint to open presentations that have been stored on it. Corporations think using an intranet is a "value-added exercise." (Who makes up these hot buzzwords, anyway?)

This entire chapter assumes that you have access to the Internet. If you do not, you should first pick up a copy of my book, *Internet Explorer 5 For Windows For Dummies,* published by IDG Books Worldwide, Inc., which shows you how to get connected to the Internet. And as a bonus, shows you how to use Internet Explorer 5.0 to access the Internet. If you purchased Office 2000, you have Internet Explorer 5 (IE5) available to use. IE5 has some really nifty tricks for using the Internet. You can find more about this software in Chapter 20.

Internet jargon you can't avoid

Unfortunately, there's no way to discuss using PowerPoint to access Internet presentations without using some farily heavy Internet terminology. Here are some basics — an overview of some of the more important Internet terms used in this chapter. (Although I'm sure many of you know these, there is always someone hiding his or her head in the sand.)

✔ **Internet:** The Internet is a huge global network that consists of literally millions of computers.

✔ **World Wide Web:** The fastest-growing segment of the Internet. The Web (as it is usually called) consists of millions of pages of information that can be displayed at will by a Web browser program.

✔ **Web browser:** A program designed to access the World Wide Web. The two most popular Web browsers are Netscape Navigator and Microsoft Internet Explorer.

✔ **HTML:** *HyperText Markup Language,* the codes used to format a page for the World Wide Web. As a casual Web user, you don't have to concern yourself with HTML. If you want to create Web pages of your own, you either need to get user-friendly Web-page creating software to side-step knowing some HTML, or, check out *HTML For Dummies,* 3rd Edition, by Ed Tittel and Steve

James (published by IDG Books Worldwide, Inc.).

You have probably noticed that there are many software applications available for creating your own Web site these days, and many user-friendly Web server communities. All you need to do to publish your own Web site is be able to breathe, able to type, and have Internet access.

✔ **Web page:** A single page of information on the World Wide Web.

✔ **Web server:** A computer that stores Web pages so the pages can be retrieved by Internet users such as yourself.

✔ **Home page:** A Web page that serves as a starting point for a collection of related Web pages (often called a *Web site*).

✔ **FTP:** File Transfer Protocol, a way of copying individual files from one Internet computer to another.

✔ **FTP site:** A server computer that stores files that can be accessed via FTP.

✔ **URL:** Uniform Resource Locator, an Internet address. A URL identifies a Web server or FTP server, plus the filename for the document or file to be retrieved. These days, folks refer to Web page addresses as URLs.

Opening a Presentation at a Web Site Using PowerPoint

Suppose that you create a PowerPoint presentation and decide to make it available to the general public via the Internet. You could do that by converting the presentation to the Internet's popular HTML format, or you can post the presentation file on the Web server so that anyone with PowerPoint can open the presentation directly from the Web server. You have to determine who your audience is, and what they are going to do with the presentation.

If you want to make your PowerPoint presentation available to other PowerPoint users on, let's say, your intranet, then saving your presentation to the Intranet in .ppt format makes sense. If you want to make your presentation available to users without PowerPoint, then saving your presentation in HTML makes sense, as users can access the presentation with only a browser. You can find more information about saving HTML presentations to the Web and using browsers to access HTML files created in PowerPoint in Chapter 20.

You can open .ppt presentations that reside on Internet Web servers by using the standard File➪Open command.

To open a presentation located on a Web server, you must know the complete address (called a URL) of the presentation that you want to open. This address will usually consist of three parts: a server address, one or more directory names, and a filename for the presentation. The address must always begin with `http://` so that PowerPoint can distinguish the address from a normal filename. And the other parts of the URL are separated by slashes.

For example, consider this address:

```
http://www.con.com/river/trouble.ppt
```

Here, the server name is `www.con.com`, the directory is `river`, and the filename is `trouble.ppt`.

When you know the URL, all you have to do to open a presentation is type its URL in the File Name field on the standard Open dialog box. Here's the complete procedure for opening a presentation at an Internet Web site:

1. **Find out the complete URL of the presentation that you want to open.**

2. **Choose the File➪Open command.**

   Alternatively, click the Open button or use the keyboard shortcut Ctrl+O. One way or the other, the Open dialog box shown in Figure 19-1 appears.

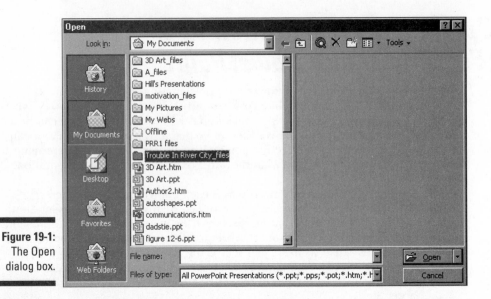

Figure 19-1:
The Open
dialog box.

3. **In the File Name field, type the URL of the presentation that you want to open.**

   For example, type `http://www.con.com/river/trouble.ppt`.

4. **Click Open.**

   If you're not already connected to the Internet, a Connect To dialog box appears so that you can make a connection.

   Copying the file over the Internet to your computer takes a few moments — perhaps a few minutes if the presentation is large. When the transfer is finished, the presentation is displayed as normal, as Figure 19-2 shows.

If you have the Web toolbar displayed, you can enter the address in the Address box, press Enter, and wa-laa! The presentation is displayed. You can find more about the Web toolbar at the end of this chapter.

You have just successfully opened a .ppt presentation residing on the Internet using PowerPoint. In Chapter 20, you learn how to save a PowerPoint presentation to the Web using the Open dialog box, in HTML format, as well as open the presentations in your browser just for kicks, too. Don't put the book down now! Everyone loves a good mystery.

PowerPoint doesn't care if the file identified by the URL is on a computer halfway around the globe, on a computer two floors up from you, or on your own computer. So long as the URL is valid, PowerPoint retrieves the presentation and displays it.

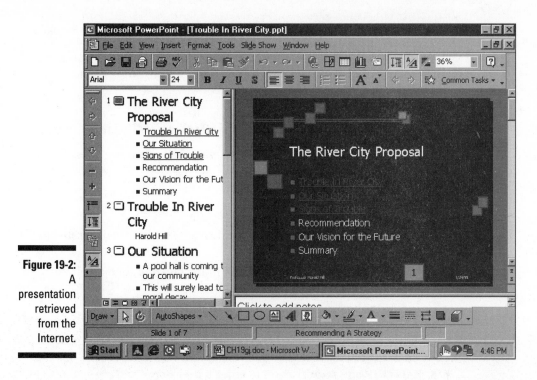

Figure 19-2:
A
presentation
retrieved
from the
Internet.

Using an FTP Site

FTP, which stands for *File Transfer Protocol,* is one of the oldest parts of the Internet. FTP is designed to create Internet libraries where files can be stored and retrieved by other Internet users.

FTP uses a directory structure that works much like Windows 95 or 98 folders. The main directory of an FTP site is called the *root.* Within the root are other directories, which may contain files, additional directories, or both. For example, a typical FTP server for a business may have directories such as Products (for storing files that contain product information), Company (for company information), Software (for software files that can be downloaded), and Docs (for documentation about the company's products).

Until Office 97, you had to use separate FTP software to retrieve files from an FTP site. Since Office 97 (and in PowerPoint 2000, of course), you can access FTP sites from the standard Open and Save As dialog boxes. Since PowerPoint 97, you can set up FTP sites so that you can access them as if they were disk drives attached to your computer.

The following section — "Adding an FTP site to your computer" — explains how you can set up an FTP site so that you can access it from within PowerPoint. The section after that — "Opening a presentation from an FTP site" — shows how to actually access an FTP site from PowerPoint.

Adding an FTP site to your computer

Before you can access files in an FTP site, you must add the address (URL) of the FTP site to your computer's list of FTP sites. To do that, follow these steps:

1. **In PowerPoint, summon the File⇨Open command.**

   This command summons the Open dialog box, which is illustrated in Figure 19-1.

2. **Click the down arrow for the Look in list box and then scroll down to select Add/Modify FTP Locations.**

   The dialog box shown in Figure 19-3 appears.

3. **Type the URL of the FTP site in the Name of FTP site field.**

   Be sure to include `ftp://` at the start of the URL.

4. **If this FTP site requires you to enter a user name and password to gain access, click the User button and then type your user name and password.**

   You have to get the name and password to use from the administrator of the FTP site you are accessing. (At many FTP sites, the user name of "Anonymous" works, with the password being your e-mail name.)

5. **Click Add.**

   The new FTP site is added.

6. **Click OK.**

   The Add/Modify FTP Locations dialog box vanishes, returning you to the Open dialog box.

7. **Click Cancel to return to PowerPoint.**

   The FTP site is now added to the list of FTP sites that are available from within PowerPoint. To open a presentation from this site or another site you have previously added, follow the steps detailed in the next section.

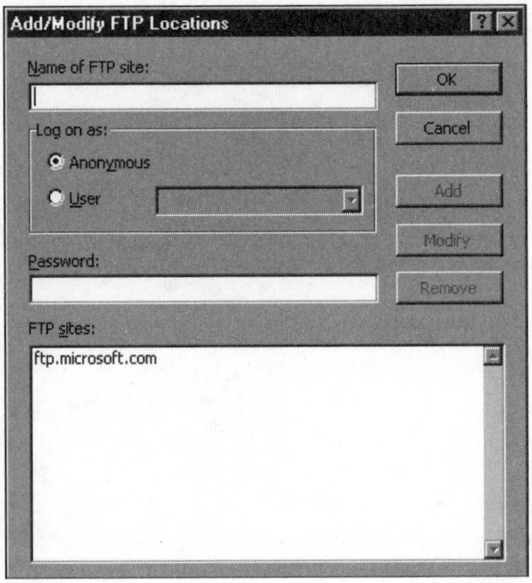

Figure 19-3:
Adding an
FTP site.

Opening a presentation from an FTP site

To open a presentation from an FTP site, follow these steps:

1. **Choose the File⇨Open command.**

   This summons the Open dialog box.

2. **Click the down arrow of the Look in list box and then scroll down to find and select the FTP site containing the presentation that you want to open.**

   Your computer hesitates for a moment as it connects with the FTP site. Then the Open dialog box is displayed, listing the directories that appear at the FTP site's root. See Figure 19-4.

3. **Select the file that you want to open.**

   To open a directory, double-click the directory's icon. Click the icon of the file you want to select.

4. **Click Open.**

   Depending on the size of your presentation, you may have to wait for a few minutes for PowerPoint to download the presentation.

You're done!

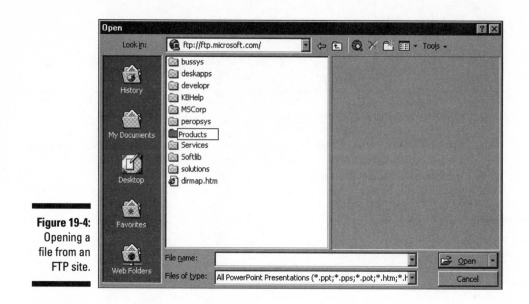

Figure 19-4:
Opening a
file from an
FTP site.

Saving a presentation to an FTP site

If you have access to an FTP site that lets you store your file (that is, if you have "write privileges" for the FTP site), you can also save a presentation directly to the FTP site from PowerPoint using the File⊅Save As command. Here is the procedure:

1. **Choose the File⊅Save As command.**

   The familiar Save As dialog box appears.

2. **Click the down arrow for the Look in list box and then scroll down to find and select the FTP site on which you want to save the presentation.**

   Your computer connects to the FTP site (this may take a moment) and then displays the FTP site's root directory in the Save As dialog box.

3. **Navigate to the directory where you want to save the file.**

4. **Type a name for the file.**

5. **Click Save.**

   The file is copied to the FTP server. Depending on the size of the file, this may take a while. If the file has dozens of slides, each with large graphics, you might have enough time to catch a quick lunch while the file is copied to the FTP server.

Using the Web Toolbar

PowerPoint 2000 (as well as the other Office 97 programs) sports a toolbar called the Web toolbar. The Web toolbar is designed to make it easier for you to view documents that contain hyperlinks or that were retrieved from the World Wide Web. Figure 19-5 shows a document with the Web toolbar active, and Table 19-1 lists the function of each button and control on the Web toolbar.

To summon the Web toolbar, choose the View⇨Toolbars⇨Web or click the Web toolbar button in the standard toolbar.

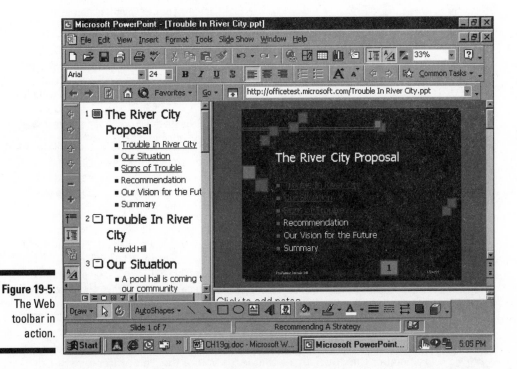

Figure 19-5:
The Web
toolbar in
action.

Table 19-1		Buttons on the Web Toolbar
Button	**Name**	**What It Does**
←	Back	Goes to the previously displayed slide.
→	Forward	Returns to the slide you went back from.

(continued)

Table 19-1 *(continued)*

Button	Name	What It Does
	Refresh Current Page	Reloads the current page.
	Start Page	Displays your designated start page.
	Search Page	Displays your designated search page.
Favorites ▾	Favorites	Displays your favorites list, similar to clicking the Look In Favorites button in an Open or Save As dialog box.
Go ▾	Go	Displays a menu that includes the Back, Forward, Start, and Search commands that correspond to the Back, Forward, Start, and Search buttons. Also includes an Open command and commands to designate the current page as your start page or search page.
	Show only Web toolbar	Temporarily hides everything on the screen except the slide area and the Web toolbar. Click this button again to get the screen back to normal.
	Address	A large combination text box and drop-down list box that shows the address of the current page. I don't picture it here in this table because it's too dang big, but you can't miss it: It takes up almost the whole right half of the Web toolbar.

TIP

If you find that you don't have all the buttons you want on your Web toolbar, remember the down arrow that leads you to the Add or Remove Buttons button. Chant, "Button, button, who's got the button?" while performing this task, and it works a lot better.

TIP

The Web toolbar is most useful when used in a slide show that is browsed by an individual rather than one that is printed out as slides or transparencies and shown with a projector. For example, suppose that you create a presentation that describes your company's employee benefits programs, and the presentation contains dozens of hyperlinks that bounce back and forth from slide to slide and perhaps even lead to other presentations. When individuals view this presentation, they'll want to activate the Web toolbar so they can use its controls to follow the presentation's hyperlinks and to go back to slides they've already viewed.

Chapter 20

Creating Web Pages with PowerPoint 2000

- -

In This Chapter

▶ Saving presentations as Web pages

▶ Publishing options

▶ Publishing a presentation or HTML file to the Web

▶ Opening a PowerPoint presentation on the Web using your browser

- -

*P*owerPoint 2000 includes a feature that can convert your presentations into a special format called *HTML (HyperText Markup Language)*. This feature is called Save as a Web Page. As you probably know, HTML is the format used to create documents viewed on the Internet's World Wide Web by programs such as Microsoft Internet Explorer or Netscape Navigator. In Office 2000, this function is no longer called Save as HTML, and there is no wizard to bother with — it isn't necessary any longer.

After you've saved a presentation as a Web page, you have converted it to HTML format, and, as you know, you can place HTML files on a World Wide Web server computer. As a result, everyone with access to the Internet can view your presentation online, using his or her own Internet access software, be it Netscape Navigator or Internet Explorer.

This chapter explores using PowerPoint as a tool for creating Web pages. And thanks to the innovations of PowerPoint 2000, the whole thing is getting far easier than it used to be.

Creating Web pages is just the beginning of having an "up-and-running" Web site. This chapter shows you what you need to know to convert PowerPoint presentations to HTML files so that they can be placed on the Web. To set up and manage your own Web site, however, you need to know much more than what's in this chapter. For more information, I recommend that you consult *HTML For Dummies,* 3rd Edition, by Ed Tittel and Steve James.

About the Save as a Web Page Feature

The Save as a Web Page feature converts PowerPoint presentations to HTML files that can be published on the World Wide Web and displayed by Web browsers such as Microsoft Internet Explorer and Netscape Navigator. By selecting Save as a Web Page in the File menu, you instantly summon the Save As dialog box that gives you access to Web publishing features. When you save a .ppt file in HTML format, PowerPoint 2000 creates a separate Web page for each slide in your presentation. All these Web pages, with the exception of the starting page, are stored in a single folder using the name of the presentation that you are converting.

For example, if you convert a presentation named Trouble in River City.ppt, the Save as a Web Page feature creates the presentation's HTML files in a folder named Trouble in River City_files. It also creates a file called Trouble in River City.htm.

In PowerPoint 97, you may remember, that the main HTML file for a converted presentation was named Index.htm. Now it is the designated name you give the presentation plus the file extension .htm.

The first thing you see when you select Save as a Web Page is the Save As dialog box shown in Figure 20-1.

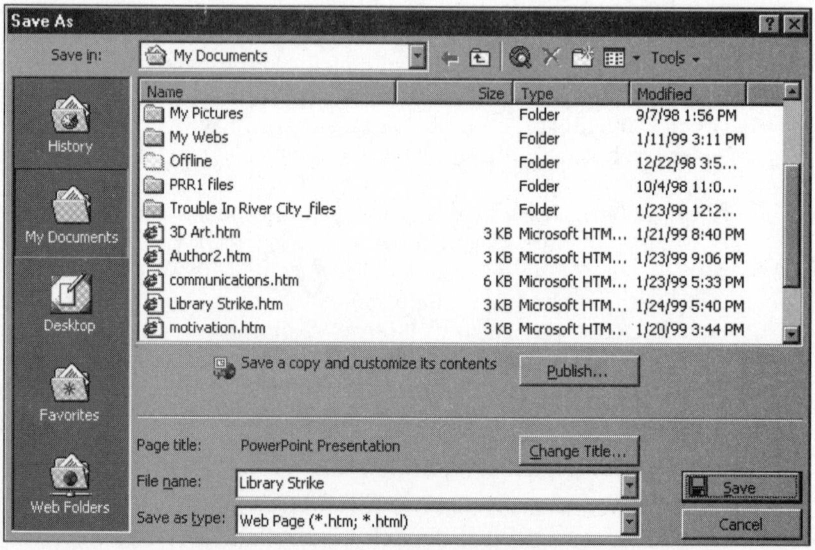

Figure 20-1:
When saving as a Web page, the Save As dialog box appears.

To save a PowerPoint presentation as a Web page, follow these steps:

1. **Select File➪Save as Web Page.**

   Notice that the name of your presentation appears in the File Name text box and that the Save as Type text box says: Web Page (*.htm; *.html).

   Now, also notice that there is a Page title and also an opportunity to change the title. The default title is always PowerPoint Presentation. You may want to change this title so that the title of the page that appears in the title bar of the browser is something more definitive and interesting.

2. **Click the Change Title button to see the Set Page Title dialog box that appears in Figure 20-2.**

Figure 20-2:
The Set
Page Title
dialog box.

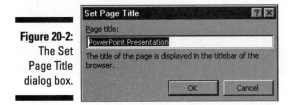

Whether or not you choose another title, you are ready to set up the publishing formatting for your presentation.

3. **Click the Publish button in the middle of the dialog box.**

   Lo and behold, the Publish as Web Page dialog box appears. Now what, you ask? Well, this handy dialog box lets you set up your Web page with all the important details necessary to make it appear according to your innermost desires.

Web Page Publishing Options

So, you are ready to publish this presentation as a Web page, are you? Well it won't be hard with the handy dandy Publish as Web Page dialog box. Here's how:

1. **Make your selections in the "Publish What?" section of the dialog box.**

   Here you decide if you are going to publish the whole presentation or just a number of slides from the presentation. Notice that you can choose to display your speaker notes. Make the appropriate selections, and you are ready to move on.

2. Click the Web Options button.

Time for a new dialog box. This dialog box, aptly named Web Options and shown in Figure 20-3, leads you through a variety of choices necessary to set up your published Web page files as you like them.

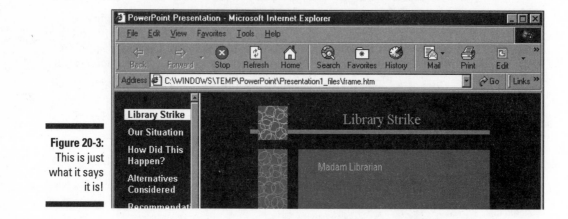

Figure 20-3: This is just what it says it is!

Here you see four different tabs: General, Files, Pictures, and Encoding. You don't have to be a Web wizard to figure this out; the default settings work for most saved presentations. The General tab allows you to make appearance selections, the Files tab makes determinations about how you files will be organized, the Pictures tab allows you to mess around with the picture files in a presentation, and the Encoding tab is set for Western European (Windows). Notice, if you click the drop-down text box, you have other choices.

3. Click OK.

You are back in the Publish as Web Page dialog box.

Now, take a gander at the browser support area. This is important. Not everyone has Internet Explorer 5. To make sure that every Tom, Dick, and Barbara can open your presentation in their browser, select All browsers listed above. Good.

4. Now, examine the Publish a Copy as section of the dialog box.

This is easy. You have another chance to change your presentation title if you wish, and you should also see the filename of the correct file in the File Name text box. If you need to, you can browse your drives for the appropriate file.

5. Click Open Published Web page in browser.

You should see Internet Explorer 5 open up majestically and display your presentation that you have saved as a HTML file like Figure 20-4.

Figure 20-4:
Bingo!

Publishing a Presentation or HTML File to the Web

Now that you've got it, what do you do with it? Here's where you need to know a little bit about the Web. You will also need Web space, whether on the Internet, or your company's intranet, in which to publish your Web page. Never fear, it's not that hard to do. Assuming you have a Web server address, here are the steps:

1. **Open your presentation that you have saved in HTML.**

   Just click on the File⇨Open and select the right .htm presentation.

2. **Select Save as Web Page from the File menu.**

3. **Now type the Web server's URL that you would like to save the .htm file to in the File Name text box.**

   Remember URL addresses always begin with http://.

4. **Click Save.**

   PowerPoint connects to the Web server and displays the folders that are currently housed on the site.

5. **Place your cursor over the File <u>N</u>ame text box and watch the name of your .htm file reappear.**

   Just like that.

6. **Click Save.**

Guess what, you're done. Now, for fun, find it using your Web browser. Type the URL address to the server you sent it to and add the name of your file, dividing the server URL and your filename (including the extension, such as Trouble.htm) by a slash. Click Go, and your file appears. Make sure you are connected to the Internet or your intranet, or it won't work.

What the heck are all those files that you see in your file folder? Thought you'd ask me. Some of the most interesting are:

✔ **GIF:** One of the most commonly used graphics formats on the Internet, but also one that results in large graphics files. If you are going to place the presentation on a corporate intranet, use this format.

✔ **JPEG:** Another popular graphics format. JPEG files are compressed, which means that some of the detail in your slides may be lost, but the slide files will be smaller. If people access your presentation over the Internet using modem connections (which are slow), this is the format to use.

✔ **PowerPoint Animation:** A new format designed specifically for PowerPoint presentations. It preserves any animations that you have created for the presentation, such as build effects, transitions, and so on. To view a presentation converted to HTML with PowerPoint Animation, people viewing the presentation must have a special program called the PowerPoint Animation Viewer installed on their computers. Fortunately, the Viewer is free and can be downloaded from the Microsoft Web site. In fact, the Viewer is automatically downloaded and installed when the user first views the presentation, so users don't have to do anything to view PowerPoint Animation presentations.

After you convert your presentation, you must upload it to your Web server's disk in order to make it available on the World Wide Web. You must copy all the files in the presentation's folder to the Web server.

Unfortunately, the procedures you have to follow to copy your files to the Web server depend on how your Web server has been set up. This is one of those times when being friends with the person responsible for administering the Web site can pay off.

Viewing a Converted Presentation

After you finish converting a presentation to HTML using the Save as HTML Wizard, you will naturally want to view it to make sure the conversion worked as you expected. To view your converted HTML presentation, just select <u>F</u>ile⇔Web Page Preview. Your Web page is instantly loaded into Internet Explorer 5.

Part V
Working with Presentations

In this part . . .

No matter how hard you try, you cannot avoid dealing with files. After all, the basic function of PowerPoint 2000, and just about any other program, for that matter, is to create files. If all you ever do is create files, pretty soon your hard disk resembles my feeble attempts at gardening: The good stuff is choked nearly to death by giant 8-foot weeds that you should have pulled out months ago. Like a garden, your hard disk — along with its directories and files — must be tended.

The chapters in this part are a file-management gardening guide. They explore the intricacies of working with PowerPoint files, making sure your files coexist peacefully with other types of files, keeping track of your files, and making sure that your files get adequate sunlight and nourishment.

Chapter 21

Online Collaborations

In This Chapter

▶ Using Presentation Broadcast

▶ Holding Web discussions

▶ Keeping in touch with e-mail subscriptions

▶ Meeting now with NetMeeting

••

*P*owerPoint has finally gotten Net savvy. In an effort to address the fast-growing trend to integrate its Office applications to the Internet, Microsoft has begun to realize that the future of computing really will rely on the ability of software to interface globally. Minus the trendy talk, the Internet is "da bomb." It continues to be the hottest, fastest, coolest, and most productive way to do business in the world. Now, when someone figures out how to rid us of SPAM, we'll all be set.

In previous editions of this book, I noted that it was nice to have a modem, and I expected that most people had some experience with the Internet. There were, however, a number of users who were not online. But now any child can and does use the Internet. Face it — if you don't have access to the Internet, you won't have anything to discuss with your friends, colleagues, or — ahem — your children.

So, get on with it. Why not finally open one of those cool "free 50-hour" deals you have been chucking in a drawer? With two shakes of a mouse's tail, you'll be online. This chapter addresses some great stuff you can do with PowerPoint and your Internet (or intranet) connection, making you a global PowerPoint user.

Using Presentation Broadcast

Remember Presentation Conference in PowerPoint 97? Wonder what happened to it? It is now Presentation Broadcast. It used to be that you and your PowerPoint-using friends could get together and view a slide show in real time. Nobody but your exclusive I-have-PowerPoint-Installed pals could join you for a conference. Not so in 2000. Now the only prerequisites for joining in are that you are breathing and that you have a Web browser. (Oh yeah, you have to have an Internet connection, too. But from now on, if you're reading this chapter, I assume that you are following directions and you have one!)

This chapter shows several of the ways PowerPoint 2000 is equipped to help you collaborate effectively using the Internet. The first thing this chapter covers is Presentation Broadcast. To use Presentation Broadcast, follow these steps:

1. **You need a presentation to broadcast and someone who cares.**

   If you don't have a presentation to broadcast, you will need one eventually, but you can schedule a broadcast using a blank presentation. Go back and look at your recently prepared presentations. Pick one. If you haven't created one, it's time to go back a few chapters and get busy. Then, get some of your colleagues to commit to viewing your broadcast. These people don't have to be across the country — they can be anywhere.

2. **Select Slide Show⇨Online Broadcast⇨Set Up and Schedule.**

   The dialog box shown in Figure 21-1 appears.

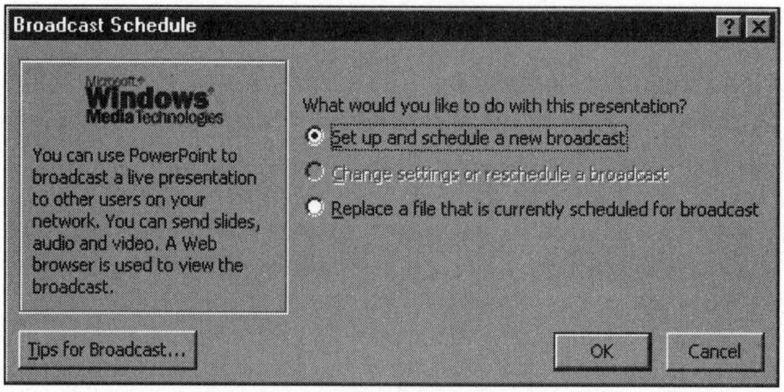

Figure 21-1:
You are
instantly
confronted
with the
Broadcast
Schedule
dialog box.

Broadcast Schedule	? ✕
Windows Media Technologies	**What would you like to do with this presentation?**
You can use PowerPoint to broadcast a live presentation to other users on your network. You can send slides, audio and video. A Web browser is used to view the broadcast.	◉ Set up and schedule a new broadcast
	○ Change settings or reschedule a broadcast
	○ Replace a file that is currently scheduled for broadcast
Tips for Broadcast...	OK Cancel

If you remember the Presentation Conference Wizard in 97, just get used to the fact that you aren't going to be babied anymore. Savvy Internet users don't need to be talked down to and patronized by a smarmy little Wizard. (Or do we?)

3. Click Set Up and Schedule a New Broadcast, and then click OK.

Suddenly a new dialog box pops up, appropriately called the Schedule a New Broadcast dialog box. Now, beginning with the default tab, Description, the Title of the presentation you have open when you select Presentation Broadcast appears. If you are scheduling from a blank presentation, you may want to open a new one and save it with the title you will be using to save yourself some steps later.

4. Add the necessary information to the Description tab of the Schedule a New Broadcast dialog box.

All of the information you are about to add gives the people who are going to view your broadcast information that shows up in the Lobby. (Note the Preview Lobby Page button.) The Lobby is a place where people stand around and talk, drink cappuccino, and hob-nob (There, I finally said "hob-nob" in print!). Actually, this page is a Web page that allows you to give preview information to your audience about your broadcast before beginning. Add your Title, Description, Speaker and Contact information here as in Figure 21-2.

Figure 21-2:
The Description tab sets up your Lobby information.

Schedule a New Broadcast ? X

| Description | Broadcast Settings |

This information will appear on the lobby page for the new broadcast:

Title: Trouble In River City

Description: This informatative broadcast will give you all you need to know to protect your son or your daughter from the arms of a jungle animal instinct--Hysteria! Friends, the idle brain is the devil's playground-Trouble!

Speaker: Harold Hill

Contact: Harold Hill   [Address Book...]

[Preview Lobby Page]   [Schedule Broadcast]   [Cancel]

As you enter your description information, make sure you spell carefully. Spell check doesn't work here. If you are a terrible speller, consider cutting and pasting a spell-checked paragraph or two here.

5. Now click Preview Lobby Page and take a look.

Notice that Microsoft Internet Explorer is automatically called up to display the Lobby page, as shown in Figure 21-3.

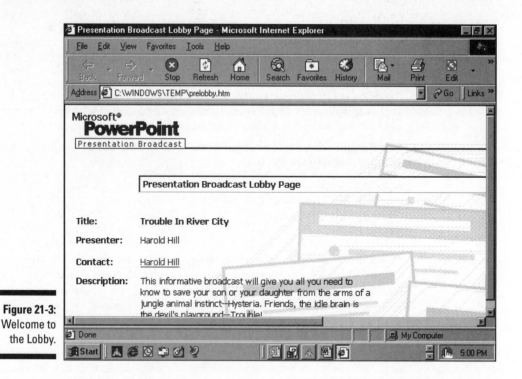

Figure 21-3:
Welcome to
the Lobby.

Now, you have to make some choices about what's going to happen when your audience is actually viewing your broadcast. If you used Presentation Conference, you remember that you couldn't send sound and video. (Well, actually, you could hear some sounds like those applied to transitions or animations, but only if an audience member's computer was set up for that.) But you couldn't use a microphone and broadcast your voice in Real Time. Set up any of the following in your broadcast settings.

✔**Audio and video:** Anything that you can see or hear over the Web is a possibility in Presentation Broadcast. But you have to check the appropriate check boxes at the top of this dialog box.

✔**Audience feedback during broadcast:** Do you want to hear what people think? If you do, this part of the dialog box allows you to set up e-mail options so that people can send their thoughts to you in e-mail. Also, if you have access to a chat server, you can conduct real-time chat during your presentation. I don't know about you, but I hate it when people whisper during my show.

✔**Recording:** This is a handy trick, and it's sure to save you some precious time. This option allows you to record your broadcast and save it somewhere convenient. No more long phone calls trying to explain what somebody missed — just direct the person to the location of the recorded broadcast and get back to work.

I ✔**Viewers can access speaker notes**: Yep. Take a look at it all in Figure 21-4.

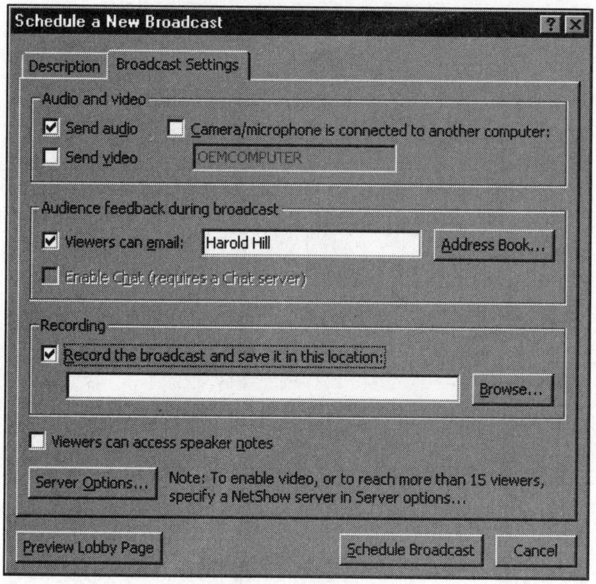

Figure 21-4:
The
Schedule
a New
Broadcast
dialog box.

Schedule a New Broadcast dialog box:

- Description / Broadcast Settings (tabs)
- Audio and video
  - ☑ Send audio   ☐ Camera/microphone is connected to another computer: OEMCOMPUTER
  - ☐ Send video
- Audience feedback during broadcast
  - ☑ Viewers can email: Harold Hill   Address Book...
  - ☐ Enable Chat (requires a Chat server)
- Recording
  - ☑ Record the broadcast and save it in this location: Browse...
- ☐ Viewers can access speaker notes
- Server Options...   Note: To enable video, or to reach more than 15 viewers, specify a NetShow server in Server options...
- Preview Lobby Page   Schedule Broadcast   Cancel

That was simple. The next part is the tricky part. Actually, it's not so bad once you are clear about a few pesky details. Read the next section to find out about the details.

Scheduling a Broadcast

Here is where all the great stuff you know about creating shared folders comes into play. (See the following sidebar.) In this section, you set up all the fussy stuff about your broadcast. Follow these steps:

1. **Click Schedule Broadcast on the bottom of the Schedule a New Broadcast dialog box.**

   The dialog box shown in Figure 21-5 appears.

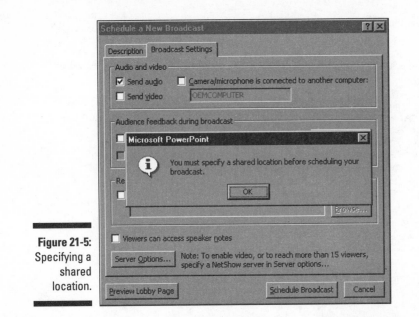

Figure 21-5:
Specifying a
shared
location.

Creating shared folders

In order to schedule a Presentation Broadcast, you need to specify a shared location folder. This little trick is easy after you find out how to jump through the various hoops required in Windows 95 or better. Basically, a broadcast requires a server to host the broadcast and a shared folder for users to be able to access shared information. The following are a few Windows tricks to help you leave work before ten in the evening.

1. Make sure File and Print Sharing is enabled on your computer. In your Control Panel, click the Network Dialog box icon. On the Configuration Tab, Click File and Print Sharing. This loads the necessary files to allow you to do this. Click OK and restart your computer for this change to take effect.

2. Before leaving this dialog box, click the Identification tab and determine the name of your computer. This will be the server name for the shared folder.

3. In Windows Explorer or My Computer, highlight the folder you want to make the shared folder. On the File menu, click Properties. Click the Sharing Tab and then click Shared As. Notice that the Share name is the name of the Shared folder you selected.

4. Decide if you want your Shared Folder to be Read-Only. You can even create a password to determine who has rights and privileges with your shared file. Click OK.

Your shared folder path is: Folder name\.

2. **Click OK and enter the shared location information in the Server Options dialog box.**

   Enter your shared location in this way: \\Servername\Shared Folder name\.

   Notice the way this looks in the Specify a Shared Location text box, as shown in Figure 21-6. Note the directions of the slash marks and the double slash marks at the beginning of the entry.

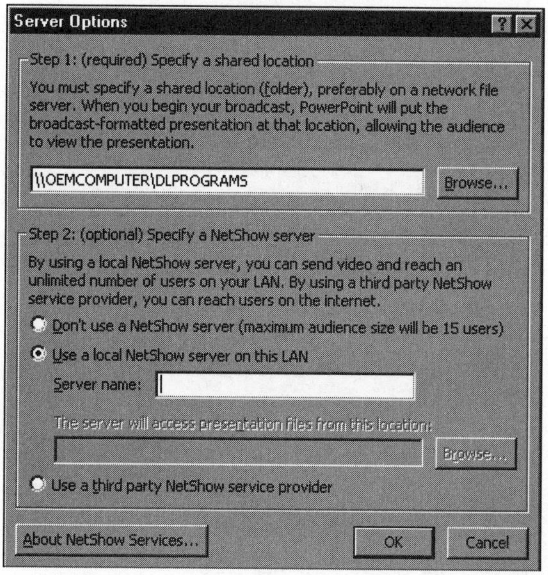

Figure 21-6:
\\Servername
\Shared
Folder name\.

Server Options

Step 1: (required) Specify a shared location

You must specify a shared location (folder), preferably on a network file server. When you begin your broadcast, PowerPoint will put the broadcast-formatted presentation at that location, allowing the audience to view the presentation.

\\OEMCOMPUTER\DLPROGRAMS   Browse...

Step 2: (optional) Specify a NetShow server

By using a local NetShow server, you can send video and reach an unlimited number of users on your LAN. By using a third party NetShow service provider, you can reach users on the internet.

○ Don't use a NetShow server (maximum audience size will be 15 users)

◉ Use a local NetShow server on this LAN

   Server name:

   The server will access presentation files from this location:

                                          Browse...

○ Use a third party NetShow service provider

About NetShow Services...   OK   Cancel

3. **Click OK and then click the Schedule Broadcast button once more.**

   PowerPoint validates your settings and plops you into the Outlook scheduler dialog box, as shown in Figure 21-7.

   You don't really think I am going to explain Outlook in this paragraph, do you? I hope not. If you are not familiar with Outlook, pick up an excellent book on the subject. I suggest *Outlook 2000 For Windows For Dummies* by Bill Dyszel. This book quickly gets you up to speed on the ins and outs of Outlook 2000 if it's new to you.

4. **Save, and you are ready to broadcast.**

   As soon as you save your Settings in the Outlook scheduler dialog box, you should close the dialog box. PowerPoint gives you the good news shown in Figure 21-8.

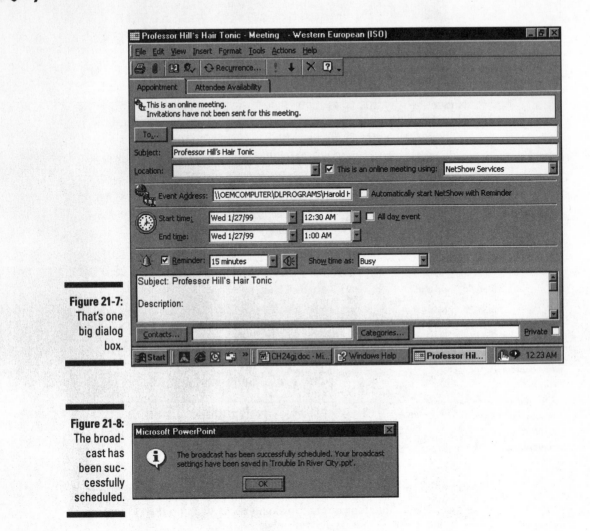

Figure 21-7:
That's one
big dialog
box.

Figure 21-8:
The broad-
cast has
been suc-
cessfully
scheduled.

5. Click OK.

When you reopen the same file, you can begin your broadcast.

6. Reopen your file.

7. Select Slide Show⇨Online Broadcast⇨Begin Broadcast.

Suddenly PowerPoint 2000 is dashing around preparing your broadcast.
It's so exciting! Like opening night! Seriously, PowerPoint connects to
NetShow and does a little encoding trick to get your broadcast ready,
and then you get to check your microphone, as shown in Figure 21-9.

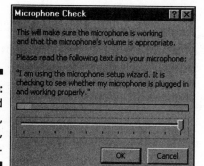

Figure 21-9:
Sound
check,
testing one,
two, three.

8. **Read the text provided on the Microphone Check dialog box.**

   After you have determined whether or not your voice is registering, you can move on.

9. **Click OK.**

10. **Click Start on the Broadcast Presentation dialog box, and break a leg.**

    Your broadcast runs just like a slide show. The right and left mouse commands remain the same.

Online Collaboration Tools — Web Discussions in PowerPoint

If you are an employee, rather than self-employed, usually you work with other people. Writers sometimes forget that other people actually exist, and they need to communicate, but they do. One great way to communicate with your colleagues is with the new PowerPoint 2000 feature called Web Discussions.

Web Discussions allow you and your workin' pals to review a presentation, and use a nifty discussion panel at the bottom of your screen to make remarks. (Remember, this feature does require that Office Server Extensions are installed on your company's Web server, but a simple phone call to your network administrator or a quick stop by his or her office with a box of Ding Dongs should help you secure the server address to connect to.)

To start a Web Discussion in PowerPoint, follow these steps:

1. **Make some friends at work.**

   You can have a discussion with yourself, but people will talk. You and your colleagues will find that it is easy to view documents from your individual computers, even if you are in the same office. This makes even more sense for branch offices miles away.

2. Choose Tools⇨Online Collaboration⇨Web Discussions.

Suddenly a dialog box appears, like the one shown in Figure 21-10, giving you the opportunity to add a discussion server. Now's the time to bribe the network administrator with those Ding Dongs.

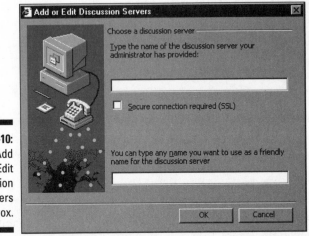

Figure 21-10:
The Add
or Edit
Discussion
Servers
dialog box.

In this dialog box, you need to enter the name of the discussion server. Notice that dialog box says ". . . your administrator has provided." Hey, those Ding Dongs did the trick! The second text box in the dialog box prompts you to type a "friendly" name for the discussion server. I guess unfriendly names are not politically correct.

3. Click OK.

Now, you are sent into the next phase of setting up your discussion, the Discussion Options dialog box appears. Notice, as in Figure 21-11, that the server you have entered appears, and after making a few selections, you will be ready to discuss to your heart's content.

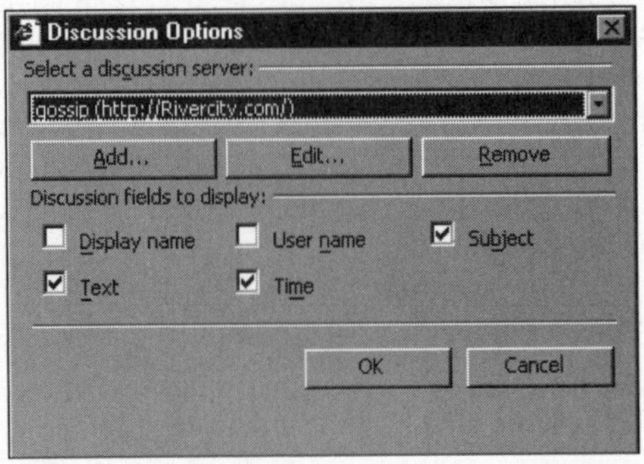

Figure 21-11:
Discussion
Options.

In this spot you can edit, add or remove your server selections as well as set up how you would like your discussion to appear. You can set up your discussion fields here including Display name, User name, and Subject, Text and Time. This is all very logical.

4. Click OK.

Watch as your screen morphs into a discussion. You begin to see others making remarks that come across your discussion pane.

Feel like making a remark? Notice the new toolbar that appears below the discussion pane, as shown in Figure 21-12. Appropriately enough, it is called the Web Discussions toolbar. This toolbar is available only at this point in PowerPoint. You cannot access it like most other toolbars through View⇨Toolbars. See Table 21-1 for a brief description of its functions.

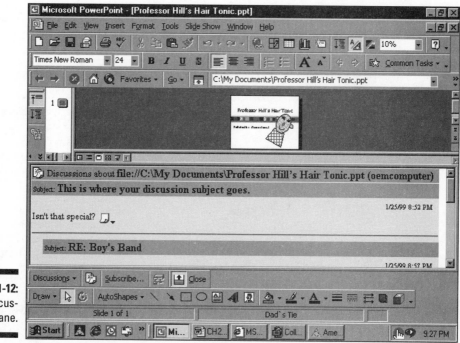

Figure 21-12:
The discussion pane.

Table 21-1	The Web Discussion Toolbar Buttons	
Description	*Button*	*What it Does*
 Discussions ▾	Discussions	Leads you to a pull-down menu of options to insert, refresh, filter, or print the discussions. Also gives you a return trip to the Discussion Options dialog box.
 [icon]	Insert Discussion	Shortcut to the same function on the Discussions pull-down menu.
 Subscribe...	Subscribe	This feature allows you to be notified by e-mail when any changes are made to a document or the contents of a file folder. Curious? Wait one more page.
 [icon]	Stop Communication	Disconnects you from the discussion server.
 [icon]	Show/Hide Discussion Pane	Clicking this button hides or displays (whichever you aren't already doing) the discussion pane. It does not disconnect you from the discussion server.
 Close	Close	Closes the whole Web Discussion, including the discussion pane, and disconnects you from the server.

5. **Click the Insert Discussion icon in the pane and become verbose.**

   You see the same floating menu as pictured in Figure 21-13. Click Reply, Edit, or Delete, and you are on your way.

Figure 21-13: Become verbose in three easy steps!

6. **Just for kicks, click Reply.**

   Type away in the resulting Enter Discussion Text dialog box.

7. **Click OK.**

E-Mail Subscriptions

Now, just for the sake of argument, pretend you are totally captivated by the document you are discussing, and you want to keep track of the changes made to it. How can you do this? It's easy with Document Subscription. This feature allows you to sign up to be notified by e-mail every time the document changes. Press the Document Subscription button on the Web Discussion toolbar (which I discuss in the previous section). The Document Subscription dialog box appears, looking just like the one shown in Figure 21-14. First you select the individual document or folder you want to keep in touch with. Then you decide the kinds of changes you want to know about. See the range of options listed in Figure 21-14.

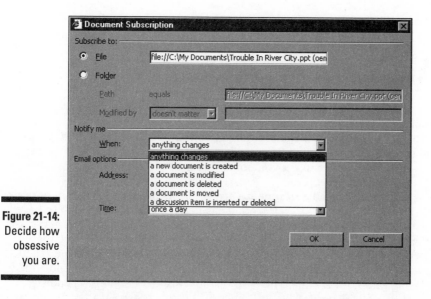

Figure 21-14: Decide how obsessive you are.

Now viewers can subscribe to e-mail. As shown in Figure 21-15, you can subscribe to change notices every time the document changes, or merely daily, or, for those who don't have enough mail already in their in-boxes, only once a week! (Those slackers.)

Document Subscription

Subscribe to:

● File   file://C:\My Documents\Trouble In River City.ppt (oen

○ Folder

   Path   equals   file://C:\My Documents\Trouble In River City.ppt (oen

   Modified by   doesn't matter

Notify me

   When: anything changes

Email options

   Address: HaroldHill@boysband.org

         (e.g. someone@microsoft.com)

   Time: once a day

         when a change occurs
         once a day
         once a week

                                     Cancel

Figure 21-15:
Decide how
much mail
you want.

That's all there is to it. Test it out and enjoy.

Meet Now with NetMeeting

You know how PowerPoint includes various tools that are actually applications in and of themselves. The Meet Now feature hooks you up with yet another — NetMeeting. You may already be familiar with NetMeeting, and if you aren't, you need to sit down and spend a day or two with it. However, here are a few basics to get you pointed in the right direction.

I'm not going to be able to squeeze in a whole *NetMeeting For Dummies* book at the end of Chapter 21. NetMeeting has been around long enough to have a mature set of features that support any size meeting and any level of complexity. It works so well, in fact, that it is fast becoming a staple in large corporate intranets and making it hard for business travelers to keep their budgets. You can figure it out just by having a friend at the other end and playing with it for a while. The Help text for this feature in PowerPoint, in NetMeeting itself, and at `www.microsoft.com/netmeeting/` are all pretty good.

What's so hot about NetMeeting, you ask? Well, for starters, it's a collaborative application that allows you and your colleagues to work on the same presentation, using a whiteboard, chat, audio, and video broadcast, and of course the Windows application of your choice. One big difference between

NetMeeting and Presentation Broadcast is that NetMeeting users can take turns driving the application. And PowerPoint in NetMeeting isn't limited to a mere slide show presentation. NetMeeting viewers get to see the presenter edit changes in PowerPoint (or Word or Excel or . . .).

In PowerPoint 2000, for the first time you are able to start up NetMeeting without ever leaving PowerPoint. Plus, there is a mini-NetMeeting toolbar to help you host your meeting without flip-flopping between windows like a salmon in Seattle's Pike's Market.

Check your company's policy on lunchtime video gaming before connecting with your pals in another time zone and setting up that chess match. Some companies frown on their employees creating virtual casinos by combining NetMeeting with a $10 piece of roulette or blackjack software.

To get there from here, you need to choose Tools⇨Online Collaboration⇨ Meet Now and identify yourself, if asked.

Now select a server to host your meeting. From the Place a Call dialog box, shown in Figure 21-16, you pick your server from the Directory text box. You should have decided on this location with your fellow collaborators when you scheduled your meeting. (Remember Meeting Scheduling 101? Who, What, Where, When, Why?) Otherwise, you will be destined to wander all of cyberspace hoping by mere fortune to bump into them. Notice that most of these NetMeeting servers have weird names such as ils.microsoft.com. ILS stands for Internet Locater Server. Don't make me explain how it works, but somehow the server software knows who is on that server and has NetMeeting running at the same time.

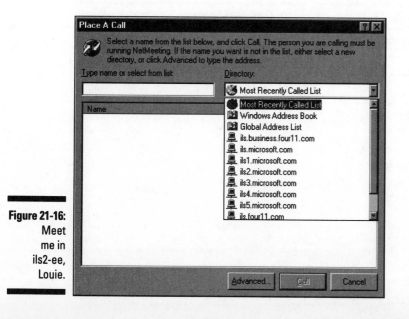

Figure 21-16: Meet me in ils2-ee, Louie.

After you choose your server, then pick your partner and do-si-do. Double-click and promenade. Your collaborators can call you, too. Kinda like a Sadie Hawkins dance.

Now you've done it. You've started a NetMeeting. The NetMeeting application launches. If this is the first time you've ever run NetMeeting, you are prompted for some profile information. It's simple to fill in. After NetMeeting is set up, you will be back in PowerPoint, but now you see a new nifty little toolbar, called Online Meeting (see Figure 21-17).

Figure 21-17:
The Online
Meeting
nifty little
toolbar.

NetMeeting has many more features than those shown on the PowerPoint 2000 Online Meeting toolbar, but PowerPoint did capture the important ones needed to conduct a simple meeting, get the job done, and go home. You can start up the Online Meeting toolbar anytime you want from View⇨Toolbars⇨ Online Meeting. It will be terribly boring, though, because all the function buttons will be grayed out. Table 21-2 tells you about the buttons in the toolbar.

Table 21-2	The Online Meeting Toolbar Buttons	
Description	**Button**	**What it Does**
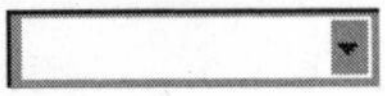 [▼]	Participant List	A pull-down menu of those folks who are actively on your call at that moment.
 🖳	Call Participant	Puts you back in the Place a Call dialog box shown in Figure 21-16. Get more people to join your meeting, sell a plan, get a large budget, see the world.

Description	Button	What it Does
	Remove Participants	There comes a time when the children have to leave the room, and now you have the button to make that happen. If you ever connect a big meeting to a publicly available server, you may find unwelcome guests you need to excuse from the room.
	Allow Others to Edit	I told you NetMeeting was cooler than Presentation Broadcast. Watch the cursor when you turn over control to someone else. His or her name floats along behind the arrow to let everyone know who is driving.
	Display Chat Window	If you don't have an audio hookup, via computer microphones and sound cards or via telephone during your meeting, use this feature to type your message to users and get their comments and feedback. If you've ever been in a chat room before, this is kid's stuff.
	Display Whiteboard	The NetMeeting Whiteboard is a multipage, multiuser drawing application for sharing graphics with your collaborators. It reminds me of the Windows Paint program on steroids (food supplements if you are Mark McGwire).
	End Meeting	I'll give you three guesses, and the first two don't count.

One difference between standard NetMeeting and launching it from within PowerPoint is that you don't need to specify which application you want to share. When launched from within PowerPoint, NetMeeting automatically assumes that you want to share PowerPoint.

If many applications are being shared in a NetMeeting, minimize or close inactive windows. The observers' screens fill up with dark boxes, and it gets confusing pretty fast.

If you are hosting a small gathering, keep your NetMeeting settings default to manually accept all calls. It's the Internet version of closing the door to your conference room. For large meetings, NetMeeting has features like Host Meeting and Automatically Accept Incoming Calls, which become more helpful.

Use the Esc key to restore control of the cursor.

NetMeeting is like craps. It's pretty intimidating the first time you try it — or even watch. Of course, so is calamari. Even if you have the feel for it, your novice collaborators (*newbies* in Net lingo) may be overwhelmed and need some handholding. Until everyone you work with is comfortable with the application, I strongly suggest you plan some extra time at the beginning of your meeting for getting everyone acclimated with how to find the server, how to share applications, how to chat, take turns on the Whiteboard, know who is driving, and so on. You may even plan a whole training/familiarization session in advance to take all the thrills and chills out of the experience and allow you to get down to work without distractions when you really need to. More than one meeting has been blown by intrigued newbies playing with the collaboration features. It's worse when that newbie is the one who is hosting the meeting.

Now get out there and host a meeting!

Chapter 22

Juggling Multiple Presentations and Stealing Slides

In This Chapter

▶ Editing several presentations all at once

▶ Stealing slides from another PowerPoint file

▶ Saving summary information

Sure, you probably already know how to click the New button to create a new file, the Open button to retrieve an existing file, or the Save button to save a file. (Refer back to Chapter 1 if you don't.) But working with files involves more than clicking these three buttons. This chapter covers the all-important and ever-so-boring topic of working with PowerPoint files. Have fun.

Editing More Than One Presentation at a Time

Some people like to do just one thing at a time: Start a task, work on it till it's done, and then put away their tools. These same people sort their canned goods by food group and have garages that look like the hardware department at Sears.

Then there are people like me, who work on no fewer than 12 things at a time, would just as soon leave canned goods in the bag arranged just the way the kid at the grocery store tossed them in, and haven't been able to park both cars in the garage since before the kids were born.

Apparently, a few of the latter type work at Microsoft because they decided to enable you to open a whole gaggle of PowerPoint files at a time. Now we're getting somewhere!

To open more than one presentation, just keep using the File⇔Open command. PowerPoint places each file you open in its own presentation window inside the PowerPoint window. This presentation window is normally maximized to fill all the available space within the PowerPoint window, so you can see only one presentation window at a time. But you can switch between windows by choosing the window you want with the Window command or by pressing Ctrl+F6 to pop from window to window.

PowerPoint enables you to display the window for each open file in three ways:

✔ **Cascaded:** The presentation windows are stacked atop one another, as shown in Figure 22-1. This arrangement enables you to see the title bar of each window. To switch to a window other than the one on top, click its title bar or any other portion of the window you can see. This step sucks the window up to the top of the stack. To cause all presentation windows to fall into a cascaded stack, choose the Window⇔Cascade command.

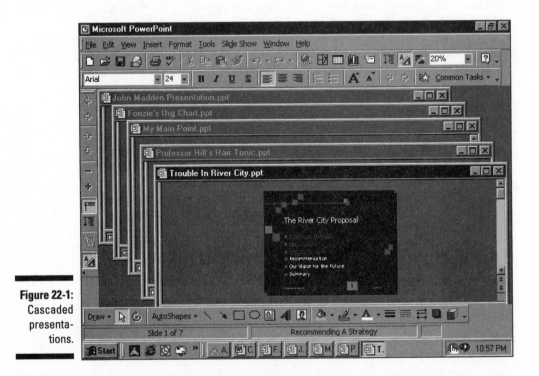

Figure 22-1:
Cascaded presentations.

✔ **Tiled:** The presentation windows are arranged side-by-side, as shown in Figure 22-2. This arrangement enables you to see a small portion of each presentation, though the more files you have open, the smaller this portion gets. To arrange all presentation windows in tiled form, use the Window⇨Arrange All command.

✔ **Minimized:** The window shrinks down to a little title bar that is just big enough to show the first part of the presentation's name and the standard window-control buttons, as shown in Figure 22-3. To shrink a presentation window to a minimized window, click the window's minimize button. To restore the window, double-click the icon.

Even though you can open umpteen presentation windows, only one is active at a time. While you work on one presentation, the others lie dormant, praying to the ASCII gods that you won't neglect them forever.

To copy something from one file to another, switch to the first file's window, copy the object to the Clipboard (by using the normal Copy command, Ctrl+C), and then switch to the second file's window and paste (Ctrl+V) away. Or use the Edit menu commands to perform the same task.

You can quickly change the size of a presentation window so that it's just big enough to show the entire slide at the current zoom factor by using the Window⇨Fit to Page command.

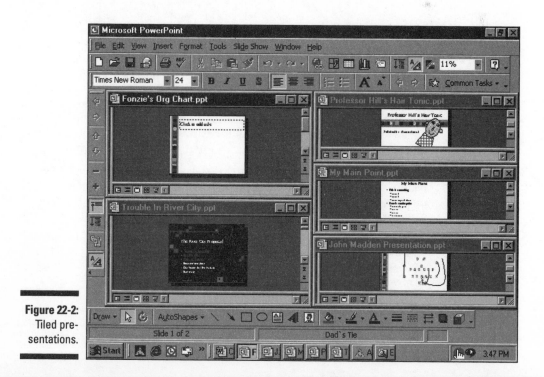

Figure 22-2:
Tiled pre-
sentations.

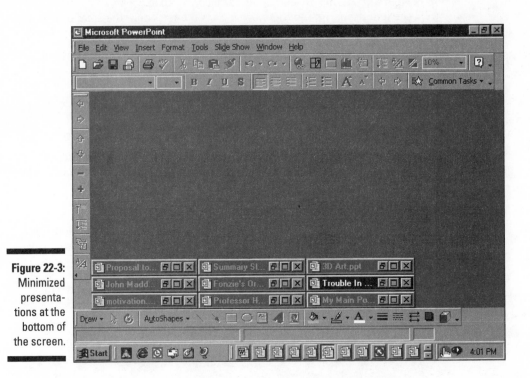

Figure 22-3:
Minimized
presenta-
tions at the
bottom of
the screen.

Here are a couple of tips for working with multiple windows:

- ✔ You can open more than one file with a single pass through the File➪Open command. Just hold down the Ctrl key while you click each file you want to open or use the Shift key to select a block of files. When you click OK, all the files you selected open, each in its own window.

- ✔ Some men especially love to use the Ctrl+F6 shortcut to flip from one window to the next. They sit there at the computer, beer in hand, flipping incessantly from window to window and hoping to find a football game or a boxing match.

- ✔ If you want to shut down a window, use the File➪Close command, press Ctrl+W, or click the window's close button. If the file displayed in the window contains changes that haven't been saved to disk, PowerPoint asks whether you want to save the file first.

Stealing Slides from Other Presentations

What do you do when you're plodding along in PowerPoint and realize that you want to copy slides from an old presentation into the one you're working on now? You steal the existing slides, that's what you do. No need to reinvent the wheel, as they say.

To steal slides from an existing presentation, you get to use the Slide Stealer — oops, it's actually called the Slide Finder — feature. To use it, follow these steps:

1. **Move to the slide you want the stolen slides to be placed after.**

2. **Conjure up the Insert➪Slides from Files command.**

    This step displays the Slide Finder dialog box shown in Figure 22-4.

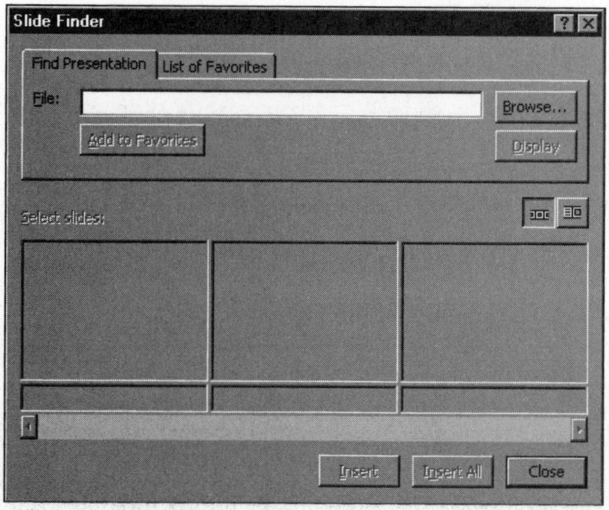

Figure 22-4:
The Slide
Finder
dialog box.

3. **Click the Browse button.**

    This brings up an ordinary, run-of-the-mill Open dialog box.

4. **Rummage around until you find the presentation you want to steal. Highlight it and click Open.**

    You return to the Slide Finder dialog box.

5. **Click Display.**

    The file opens and displays the first few slides of the presentation, as shown in Figure 22-5.

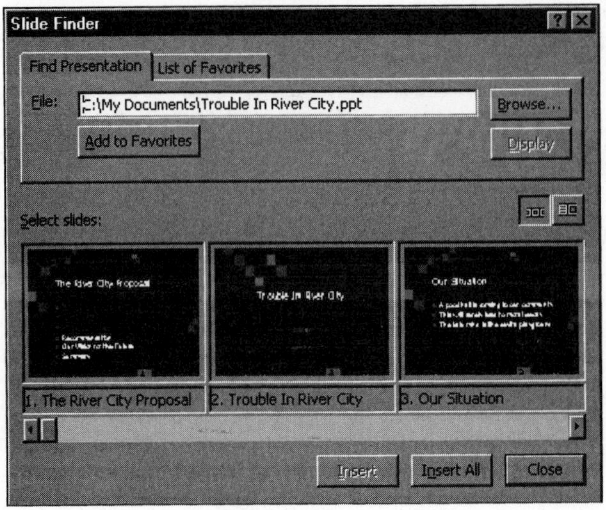

Figure 22-5:
The Slide
Finder
cases a
presentation.

6. **Select the slides you want to copy.**

   Click once to select a slide. When you select a slide, a heavy border appears around the slide so you'll know it's selected. You can select more than one slide by simply clicking each slide you want to select. Use the scroll bar that appears beneath the slide images to scroll through all of the slides in the presentation.

   If you click a slide by mistake, click it again to deselect it.

7. **Click Insert to insert the slides you selected.**

   The slides are inserted into the document, but the Slide Finder dialog box remains on the screen.

8. **Repeat Steps 3 through 7 if you want to insert slides from additional presentations.**

9. **Click Close to dismiss the Slide Finder dialog box.**

   You're done.

Here are a few points to ponder as you drift off to sleep tonight, wondering in amazement that PowerPoint lets you plagiarize slides from other people's presentations:

✔ As the slides are copied into the presentation, they are adjusted to match the master slide layout for the new presentation. Embedded charts are even updated to reflect the new color scheme.

✔ If you want to insert all of the slides from a presentation, you can dispense with Steps 5 through 7. Just click Insert All to copy all of the slides from the presentation.

✔ If you find that you frequently return to a particular presentation to steal its slides, add that presentation to the Slide Finder's list of favorites. To do that, click the Browse button and open the presentation. Then, click the Add to Favorites button. Thereafter, you can click the List of Favorites tab to display your list of favorite presentations.

✔ Stealing slides is a felony in most states, and if you transmit the presentation across state lines by way of a modem, the feds may get involved — which is good, because it pretty much guarantees that you'll get off scot-free.

Exploring Document Properties

PowerPoint stores summary information, known in Windows 95/98 lingo as *document properties,* with each PowerPoint presentation file you create. Document properties include the filename and directory, the template assigned to the file, and some information you can type: the presentation's title, subject, author, keywords, and comments.

If you use PowerPoint much of the time and have trouble remembering which file is which, the summary info can help you keep your files sorted. The summary info is also handy if you know that you created a presentation about edible spiders last year but can't remember the filename. Just use the File⇨Open command to search for all files with the keyword *spider* in the summary info. (Using the File⇨Open command to search for files is covered in Chapter 23.)

To view or set the document properties for a presentation, follow these steps:

1. **Open the file if it isn't already open.**

2. **Conjure up the File⇨Properties command.**

   The Properties dialog box appears.

3. **Type whatever summary info you want to store along with the file.**

   The Title field in the Summary info dialog box is automatically filled in with whatever you type in the first slide's title placeholder, and the Author field is filled in with your name. (PowerPoint asked for your name when you installed it, remember?)

4. **When you're done, click OK.**

5. **Save the file (Ctrl+S or File⇨Save).**

When you fill out the Summary information, spend a few moments thinking about which keywords you may use to look for the file later on. Choosing descriptive keywords makes the file much easier to find.

Also, explore the other tabs on the Properties dialog box. You find all sorts of interesting information about your presentation there.

If you want to include summary information with every PowerPoint file you create, use the Tools⇨Options command and check the Prompt for file properties option on the Save tab (see Figure 22-6). This causes the Properties dialog box to be displayed whenever you save a new file so you can type the summary information for the file.

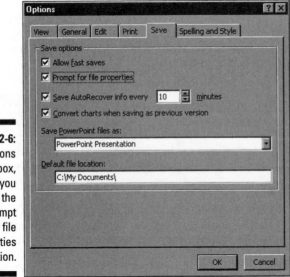

Figure 22-6:
The Options dialog box, where you can set the Prompt for file properties option.

Chapter 23

Sharing Information with Other Programs

*I*n the spirit of NAFTA, this chapter shows you how to exchange data with files created by other programs. Sure, it would be nice if you could build a brick-walled protectionist fortress around yourself and never even acknowledge the existence of other programs, but that wouldn't be — as a former president would say — prudent. Other programs are here to stay, so you had better learn to get along.

The technical term for loading a file created by some other program and converting it to the PowerPoint 2000 format is, appropriately enough, *importing*. You can import all sorts of file types into PowerPoint: Word for Windows documents, other word-processing documents, generic DOS text files, and even Excel and many other applications, too.

The converse of importing, naturally, is *exporting*. PowerPoint can import more file formats than it can export. I guess the folks at Microsoft want you to convert the competition's files to PowerPoint but not the other way around.

Once nice thing about PowerPoint 2000, as well as all of the other applications in Office, is the ability to save backwards. And no, this doesn't mean spinning around in your swivel chair and clicking the Save button. It means that you can save PowerPoint 2000 files to the older versions of PowerPoint that your less hip colleagues are running.

Importing a Foreign File

You have just spent three weeks writing a detailed proposal for a new project, and your boss has just decided that he wants *you* to make the presentation. He expects you to create top-quality 35mm slides based on the proposal, a 60-page Word for Windows document. What do you do?

If you have low self-esteem, you hide in the closet for a week or two. Otherwise, you just import the document into PowerPoint and get to work. With luck, the PowerPoint text-conversion routines recognize headings in the document and convert them to an outline suitable for presentation. It doesn't always work the way you hope, but it's a start, anyway.

PowerPoint can import not only Word for Windows files but also other file types. Here's the complete list of text file types PowerPoint admits:

- **Word for Windows:** PowerPoint works with the Word for Windows outline feature to convert a document to a presentation. Each level-1 heading starts a new slide, with lower-level headings converted to slide text. Paragraphs not assigned a heading style are ignored.

- **Other word-processing software:** To import a document created by another word-processing software, first use that application's conversion feature to store the document as a Rich Text Format (RTF) file. If the word-processing program uses heading styles, they are properly converted to PowerPoint outline levels. If not, PowerPoint guesses at the outline structure by examining how paragraphs are indented.

- **DOS text files:** PowerPoint can read plain, old-fashioned DOS text files, sometimes called *ASCII files*. (ASCII is pronounced *ask-ee*.) Most word-processing software can save files in ASCII format, and the Windows Notepad program and the DOS Edit command work with ASCII files. PowerPoint looks for tabs at the beginning of each line to figure out how to construct an outline from the file.

- **Competitors' presentation files:** PowerPoint converts presentation files created by Harvard Graphics or Lotus Freelance.

Creating a presentation from a foreign file

This procedure shows you how to create a new presentation from a foreign file:

1. **Choose the File⇨Open command.**

   The Open dialog box appears.

2. Pick the file type.

Scroll through the Files of Type list box until you find the one you want (see Figure 23-1).

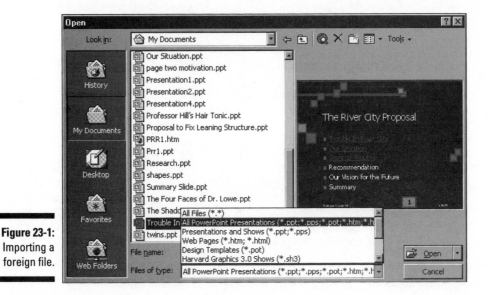

Figure 23-1: Importing a foreign file.

3. Choose the file you want to import.

You may have to rummage about to find it.

4. Click Open.

If you are running the feature for the first time, PowerPoint needs to install it. You see a little dialog box like the one shown in Figure 23-2. Installing takes a second, so you have time to quickly refresh your coffee.

Figure 23-2: PowerPoint installs the necessary files.

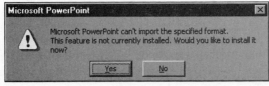

The file is imported. PowerPoint does its best to construct a reasonable outline from the file.

5. **Apply a template.**

   Choose the Format⇨Apply Design command and select an appropriate template.

6. **Edit the outline.**

   The outline imported from the file probably needs work. Have fun.

Don't expect perfection when you import a document. PowerPoint does its best to guess at the outline structure of the document, but sometimes it gets confused. Be patient and be prepared to do some heavy editing.

The PowerPoint customs officers don't allow immigrant word-processing files to bring their graphics with them. You have to copy any charts or pictures you want to include in the presentation. The easiest way to do that is to fire up both the word processor and PowerPoint at the same time and then copy graphics from the word-processing document to PowerPoint by way of the Clipboard. (You can press Ctrl+C to copy and Ctrl+V to paste, remember?)

Inserting slides from an outline

You can insert slides from an outline directly into an existing presentation by using the Insert⇨Slides from Outline command. Here's the procedure:

1. **Move to the slide that you want your new slides to follow.**

   For best results, switch to Outline view or Slide Sorter view.

2. **Activate the Insert⇨Slides from Outline command.**

   The Insert Outline dialog box, shown in Figure 23-3, appears.

3. **Select the file that contains the outline you want to copy.**

4. **Click Insert.**

5. **Review the outline and edit as necessary.**

   It probably won't work exactly as you expect, but it should be close.

The outline can be a Word for Windows document, a document exported from another word processor in Rich Text Format (RTF), or a plain ASCII file.

PowerPoint formats the new slides using the master slide that's already in place.

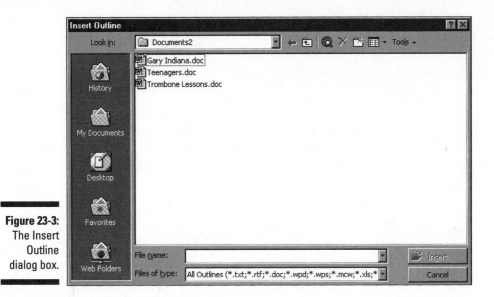

Figure 23-3:
The Insert
Outline
dialog box.

Exporting an Outline

PowerPoint enables you to save a presentation's outline by using Rich Text Format (RTF), a document format that is recognized by just about every word-processing program ever written. Here's the procedure:

1. **Activate the File⇨Save As command.**

   The Save As dialog box appears.

2. **Choose Outline/RTF (*.rtf) in the Save as Type list box.**

3. **Type a filename.**

4. **Click Save.**

To open the outline file by using Microsoft Word for Windows, just use the File⇨Open command. Choose RTF as the file type to search for. Word automatically recognizes that the file is stored in RTF format and offers to convert it.

To open the outline file with other word processors, you may have to use an Import command or a separate conversion program.

Saving Slides as Graphics Files

Just spent hours polishing a beautiful slide and wish that you could find a way to save the slide as a graphics file so that you can import it into another program, such as Word for Windows or a desktop-publishing program? You've come to the right place. Fancy that.

PowerPoint has the capability to save any slide in a presentation as a separate graphics file by using one of four formats: Windows Metafile (WMF), Graphics Interchange Format (GIF), Joint Photographic Experts Group (JPEG), or Portable Network Graphics. Just follow these steps:

1. **Open the presentation and move to the slide you want to save as a graphic.**

   You can do this in Slide view or in Slide Sorter view — whatever suits your fancy.

2. **Choose the File⇨Save As command.**

3. **Pick the graphics file format you want to use in the Save as Type drop-down list box.**

   Choose Windows Metafile (*.wmf), GIF (*.gif), JPEG File Interchange Format, (*.jpg), or Portable Network Graphics (*.png).

4. **The filename and extension are automatically loaded.**

   The extension is automatically appended to the end of the filename, so you don't have to type it.

5. **Click Save.**

Chapter 24

Managing Your Files

● ●

In This Chapter

▶ Using filenames you can remember

▶ Using folders wisely

▶ Finding lost files

▶ Copying files

▶ Creating new folders

▶ Deleting files

▶ Creating new folders

▶ Backing up your files

● ●

My first computer had two disk drives; each drive held 360K of data. A year later, I had a gargantuan 10MB hard disk and wondered how I would keep track of two or three hundred files that I would store on the disk. (I never thought I would fill it up, either.) Today I have more than 6,000MB of disk space, with more than 20,000 files. It's a miracle I can find anything.

This chapter talks about the mundane task of managing your files: keeping track of where they are, giving them names that help you remember what they contain, and — perhaps most important — backing them up.

Organizing Your Files

The first step in managing your files is organizing them so that you can find them. You must do only two things to organize your files, but you must do them both well: use filenames you can remember and use folders wisely.

Using filenames that you can remember

One of the best things about Windows 95 or 98 is that you have finally been freed of the sadistic eight-character file-naming conventions foisted upon you by the DOS moguls many years ago. With Windows 95/8, filenames can be as long as you want or need them to be (within reason), so instead of names like CNEXPO99.PPT, you can give your presentations names like COMPUTER NERD EXPO 99.PPT.

The best advice I can offer about using long filenames is to start using them right away. Most people are in the habit of assigning short, cryptic names to their files. Breaking that habit takes some conscious effort. Using long filenames seems strange at first, but trust me: You get used to them.

It used to be that the biggest problem with using long filenames was that not everyone had Windows 95 yet, so not everyone used them. Now, it's getting rarer and rarer to find someone that doesn't run with at least Windows 95, so eventually this will be a non-issue. If you assign a long filename to a file and then copy that file to a diskette and take it to a computer that doesn't have Windows 95, the long filename will seem to have vanished, replaced by a cryptic eight-character approximation of the long filename. For example, COMPUTER NERD EXPO 99PPT becomes COMPUT~1.PPT. The file is still accessible, but the long filename is not. If you need proof of this but don't know anyone who doesn't have Windows 95, attach a file to e-mail and enjoy the cryptic name. But hurry — something tells me that Microsoft's intuitive file-naming system will one day be computer industry norm.

Until this problem is a faded memory, whenever possible, you may want to try to jam as much important information as possible into the first six characters of the filename. For example, suppose you have two files: COMPUTER NERD EXPO 95.PPT and COMPUTER NERD EXPO 96.PPT. The short-form filenames for these two files will be COMPUT~1.PPT and COMPUT~2.PPT. From these filenames, it's hard to tell which is the '95 version and which is for '96. Suppose, however, that you had named the files 95 COMPUTER NERD EXPO.PPT and 96 COMPUTER NERD EXPO.PPT. Then the short filenames would be 95COMP~1.PPT and 96COMP~1.PPT. Here are a few additional file-naming pointers:

- ✔ If your presentation includes speaker notes, add the filename to the bottom of the page on the Notes master. That way, the filename is printed on each speaker notes page, which makes it easier to file later.

- ✔ Be consistent about how you name files. If AREXPO98.PPT is the presentation file for Arachnid Expo '98, use AREXPO99.PPT for next year's Expo.

- ✔ If you are going to store a file on the Internet, don't use spaces or other special symbols in the filename.

TIP

✔ PowerPoint 2000 has a large variety of ways you can name a file. Don't let this throw you; it really isn't confusing. Just remember that when anything is altered, the alteration is usually pointing in one direction — to the Internet! If you click Save As and then click the Save as Type text box, you see that besides the names of the different types of files, Microsoft also gives you the file extensions for each. Besides .ppt, there is .htm, and .html and even .pot. The Save as Web Page option has changed even more. Check out the ins and outs of this altered feature in Chapter 20. Now that users find themselves preparing files for the Internet more frequently, the days when you simply saved everything to .ppt are gone. Refresh your understanding of Chapter 20 now, if you are making an Internet presentation.

Using folders wisely

The biggest file-management mistake most beginners make is to dump all their files in one folder. This technique is the electronic equivalent of storing all your tax records in a shoe box. Sure, all the files are there, but finding anything is next to impossible. Show the shoe box to your accountant on April 14, and you'll be lucky if he or she stops laughing long enough to show you how to file for an extension.

Use folders to impose organization on your files. Don't just dump all your files into one folder. Instead, create a separate folder for each project and dump all the files for each project into its folder. Suppose that you're charged with the task of presenting a market analysis every month. You can create a folder named MARKET ANALYSIS to store the PowerPoint files for these reports. Then each month's PowerPoint file is named by using the month and year: 99 JANUARY.PPT, 99 FEBRUARY.PPT, 99 MARCH.PPT, and so on. (If you're not up to snuff on how folders work, see the sidebar, "Don't read this folder stuff if you can avoid it.")

Windows 95, or better, enables you to create folders within folders to give your hard disk even more organization. Carrying our market-analysis presentation one step further, suppose that you need quite a few files to assemble each report: perhaps a master PowerPoint presentation file, several Excel worksheet files, a Word document or two, and who knows what else. To keep these files separate, you can create subfolders named JANUARY 99, FEBRUARY 99, MARCH 99, and so on within the MARKET ANALYSIS folder. All the files required for a given month's market analysis are stored in the appropriate subfolder. Very slick, eh?

TIP

You can read the steps for creating a new folder later in this chapter, under the heading "Creating a New Folder." Isn't that clever?

This list includes some tips for working with folders:

- ✔ Every disk has a *root (or top level) directory,* a special folder that should not be used to store files. The root directory is kind of like a fire lane, which should be kept free for emergency vehicles at all times. In short, don't use the C:\ directory to store files.

- ✔ Don't store PowerPoint presentation files in the \Microsoft Office or \Office folder. These folders are where all PowerPoint program files belong. You don't want your own files mingling with them.

- ✔ There's no reason you can't store files that belong to different application programs together in the same folder. Each file's extension identifies the program that created the file. No need to segregate. Most Office 2000 Open dialog boxes filter by type anyway.

- ✔ Don't forget to clean out your folders periodically by deleting files that you no longer need. It also may be interesting to clean out your Recycle Bin — who knows what you have in there!

There is no limit to the number of files you can store in a folder, nor is there a limit to the number of folders you can create. The only exception to this rule is that the root folder can have no more than 512 files and folders. That's why you should keep the root folder free from unnecessary files.

Don't read this folder stuff if you can avoid it

A *folder* is the means by which Windows keeps track of the files on your hard disk. Without folders, your hard disk would resemble the yarn basket after the cat ran amok.

The terms *directory* and *folder* are used interchangeably because until Windows 95, folders were called directories. The good folks at Microsoft thought that changing the name *directory* to *folder* would somehow make Windows 95/8 easier to use. Just like they have taken to calling saving in HTML saving as a Web page, they figure the basic user likes things user-friendly. Go figure.

Every file on a disk must have a *directory entry,* which is nothing more than a notation in a folder that lists the file's name and its location on disk. Think of the folder as a guest registry for a bed-and-breakfast, and you have the idea. The guest registry lists the name of each occupant and the occupant's room number. In a similar way, a disk folder lists each file by name and its disk "room number."

Every disk has a least one folder, called the *root directory.* You can create additional folders to store your files in an orderly fashion.

Using the File⇨Open Command

The most direct way to open a presentation is to use the File⇨Open command. You have three ways to summon this command:

- ✔ Choose the File⇨Open command from the menus.

- ✔ Click the Open button in the standard toolbar.

- ✔ Press Ctrl+O or Ctrl+F12. Ctrl+O is the more intuitive keyboard shortcut for the File⇨Open command — *O* is for *Open* — but Ctrl+F12 is left over from the early days of Windows, before Microsoft programmers decided that keyboard shortcuts should make sense. Rather than drop an antiquated and senseless keyboard shortcut in favor of one that makes sense and is consistent across all Windows applications (or at least is supposed to be), the developers at Microsoft decided to leave *both* keyboard shortcuts in place. You can amaze your colleagues by showing them the many ways to open a file! Sounds like something Dilbert would do.

However you do it, the Open dialog box shown in Figure 24-1 appears. If you're an experienced PowerPoint user, you'll notice right away that this dialog box has changed again! Notice the Web-friendly sidebar that allows you to click icons for popular file destinations. In particular, long filenames are supported.

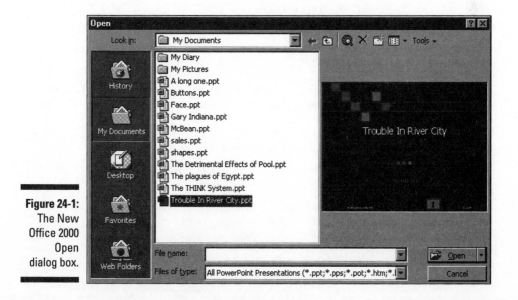

Figure 24-1:
The New
Office 2000
Open
dialog box.

Notice that the Open dialog box has changed pretty significantly since Office 97. Conveniently, all the Office products use the same Open dialog box.

There's a place for us

On the left-hand side of this dialog box, a column of five large buttons helps you quickly navigate to the most popular places to find files you want to open. Appropriately, this column is called the Places Bar. Nothing in the dialog box uses the words "Places Bar," but if you've had as many conversations with the Office Assistant as I have had, then you sort of pick up these things. I suggest you use the expression "Places Bar" three times a day at work until everyone is impressed with your depth of understanding. From top to bottom, the places are:

- **History:** A collection of the most recent files you have used.
- **My Documents:** The default location for saving Microsoft Office files.
- **Desktop:** Many people like to keep files currently in work on their desktop to make them easy to find.
- **Favorites:** I guess it goes without saying that if a file is a favorite, then you'll probably want to open it again.
- **Web Folders:** A new Office 2000 feature, Web Folders is a part of the focus on Web integration in the new Office Suite.

Changing views

The Views button in the Open dialog box leads you to a choice of four different views of your documents. The four view buttons in the Views pull-down menu let you make the switch:

- **List:** Displays a list of folders and documents with icons.
- **Details:** Displays a list of folders and documents with details, including the filename, type, size, and creation date.
- **Properties:** Displays a panel showing various properties for the selected file, including the title, author, template, word count, and other useful information.
- **Preview:** Displays a preview of the selected file.

A fifth choice on the pull-down menu is Arrange Icons. It does the same thing you probably already know about the Windows Explorer Arrange Icons feature. You can sort the files by name, type, size, date, and sign of the zodiac.

Deleting and renaming files and folders

You can delete and rename files and folders from the Open dialog box. Here's how:

- ✔ To delete a file or folder, simply select the file or folder and press the Delete key.

- ✔ To rename a file or folder, select the file or folder by clicking it once and then click the filename again. A text editing box appears around the file or folder name, allowing you to edit the name. (Don't click too quickly, or PowerPoint thinks that you double-clicked and opens the file or folder.)

If you are click-speed impaired, try clicking the right mouse button just once and choose Rename.

Playing favorites

The Open dialog box has changed a bit when it comes to the Favorites function. The Look in Favorites button has been redrawn and moved to the Places Bar (notice how I subtly threw in the term at an appropriate point?). Also the Add to Favorites button is gone. What to do?

You can still add files and folders to your Favorites folder, but you have to know the territory. You can get to the location shown in Figure 24-2 by following these simple steps.

1. **Choose View➪Toolbars➪Web.**

2. **Pull down the Favorites menu.**

3. **Choose Add to Favorites.**

Your file or folder is now contained in your Favorites list. Want proof? Click the Favorites folder on the Places Bar. There you will find it.

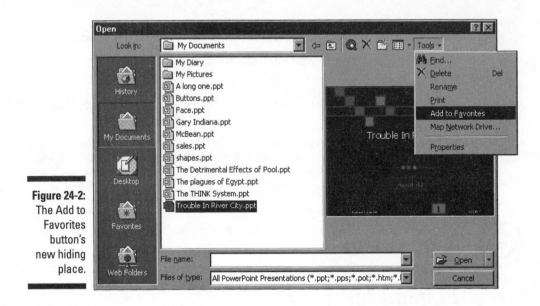

Figure 24-2:
The Add to
Favorites
button's
new hiding
place.

Finding Lost Files

You can perform simple document searches by using fields that are available right on the Open dialog box. The following paragraphs describe these fields:

- ✔ **File Name:** Ordinarily, this field is left blank so that PowerPoint displays all the files in the folder that meet the criteria specified in the Files of Type, Text or Property, and Last Modified fields. You can, however, type a wildcard filename in this field to limit the files that are displayed. A *wildcard* filename includes an asterisk that stands for one or more unknown portions of the filename. For example, if you type **bob*** and press the Enter key, only those documents whose filenames begin with the letters *bob* are displayed.

- ✔ **Files of Type:** This field lets you select the type of files to be listed in the Open dialog box.

Don't give up if you can't find the file you just know is out there using these simple filters. Windows Explorer can provide advanced search features such as date, file contents, and all levels of subdirectories.

Copying Files

Both the File⇨Open and File⇨Save As commands let you make copies of your files. All you have to remember are the ubiquitous Ctrl+C and Ctrl+V short-cuts for Copy and Paste. Follow these easy, step-by-step instructions:

1. **Conjure up the File⇨Open or File⇨Save As command.**

2. **Press Ctrl+C to copy the file.**

3. **Navigate to the folder to which you want the file copied.**

4. **Press Ctrl+V to paste the file into the folder.**

Creating a New Folder

It happens to me all the time: I'm working on a new presentation, and when I'm ready to save it, I decide that I want to create a new folder for it. Back in the old Windows 3.1 days, you had to switch to Program Manager, launch File Manager, (now called Windows Explorer) create the new folder, exit File Manager, and then switch back to PowerPoint and save the file in the new folder. Bother.

Mercifully, PowerPoint 2000 now allows you to create a new folder right in the Save, Save As, and Open dialog boxes. All you have to do is click the New Folder button and type a name for the new folder, and — voilà! — no more File Manager/Explorer.

Deleting Files

Don't need a file anymore? Free up the valuable disk space it occupies by deleting it. All you have to do is select the file in the Open or Save As dialog box and press the Delete key. Poof! The file is history.

Backing Up Your Files

When was the last time you changed the oil in your car, took your dog for a walk, or backed up the files on your hard disk? The neglect of any of these three tasks can have disastrous consequences. This isn't the time or place for a stern lecture about the importance of backing up, though, so I'll spare you the soapbox lecture.

One way to back up a file is to use the PowerPoint Save As command to save a copy of the file to a floppy disk.

But the best way to back up your files is to use an Official Backup Program. Fortunately, Windows 95 and higher comes with a fairly decent backup program that can back up your files to diskettes or to a tape drive, if you're lucky enough to have one. You'll find the Windows backup program buried in the Start menu under Programs, Accessories, System Tools. (If you can't find Microsoft Backup in your Start menu, it may not have been installed when you installed Windows 95 or 98. You'll have to rerun the Windows setup program to install Microsoft Backup from your installation CD or diskettes.)

Keep in mind these hints about backing up your files:

✔ Remember what I said about this not being the time or place for a lecture? I lied. Back up your files every day. You never know when a stray asteroid will strike your city and possibly wipe out all human life and erase your files, too. So don't put it off! Back up today!

✔ Always have plenty of disks on hand for backups.

✔ You don't have to back up every file on your hard disk every day. Just back up the files you changed that day. Microsoft Backup has a slick feature called *incremental backup* that does precisely that, and it does it automatically so that you don't even have to think about it.

✔ Not lucky enough to have a tape drive? With prices what they are, you should seriously consider it. You can purchase a tape drive capable of backing up 350MB of data on a single tape for under $150 these days.

✔ You'll sleep much better tonight if you back up your files today.

Chapter 25

Creating 35mm Slides

· ·

· ·

*Y*ou can convert PowerPoint 2000 slides easily to 35mm color slides, but unless you have your own photo processing equipment, you have to deal with a photo lab to get the job done. It isn't cheap (here in California, it costs $7–$10 per slide), but the slides look great.

This chapter briefly covers what you need to know to take your presentation to a local photo lab for processing. But most of the chapter is devoted to using Genigraphics — without a doubt the most convenient way to get 35mm slides out of PowerPoint.

Using a Local Photo Lab

One way to produce 35mm slides from a PowerPoint presentation is to take the presentation files to a local photo lab with the equipment to create the slides. Call the lab first to find out the cost and to check on any special requirements it may have, such as whether you need to embed TrueType fonts when you save the file and how the lab prefers you to save the file.

To be safe, always embed TrueType fonts.

You can find photo labs that can produce computer output listed in the *Yellow Pages* under Computer Graphics, or perhaps under Photo Finishing. Call several labs and compare costs and find out how quickly each can finish the job.

Use the PowerPoint File⇨Save As command to save the presentation to disk. Take two copies of the presentation file — on separate disks — to the photo shop. Nothing is more frustrating than driving across town only to discover that something's wrong with your disk. Or you can always attach your file to an e-mail and send it to the photo shop, if the shop is set up to receive files electronically.

Carefully proof your slides by using the PowerPoint Slide Show view. Run the spell checker. At $10 per slide, you don't want many typos to slip by.

Using Genigraphics

Genigraphics is a company that specializes in computer graphics and managed to get its software bundled with PowerPoint. If you can't find a local shop that can do the job, Genigraphics is always available. You can send the company your presentation on disk, or you can send it via modem. PowerPoint even comes with a built-in command that automatically sends your presentations to Genigraphics.

Genigraphics accepts major credit cards or can bill you COD. If you've got clout, you may convince them to open an account. For really big presentations, they offer convenient 15- or 30-year mortgages with fixed or adjustable rates.

Sending a presentation to Genigraphics for printing is easy. If you have a modem, follow these steps:

1. **Open your presentation.**

    Use the File⇨Open command to find and open your file.

2. **Use the File⇨Page Setup command to set the slides to 35mm, Landscape.**

3. **Click OK.**

4. **Choose the File⇨Send To⇨Genigraphics command.**

    The Genigraphics Wizard appears, as shown in Figure 25-1.

    If you cannot find the File⇨Send To⇨Genigraphics command, you need to install it. Rerun the PowerPoint 2000 or Office 2000 setup program.

5. **Click Next>.**

    The Wizard starts asking questions. See Figure 25-2, the first dialog box that appears, in which the Wizard wants to know what kind of output you want to create: 35mm slides, transparencies, posters, and so on.

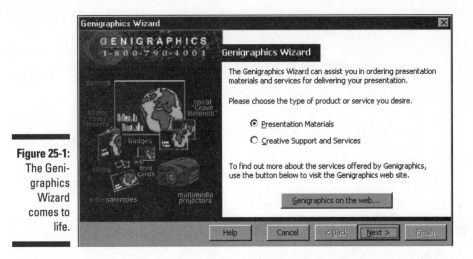

Figure 25-1:
The Geni-
graphics
Wizard
comes to
life.

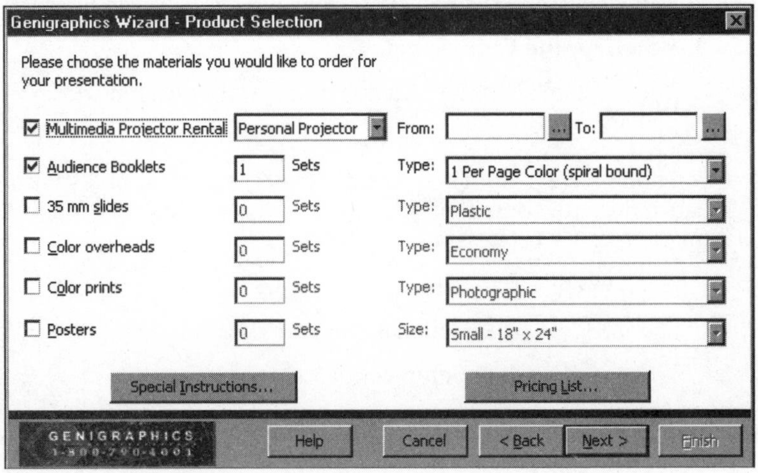

Figure 25-2:
The Geni-
graphics
Wizard
starts
asking
questions.

6. **Answer the questions and click Next>.**

   More questions appear.

7. **Keep answering questions and clicking Next>.**

   This process goes on for a while. Genigraphics needs a lot of information: how you want the slides created, how you want them shipped,
   where you want them shipped to, and — most importantly — how
   you're going to pay for them. There's no way around it: You're going to
   have to give them a credit card number.

One big decision you have to make is how quickly you need the slides. If you have procrastinated until the day before the big presentation, you have to pay a premium to get the slides processed overnight. At the time I wrote this, next-day processing cost $7.50 per slide. If you have a few days to spare, you can get by with second-day processing for $6.50 per slide. And if you have 7–10 days, you can use the Plan-Ahead method, which costs only $4.50 per slide.

Another important question you are asked is whether you want a separate slide for each build line. (A build displays bullet lines progressively, adding one line at a time.) This can make a huge difference in the cost. For example, suppose your presentation consists of 12 slides, and you put it off until the day before the big event. At $7.50 each, 12 slides will cost you over $100. But if each slide has five bullets and you want a separate slide for each build, you're talking about 60 slides at a cost of more than $500. Those build effects aren't cheap.

8. **When you have answered all the questions, click Finish.**

   As you check out the Genigraphics Wizard, notice that you have lots of options to send the shop your file, including via the Internet.

9. **Watch for the FedEx truck.**

   The finished slides should appear at your doorstep within the stated delivery time.

If you don't have a modem, you can direct the Genigraphics Wizard to create a diskette containing your presentation. Then mail the diskette to Genigraphics for processing.

Chapter 26

It's Show Time — PowerPoint Live!

You can play some really slick tricks during an on-computer slide show with PowerPoint 2000. You can use the mouse (or keyboard) to move from slide to slide, to go back to a slide that you've already shown, or to skip a slide. And you can use the mouse to doodle on your slides, underlining or circling key points as you go (I call this the "John Madden Effect," in honor of the former football coach who circles plays with great relish on telecasts). This chapter shows you how to employ these nifty tricks to bedazzle your audience.

But before you go to the play-by-play section of this chapter, consider your audience. PowerPoint culture is changing as Internet and intranet broadcasting becomes more common and as projection devices become staples in everyone's office. There are really three ways you can present a slide show:

1. **In a one-on-one meeting.**

2. **In a large group setting with a data projector (or an overhead projector).**

3. **Using Presentation Broadcast (explained in Chapter 21).**

For all three types of slide show there are many similarities. This chapter focuses on live presentations. For presentations on your intranet or Internet, see Chapter 21. First, you always have to set up your show.

Setting Up a Slide Show

To set up a slide show so it can be presented on your computer, conjure up the Slide Show⇨Set Up Show command. This summons the Set Up Show dialog box, shown in Figure 26-1. With this dialog box, you can twiddle with the various options that are available for presenting slide shows. (Remember, you won't be able to summon this command in the Slide Show drop-down menu unless you have opened a presentation.)

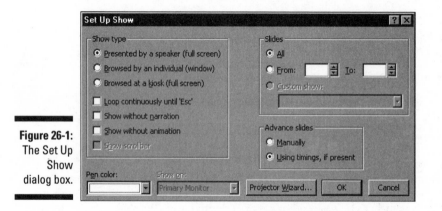

Figure 26-1:
The Set Up
Show
dialog box.

With the options on the Set Up Show dialog box, you can do the following:

✔ Configure the presentation for one of three basic slide show types: Presented by a Speaker (Full Screen), Browsed by an Individual (Window), or Browsed at a Kiosk (Full Screen).

✔ Choose Loop Continuously until Esc to set up the show to loop indefinitely, so that when the show reaches the last slide, it automatically starts over again at the first slide.

✔ Choose to show the slide show without narrations or animations.

✔ Choose All to include all slides in the slide show.

✔ Choose From and supply starting and ending slide numbers to display a range of slides.

✔ Choose Custom Show if you have set up any custom shows within your presentation. (See the section "Using Custom Shows" later in this chapter for more information.)

✔ Choose Manually to advance from slide to slide by pressing the Enter key, pressing the spacebar, or clicking the mouse button.

✔ Choose Using Timings, if present to advance automatically using the timings specified for each slide.

If you're a stickler for detail, you probably notice that the PowerPoint 2000 Set Up Show dialog box has altered slightly from its predecessor. A friendly little button is directly below Advance Slides. This is the Projector Wizard (see Figure 26-2). (Pretty soon, all you are going to need to know to run any Microsoft application is how to read!)

This Wizard leads you calmly and carefully through the ins and outs of connecting your computer to a data projector. Although these instructions may seem simple to some, the complexity of instructions is directly proportional to the number of restless audience members you have waiting in front of you.

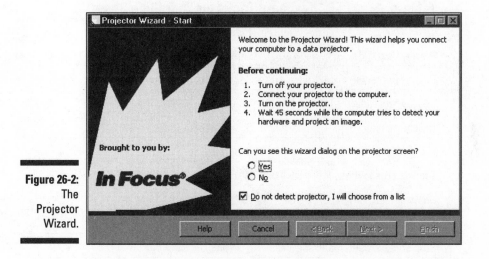

Figure 26-2: The Projector Wizard.

Answer the simple question: "Can you see your desktop image on the projector screen?" and proceed along by clicking Next. The Wizard leads you through all aspects of setting up your projector, including a sound check.

Starting a Slide Show

When you start a slide show in a one-on-one or small group setting without a projector, beginning is just a click away.

To start a slide show immediately, click the Slide Show button (shown in the margin). If you have set up a full-screen slide show, PowerPoint replaces the entire screen with the first slide of the slide show. To advance to the next slide, click the mouse, press Enter, the down arrow, the Page Down key, or the spacebar. You can also start a slide show by choosing the View⇨Slide Show command or the Slide Show⇨View Show command.

Keyboard and mouse tricks for your slide show

During an on-screen slide show, you can use the keyboard and mouse to control your presentation. Tables 26-1 and 26-2 list the keys and clicks you can use.

Table 26-1	Keyboard Tricks for Your Slide Show
To Do This	*Press Any of These Keys*
Display next slide	Enter, spacebar, Page Down, N
Display preceding slide	Backspace, Page Up, P
Display first slide	1+Enter
Display specific slide	Slide number+Enter
Toggle screen black	B, period
Toggle screen white	W, comma
Show or hide pointer	A, = (equals sign)
Erase screen doodles	E
Stop or restart automatic show	S, + (plus)
Display next slide even if hidden	H
Display specific hidden slide	Slide number of hidden slide+Enter
Change pen to arrow	Ctrl+A
Change arrow to pen	Ctrl+P
End slide show	Esc, Ctrl+Break (the Break key doubles as the Pause key), – (minus)

Table 26-2	Mouse Tricks for Your Slide Show
To Do This	*Do This*
Display next slide or build	Click
Call up menu of actions	Right-click
Display first slide	Hold down both mouse buttons for two seconds
Doodle	Press Ctrl+P to change the mouse arrow to a pen and then draw on-screen like John Madden

The John Madden effect

If you've always wanted to diagram plays on-screen the way John Madden does, try using the pen during a slide show. Here's how:

1. **Start a slide show.**

2. **When you want to doodle on a slide, press Ctrl+P.**

   The mouse arrow pointer changes to a pen shape.

3. **Draw away.**

   Figure 26-3 shows an example of a doodled-upon slide.

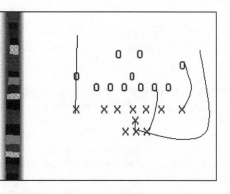

Figure 26-3:
John Madden would love PowerPoint 2000.

4. **To erase your doodles, press E.**

Drawing doodles like this requires good mouse dexterity. With practice, you can learn to create all kinds of interesting doodles. Work on circling text or drawing exclamation or question marks, smiley faces, and so on.

Keep these tasty tidbits in mind when doodling:

✔ To hide the mouse pointer temporarily during a slide show, press *A* or =. The pointer returns the moment you move the mouse, or you can press *A* or = again to summon it back.

✔ If you use the pen, be sure to say "Bam" and "Pow" a lot.

✔ To turn off the Doodle button, press the equals sign (=) on your keyboard.

You can also right-click the mouse for a floating menu of these choices, however this might be a little more distracting for your audience than the keystrokes as the audience will suddenly be privy to all your fancy footwork. But, do notice that the menu allows you to change pen colors and a few other tricks. You can set up the pen color before you begin your presentation so as not to distract by selecting Slide Show➪Set up Show➪Pen. If you have a remote mouse and you won't have access to your keyboard during your presentation, I suggest you investigate the floating menu method.

Rehearsing Your Slide Timings

You can use the PowerPoint Rehearsal feature to rehearse your presentation. The rehearsal lets you know how long your presentation takes, and it can even set slide timings so that the slides automatically advance based on the timings you set during the rehearsal.

To rehearse a slide show, summon the Slide Show➪Rehearse Timings command. This starts the slide show, with a special Rehearsal dialog box visible, as shown in Figure 26-4.

Now rehearse your presentation. Click the mouse or use keyboard shortcuts to advance slides. As you rehearse, PowerPoint keeps track of how long you display each slide and the total length of your presentation.

When you dismiss the final slide, PowerPoint displays the dialog box shown in Figure 26-5. This dialog box gives you the option of applying the timings recorded during the rehearsal to the slides in the presentation or ignoring the rehearsal timings. If you were satisfied with the slide timings during the rehearsal, click Yes.

If you mess up during a rehearsal, click the Repeat button. Clicking this button restarts the rehearsal from the beginning.

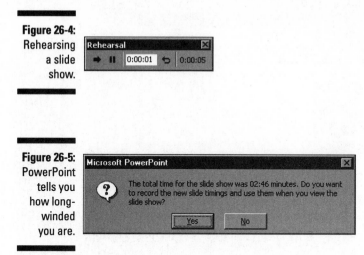

Figure 26-4:
Rehearsing
a slide
show.

Figure 26-5:
PowerPoint
tells you
how long-
winded
you are.

Taking Your Show on the Road

PowerPoint comes with a program called the *PowerPoint Viewer* that enables you to run a PowerPoint slide show on a computer that doesn't have a full-fledged copy of PowerPoint. You can't create, edit, or print presentations by using Viewer, but you can run on-screen slide shows just as if you were using the full PowerPoint program.

Using the Pack and Go Wizard

The easiest way to use the PowerPoint Viewer is to use the Pack and Go Wizard, a special PowerPoint command that copies a complete presentation onto a diskette, along with any supporting files required by the presentation — such as fonts — and a copy of the PowerPoint Viewer.

Here's the procedure for using the Pack and Go Wizard:

1. **Open the presentation you want to copy to diskette.**

2. **Choose the File⇨Pack and Go command.**

   The Pack and Go Wizard appears, as shown in Figure 26-6.

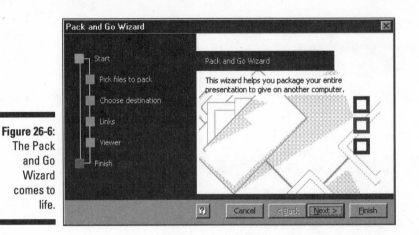

Figure 26-6:
The Pack
and Go
Wizard
comes to
life.

3. Click Next.

The Pack and Go Wizard asks which presentation you want to include, as shown in Figure 26-7. If you want, check Other presentation(s) and click the Browse button.

4. Click Next.

The Pack and Go Wizard asks whether you want to copy the presentation to drive A or a different drive.

5. Change the drive letter if necessary and then click Next.

The Pack and Go Wizard asks if you want to include linked files and TrueType fonts. Clicking both of these options is usually a good idea.

6. Click Next yet again.

This time, the Pack and Go Wizard asks whether you want the PowerPoint Viewer included on the disk.

Figure 26-7:
The Pack
and Go
Wizard asks
which
presentation
to include.

7. **Click Next one more time.**

   Finally, the last screen of the Pack and Go Wizard appears.

8. **Insert a diskette in the diskette drive.**

9. **Click Finish.**

   If prompted, insert the PowerPoint or Office CD or diskette.

10. **Get a cup of coffee.**

    Copying the presentation and the PowerPoint Viewer to diskette can take a few minutes. Be patient.

Loading a packed presentation on another computer

You cannot run a presentation directly from the disk created by the Pack and Go Wizard. Instead, you must first copy the presentation from the diskette to another computer's hard drive. To do that, simply run the Pngsetup program, which the Pack and Go Wizard automatically copies to the diskette. After you run the Pngsetup program, you can run the presentation by using the Viewer, as described in the next section.

Running a slide show by using the Viewer

Here's the procedure for displaying a slide show using the Viewer:

1. **Start PowerPoint Viewer.**

   Double-click its icon, which should be found on the folder you copied the presentation to when you ran the Pngsetup program from the diskette.

2. **Select the presentation you want to show.**

   Figure 26-8 shows the dialog box that PowerPoint Viewer displays. Use it to rummage through your files until you find the presentation you want.

3. **Click Show.**

   On with the show. Break a leg, kid.

Once the show is under way, you can use any of the keyboard or mouse tricks described in the section "Starting a Slide Show." You can even doodle on-screen à la John Madden.

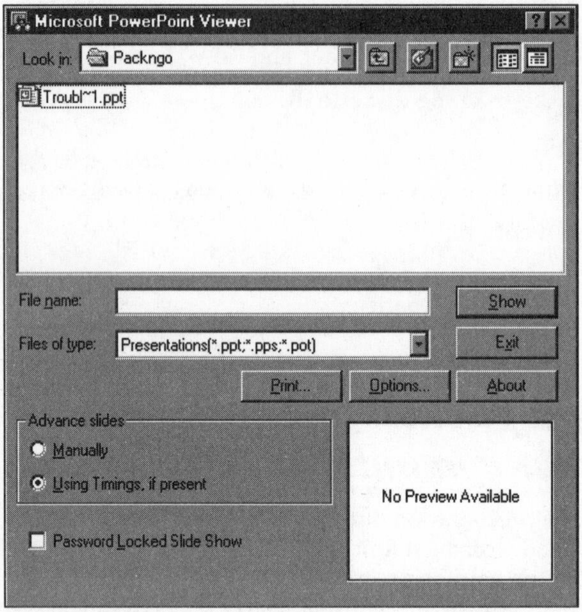

Microsoft PowerPoint Viewer

Look in: 🗀 Packngo

🗎 Troubl~1.ppt

File name:

Files of type: Presentations(*.ppt;*.pps;*.pot)

Show

Exit

Print... Options... About

Advance slides
○ Manually
◉ Using Timings, if present

No Preview Available

☐ Password Locked Slide Show

Figure 26-8:
The
PowerPoint
Viewer
dialog box.

If you have the full PowerPoint program, there's not much point in using the Viewer program instead. Viewer is designed for use on computers that don't have a copy of PowerPoint. Microsoft politely grants permission for you to copy the Viewer program to as many computers as you want. You can give it to your friends and associates. It would make a great birthday present for your mother-in-law.

If you use a desktop computer to create PowerPoint presentations and a laptop or notebook computer to run them, you don't have to install the full PowerPoint program on the laptop or notebook computer; just use the Pack and Go Wizard to transfer the presentation and the Viewer program to the notebook computer.

Giving a friend a copy of the PowerPoint Viewer program along with a presentation is perfectly legal. In fact, Microsoft specifically gives you permission to do so. This free-for-all applies only to PowerPoint Viewer, though. Don't make copies of the complete PowerPoint program for your friends unless you want to go to directly to jail (do not pass Go, do not collect $200).

If you want to set up a computer to run a slide show over and over again all day, click the Loop Continuously Until Esc box.

If you set up an unattended presentation, be sure to hide the keyboard and mouse or unplug them from the computer after you get the slide show going. Leaving a keyboard unattended is like inviting all the computer geeks within five miles to step up to your computer and find out which games you have.

If you're going to run a slide show on a computer other than the one you used to create the presentation, you need to make sure that the other computer has all the fonts that your presentation uses. If it doesn't, or if you're not sure, use the File⇨Save As command to save the file and check the Embed TrueType Fonts button. Doing so stores a copy of the fonts used by the presentation in the presentation file.

The Meeting Minder

PowerPoint includes a nifty feature called the *Meeting Minder,* which allows you to take notes during a presentation. To use the Meeting Minder, right-click the mouse during a slide show and choose the Meeting Minder command. The dialog box shown in Figure 26-9 appears.

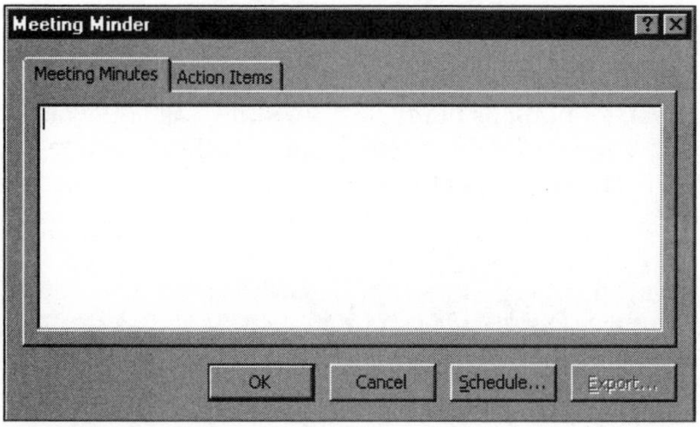

Figure 26-9:
The Meeting
Minder.

As you can see, the Meeting Minder has two tabbed areas. You can use these areas as follows:

- **Meeting Minutes:** Click the Meeting Minutes tab to keep minutes during a meeting. When you are finished, you can then click the Export button and convert the minutes to a Word document.

- **Action Items:** Click the Action Items tab to record items that require action following the meeting. Anything you type here is added to the last slide of the presentation, titled "Action Items." That way, the action items are automatically displayed at the end of the presentation.

Running a Presentation over a Network

PowerPoint 2000 allows you to run presentation conferences over a computer network, which basically means that you can run a slide show and invite other network users to view the slide show on their computers. Because this new PowerPoint 2000 feature uses Web technology to give it its "oomph," all viewers around the world or down the hall need to view your broadcast is a browser. For more information about this Presentation Broadcast Web-phenomenon, check out Chapter 21.

Using Custom Shows

Custom Shows is a feature for PowerPoint 2000 that lets you create several similar slide shows stored in a single presentation file. For example, suppose you are asked to give presentations about company benefits to management and non-management staff. You could create a presentation containing slides for all the company benefits and then create a custom show containing only those slides describing benefits that are available to non-management staff. This custom slide show could leave out slides such as "Stock Option Plans," "Golf Days," and "Boondoggles." You would then show the complete presentation to management but show the custom show to non-management staff.

A presentation can contain as many custom shows as you want. Each custom show is simply a subset of the complete presentation — made up of selected slides from the complete presentation.

Creating a custom show

To create a custom show, follow these steps:

1. **Choose the Sli̲de Show⇨C̲ustom Shows command.**

   This displays the Custom Shows dialog box as shown in Figure 26-10.

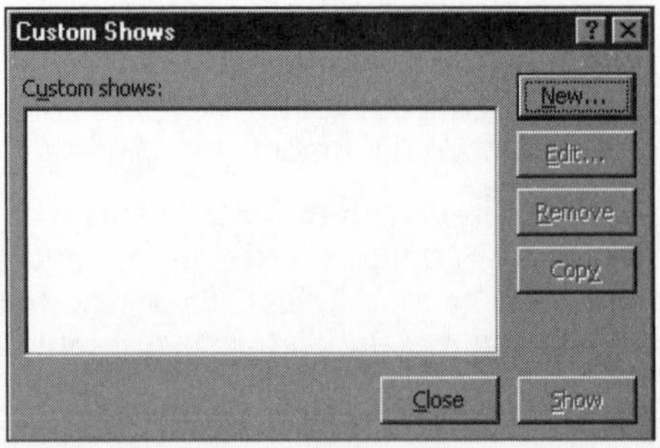

Figure 26-10:
The Custom
Shows
dialog box.

Custom Shows	? ☒
Cu̲stom shows:	N̲ew...
	Edi̲t...
	R̲emove
	Cop̲y
	C̲lose S̲how

2. **Click the New button.**

   The Define Custom Show dialog box appears, as shown in Figure 26-11.

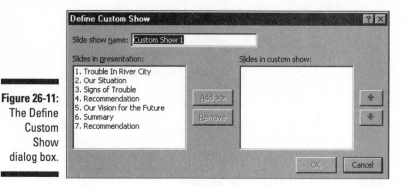

Figure 26-11: The Define Custom Show dialog box.

3. **Type a name for the custom show in the Slide Show Name field.**

4. **Add the slides you want to appear in the custom slide show.**

   All of the slides available in the presentation are listed in the list box on the left side of the Define Custom Show dialog box. To add a slide to the custom show, click the slide you want to add, and then click Add. The slide you added appears in the list box on the right side of the Define Custom Show dialog box.

   To remove a slide you've added by mistake, click the slide you want to remove in the list box on the right side of the Define Custom Show dialog box, and then click Remove.

5. **Click OK.**

   You return to the Custom Shows dialog box.

6. **Click Close to dismiss the Custom Shows dialog box.**

Showing a custom show

To show a custom show, first open the presentation that contains the custom show. Then, choose the Slide Show➪Custom Shows command to summon the Custom Shows dialog box. Click the custom show you want, and then click the Show button.

You can also call up a custom show during a slide show by right-clicking the mouse anywhere in the presentation, then choosing the Go➪Custom Shows command and clicking the custom show you want to display.

Part VI
The Part of Tens

The 5th Wave   By Rich Tennant

DAD ADDS MULTIMEDIA SOUND AND GRAPHICS TO THE TRADITIONAL CAMPFIRE GHOST STORY.

In this part . . .

PowerPoint 2000 has some really spiffy new bullets now, so how fitting indeed that this book should end with a bevy of chapters that aren't much more than glorified bulleted lists. Each chapter in this part covers ten (more or less) things worth knowing about PowerPoint. Without further ado, here they are, direct from the home office in Fresno, California.

Chapter 27

Ten New Features in PowerPoint 2000

• •

*I*f you're an experienced PowerPoint 97 user just upgrading to PowerPoint 2000, you probably turned to this chapter first. It lists the ten most important new features of PowerPoint 2000 for Windows.

Tri-Pane View

PowerPoint 2000 has changed the desktop! In an effort to make PowerPoint (as well as every other application in Office 2000) friendlier, Microsoft has created the new Tri-pane desktop (see Figure 27-1). Imagine it like this: Everything you use to create your presentation is suddenly at your fingertips. The Slide view, the Outline view, and the Notes view are all accessible at once, and all you have to do to work in any of the three views is click and drag the pane borders, and wa-laa — you are ready to create!

More "IntelliSense"

Just when you thought it was safe to return your late video copy of *2001: A Space Odyssey* to the video store, it's happened! More IntelliSense. If you have been on a long vacation, you may need to be reminded that IntelliSense is the cute little phrase that means the application you are using is designed to make "intelligent choices." In the case of PowerPoint 2000 (and all the applications in the suite), this new IntelliSense twist means that your used-to-be-stable toolbars are now equipped to make decisions about how you use them and supply you with the features you use the most. Yikes. The good news is you can find the missing buttons by clicking little down arrows on the toolbar that lead you to the stuff you're missing. As you use the toolbar, the features you use the most appear. If you feel like it, you can reset the function and start again.

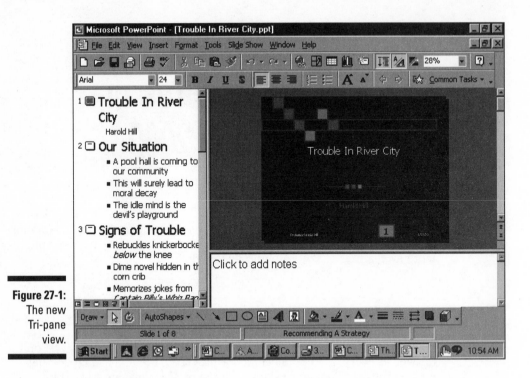

Figure 27-1:
The new
Tri-pane
view.

AutoFit Text

If you are a perfectionist, or even reasonably sensible, you like your presentation to fit on the page. Prior to now, that was sometimes a big problem, especially if you were at all verbose. Now with AutoFit text, the text you type is automatically resized to fit the slide you are working on. This means that PowerPoint will automatically change the font size to fit.

Snazzy Bullet Features

Anyone who uses PowerPoint knows how vital it is to emphasize information with bullets. Why? Well, because:

✔ Bullets make your point concisely.

✔ Bullets keep your audience focused on your point.

✔ Bullets keep you focused on your point.

Additionally, with PowerPoint 2000, bullets have become even snazzier (see Figure 27-2). Now, you can take advantage of all the new graphic bullets (which are especially nice as you use the Web to display your presentations in your intranet or the Internet). Additionally, bullets are also AutoNumbered.

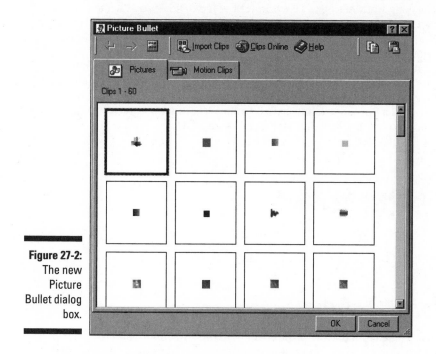

Figure 27-2:
The new
Picture
Bullet dialog
box.

Presentation Broadcast

Presentation Broadcast has to be one of the niftiest features PowerPoint 2000 has to offer. This feature enables you to run a multimedia slide show over the Internet (or your company's intranet). What makes this feature especially interesting is that now, unlike in earlier versions of PowerPoint, you can send video and audio as part of your presentation, and your viewers need only a browser (Internet Explorer 4.0 or better) to enjoy the show! Additionally, you can enable a chat function so that viewers can respond during the show, or you can allow them to e-mail you. This function works for any owner of PowerPoint for up to 15 audience members; after that, you need to specify a server for larger (perhaps corporate) groups.

Web Discussions

In Microsoft's effort to make doing business using PowerPoint global for users, it has added NetMeeting as a highly useful online collaboration tool. By accessing NetMeeting in PowerPoint (you can find it by clicking Tools➪ Online Collaboration), you can instantly collaborate with colleagues all over the globe. This feature allows you to share slides or any other document you choose with colleagues and interact in real time through the use of a chat function or the ability to draw on the "White board" — kind of like when you used to sit around in a conference room and hash out ideas with colleagues on the chalkboard. Hence the expression, "Back to the old drawing board." You can find a floating toolbar called Online Meeting that gives you the necessary tools to use the function fast (see Figure 27-3).

Figure 27-3:
The Online
Meeting
toolbar.

PowerPoint Tables

If you are a seasoned PowerPoint user, you have probably had to insert a table into your presentation numerous times. You have also had the experience of having to get out of PowerPoint, open Word or Excel to create the table, copy the table to the Clipboard, reopen PowerPoint, insert your Word or Excel table, and then format it appropriately. No more! Now, PowerPoint has its own built-in Tables feature. You can create complete tables in PowerPoint without the fuss!

Fit-To-Window Browser Compatibility

I was reading something from Microsoft the other day, and it said we are having a "Web revolution." Don't worry, I don't think you will have to arm yourself with anything more dangerous than this book. What the folks at Microsoft really mean is that they believe that the World Wide Web is revolutionizing the way we do business in the global marketplace, and they want their customers to be on top of it all. Hence, in this version of PowerPoint you see cool stuff like Web-based PowerPoint presentations that automatically check and select the right browser version. This fit-to-window feature automatically fits the presentation to the viewer's browser window.

Expanded Clipboard

Remember when you used to copy text or pictures for presentations and you had to go through the tedious process of copying something and placing it, and then looking for something else and repeating the process until your poor little fingers were weary? Now, the Clipboard has been expanded to hold 12 different pieces of text or pictures so you can copy and paste to your heart's delight! The new Clipboard function, shown in Figure 27-4, has its own Clipboard toolbar that pops up to let you manipulate your text or pictures easily.

Figure 27-4:
The
Clipboard
toolbar
makes it
easy to see
what a
copycat
you are!

Improved Web Compatibility

When you stop to think about it, what are the main things you need to make your PowerPoint presentations work on the Web? Well, first it would be nice if you could save in HTML, and it would also be handy if you could save your presentation to the Web. Also, it would be handy if somehow those people viewing your presentation on the Web could see something like what you thought you were sending them, and it would be nice if the slide adjusted to fit their browser window. It might also be a thrill if your viewers had some way to navigate around the slide show — maybe a navigation bar. What if you could receive notification through e-mail every time a document published on your intranet was edited? Could it be? Yes! PowerPoint 2000 makes this all possible with expanded Web compatibility features.

Chapter 28

Ten Things That Often Go Wrong

• •

*T*here are probably closer to 10,000 things that can go wrong when you're working with PowerPoint 2000, but these ten are among the things that go wrong most often.

I Can't Find My File!

You spent hours polishing that presentation and now you can't find the file. You know that you saved it, but it's not there! The problem is probably one of two things: Either you saved the file in a folder other than the one you thought you did, or you used a different name to save it than you intended. The solution? Use the File⇨Open command's search features. See "Finding Lost Files" in Chapter 23 for more details. Also, for a quick look, click the History icon in the upper-left–hand corner of the Open dialog box. You'll see the history of your recently used files, displaying the contents of an appropriately titled folder: Recent.

I've Run Out of Disk Space!

Nothing is more frustrating than creating a fancy PowerPoint presentation and then discovering that you're completely out of disk space. What to do? Start up a My Computer window and rummage through your hard disk, looking for files you don't need. Delete enough files to free up a few megabytes and then press Alt+Tab to move back to PowerPoint and save your file. I did this just a few days ago; I had to delete a bunch of sound files I recorded from the movie *Young Frankenstein*. (It was either them or the Word for Windows document files for the first few chapters of this book. Not an easy decision.)

If your disk is full and you can't find more than a few files to delete, try double-clicking on the Recycle Bin icon and choosing the File⇨Empty Recycle Bin command. This often frees up additional disk space. If that doesn't do the job, consider activating the Windows 98 disk compression program, DriveSpace 3, found in the Start menu under the Accessories and System Tools selections.

I've Run Out of Memory!

Many computers with only 16MB of internal memory are running Windows 95, or better, these days. Although that is enough to run PowerPoint, 32MB is a more reasonable minimum, and even 128MB isn't an outrageous amount of memory these days. Now that it's possible and probable that you may be online and using PowerPoint at the same time, make sure that you have enough memory to keep the time that tasks take to the minimum. The additional memory helps your computer to not give up and crash from the overload of open applications. Memory is cheap! Why not make sure you have enough?

PowerPoint Has Vanished!

You're working at your computer, minding your own business, when suddenly — whoosh! — PowerPoint disappears. What happened? Most likely, you clicked some area outside the PowerPoint window or you pressed Alt+Tab or Alt+Esc, which whisks you away to another program. To get PowerPoint back, press Alt+Tab. You may have to press Alt+Tab several times before PowerPoint comes back to life.

PowerPoint can also vanish into thin air if you use a screen saver program. Try giving the mouse a nudge to see whether PowerPoint reappears.

I Accidentally Deleted a File!

Just learned how to delete files and couldn't stop yourself, eh? Relax. It happens to the best of us. Odds are that you can get the deleted file back if you act fast enough. Double-click the Recycle Bin icon that sits on your desktop. There, you'll probably find the deleted file. Copy it back to the folder where it belongs.

It Won't Let Me Edit That!

No matter how hard you click the mouse, PowerPoint won't let you edit that doohickey on-screen. What gives? The doohickey is probably a part of the Slide Master. To edit it, use the View⇨Master⇨Slide Master command. This step displays the Slide Master and enables you to edit it.

Something Seems to Be Missing!

You just read the chapter about Equation Editor, but nothing happens when you try to use it. PowerPoint 2000 (as well as the rest of the applications in the suite) has a new feature called Install on Command. Most likely, you have to try to use the command once, and installation will begin upon your first try.

What Happened to My Clip Art?

You just purchased and installed an expensive clip art collection that has 500 stunning photographic-quality images from Dick Clark's Rockin' New Year's Eve Millennium Count Down, but you can't find them in the Clip Gallery. Where did they go? Nowhere. You just have to tell Clip Gallery about them. Fire up the Gallery by clicking the Insert Picture button or by selecting Insert➪Picture➪Clip Art. Then click the Import Clips button. Then insert the filename of the images you are looking to add in the File Name text box, click the appropriate clip import option, and click Import.

One of the Toolbars (Or Toolbar Features) Is Missing!

Now that PowerPoint 2000 features the wonderful, if frightening, Personalized Menus and Toolbars function, you may notice that the toolbars and menus jus' ain't what they used to be! You reach for the Bold button, but it's not there. In fact, the whole Formatting toolbar seems to be missing. What gives? Perhaps it's the new IntelliSense feature deciding which buttons on your toolbar you use 95 percent of the time. Luckily, menu choices are at the end of each menu, and down arrow buttons on the toolbars enable you to see all the toolbar and menu commands so that you can select what is missing.

If your toolbar is missing altogether, you can't see all the choices available to you. Aside from the Standard and Formatting toolbars, you will sometimes have to summon a toolbar if it somehow gets lost. It happens all the time, so don't feel bad. Just look in the mirror and say to yourself, "It's not my fault that the toolbar disappeared. It happens even to experts like that nice Mr. Lowe, who wrote a whole book about PowerPoint. I shouldn't blame myself. After all, I'm good enough, I'm smart enough, and, doggone it, people like me."

Then use the View➪Toolbars command to reactivate the missing toolbar.

You may also want to check out the Standard toolbar and select Tools⇨ Customize⇨Options. By doing so, you have an opportunity to check a text box that combines the Standard and Formatting toolbar on one line! Some people have been known to go clinically insane when this text box was checked without their knowledge. Don't be caught unaware!

All the Text Is the Same!

This problem happens in Outline view when you click the Show Formatting button. Just click Show Formatting again to restore text formatting, such as font, point size, italics, and so on.

Chapter 29

Ten PowerPoint Shortcuts

• •

*Y*ou can do just about anything you can do with PowerPoint 2000 by
hacking your way through the menus or clicking the correct toolbar
button. But a few shortcuts are worth knowing about.

Keyboard Shortcuts for Multiple Windows

 Most Windows programs that enable you to open multiple documents,
including Word for Windows and Excel, work the same way PowerPoint
works. So memorizing the menu commands and keyboard shortcuts for working with more than one presentation window in PowerPoint pays off because
you use the same menu commands and keyboard shortcuts in other
programs.

Shortcut	Action
Ctrl+F6	Moves you to the next presentation window
Shift+Ctrl+F6	Moves you to the previous presentation window
Ctrl+F10	Maximizes a presentation window
Ctrl+F5	Returns a window to its normal size
Ctrl+F4	Closes a document window

Right-Click Anywhere to Get a Quick Menu

You can right-click just about anything with the mouse button to get a quick menu of common things you can do to the object. Try it — it's kind of fun.

Ctrl+X, Ctrl+C, or Ctrl+V to Cut, Copy, or Paste

Just about all Windows applications respond to these keyboard shortcuts.

Shortcut	Action
Ctrl+X	Cuts the selection to the Clipboard.
Ctrl+C	Copies the selection to the Clipboard.
Ctrl+V	Inserts the contents of the Clipboard.

Note: Before you use Ctrl+X or Ctrl+C, select the object you want to cut or copy.

Ctrl+Z to Undo a Mistake

Oops! Didn't mean to double-click there? Don't panic. Press Ctrl+Z, and whatever you did last is undone.

Ctrl+B or Ctrl+I for Bold or Italics

Like most Windows applications, PowerPoint accepts the following keyboard shortcuts for text formatting:

Shortcut	Action
Ctrl+B	Bold
Ctrl+I	Italic
Ctrl+U	Underline
Ctrl+spacebar	Return to normal format

Note: Before using these shortcuts, highlight the text that you want to format.

Ctrl+S to Save a File

Press Ctrl+S to save the current presentation to a file. The first time you save a new file, PowerPoint displays the Save As dialog box, in which you can assign a name to the file. Thereafter, Ctrl+S saves the file by using the same name.

Ctrl+G to Show the Guides

Need help aligning drawn objects? Press Ctrl+G to display the guides. You can then drag the guidelines around and snap objects to them.

Shift While Drawing to Constrain Objects

If you hold down the Shift key while drawing an object, the object is drawn either perfectly straight or perfectly round. Circles will be circles, squares will be squares, and lines will stick to 45-degree angles.

Alt+Esc, Alt+Tab, or Ctrl+Esc to Switch to Another Program

This isn't really a PowerPoint shortcut; it's a Windows shortcut. To switch to another application that you have minimized or that is hiding behind your active window, use one of these keyboard combinations:

- ✔ **Alt+Esc:** Switches to the next program in line.
- ✔ **Alt+Tab:** Displays the name of the next program in line. While holding down the Alt key, keep pressing Tab until the name of the program you want appears. Release both keys to switch to that program.
- ✔ **Ctrl+Esc:** Pops up the Start menu, from which you can start other programs.

F1 — The Panic Button

Stuck? Press F1 to activate PowerPoint Help. With luck, you can find enough information to get you going. Help is *context sensitive,* which means that it tries to figure out what you were doing when you pressed F1 and gives you specific help for that task.

Index

From PCs to Personal Finance, We Make it Fun and Easy!

ISBN 0-7645-0594-7
$19.99 US/$28.99 CAN

ISBN 0-7645-5231-7
$19.99 US/$27.99 CAN

For more information, or to order, please call 800.762.2974.

www.hungryminds.com
www.dummies.com

Dummies Books™
Bestsellers on Every Topic!

GENERAL INTEREST TITLES

BUSINESS & PERSONAL FINANCE

Title	Author	ISBN	Price
Accounting For Dummies®	John A. Tracy, CPA	0-7645-5014-4	$19.99 US/$27.99 CAN
Business Plans For Dummies®	Paul Tiffany, Ph.D. & Steven D. Peterson, Ph.D.	1-56884-868-4	$19.99 US/$27.99 CAN
Business Writing For Dummies®	Sheryl Lindsell-Roberts	0-7645-5134-5	$16.99 US/$27.99 CAN
Consulting For Dummies®	Bob Nelson & Peter Economy	0-7645-5034-9	$19.99 US/$27.99 CAN
Customer Service For Dummies®, 2nd Edition	Karen Leland & Keith Bailey	0-7645-5209-0	$19.99 US/$27.99 CAN
Franchising For Dummies®	Dave Thomas & Michael Seid	0-7645-5160-4	$19.99 US/$27.99 CAN
Getting Results For Dummies®	Mark H. McCormack	0-7645-5205-8	$19.99 US/$27.99 CAN
Home Buying For Dummies®	Eric Tyson, MBA & Ray Brown	1-56884-385-2	$16.99 US/$24.99 CAN
House Selling For Dummies®	Eric Tyson, MBA & Ray Brown	0-7645-5038-1	$16.99 US/$24.99 CAN
Human Resources Kit For Dummies®	Max Messmer	0-7645-5131-0	$19.99 US/$27.99 CAN
Investing For Dummies®, 2nd Edition	Eric Tyson, MBA	0-7645-5162-0	$19.99 US/$27.99 CAN
Law For Dummies®	John Ventura	1-56884-860-9	$19.99 US/$27.99 CAN
Leadership For Dummies®	Marshall Loeb & Steven Kindel	0-7645-5176-0	$19.99 US/$27.99 CAN
Managing For Dummies®	Bob Nelson & Peter Economy	1-56884-858-7	$19.99 US/$27.99 CAN
Marketing For Dummies®	Alexander Hiam	1-56884-699-1	$19.99 US/$27.99 CAN
Mutual Funds For Dummies®, 2nd Edition	Eric Tyson, MBA	0-7645-5112-4	$19.99 US/$27.99 CAN
Negotiating For Dummies®	Michael C. Donaldson & Mimi Donaldson	1-56884-867-6	$19.99 US/$27.99 CAN
Personal Finance For Dummies®, 3rd Edition	Eric Tyson, MBA	0-7645-5231-7	$19.99 US/$27.99 CAN
Personal Finance For Dummies® For Canadians, 2nd Edition	Eric Tyson, MBA & Tony Martin	0-7645-5123-X	$19.99 US/$27.99 CAN
Public Speaking For Dummies®	Malcolm Kushner	0-7645-5159-0	$16.99 US/$24.99 CAN
Sales Closing For Dummies®	Tom Hopkins	0-7645-5063-2	$14.99 US/$21.99 CAN
Sales Prospecting For Dummies®	Tom Hopkins	0-7645-5066-7	$14.99 US/$21.99 CAN
Selling For Dummies®	Tom Hopkins	1-56884-389-5	$16.99 US/$24.99 CAN
Small Business For Dummies®	Eric Tyson, MBA & Jim Schell	0-7645-5094-2	$19.99 US/$27.99 CAN
Small Business Kit For Dummies®	Richard D. Harroch	0-7645-5093-4	$24.99 US/$34.99 CAN
Taxes 2001 For Dummies®	Eric Tyson & David J. Silverman	0-7645-5306-2	$15.99 US/$23.99 CAN
Time Management For Dummies®, 2nd Edition	Jeffrey J. Mayer	0-7645-5145-0	$19.99 US/$27.99 CAN
Writing Business Letters For Dummies®	Sheryl Lindsell-Roberts	0-7645-5207-4	$16.99 US/$24.99 CAN

TECHNOLOGY TITLES

INTERNET/ONLINE

Title	Author	ISBN	Price
America Online® For Dummies®, 6th Edition	John Kaufeld	0-7645-0670-6	$19.99 US/$27.99 CAN
Banking Online Dummies®	Paul Murphy	0-7645-0458-4	$24.99 US/$34.99 CAN
eBay™ For Dummies®, 2nd Edition	Marcia Collier, Roland Woerner, & Stephanie Becker	0-7645-0761-3	$19.99 US/$27.99 CAN
E-Mail For Dummies®, 2nd Edition	John R. Levine, Carol Baroudi, & Arnold Reinhold	0-7645-0131-3	$24.99 US/$34.99 CAN
Genealogy Online For Dummies®, 2nd Edition	Matthew L. Helm & April Leah Helm	0-7645-0543-2	$24.99 US/$34.99 CAN
Internet Directory For Dummies®, 3rd Edition	Brad Hill	0-7645-0558-2	$24.99 US/$34.99 CAN
Internet Auctions For Dummies®	Greg Holden	0-7645-0578-9	$24.99 US/$34.99 CAN
Internet Explorer 5.5 For Windows® For Dummies®	Doug Lowe	0-7645-0738-9	$19.99 US/$28.99 CAN
Researching Online For Dummies®, 2nd Edition	Mary Ellen Bates & Reva Basch	0-7645-0546-7	$24.99 US/$34.99 CAN
Job Searching Online For Dummies®	Pam Dixon	0-7645-0673-0	$24.99 US/$34.99 CAN
Investing Online For Dummies®, 3rd Edition	Kathleen Sindell, Ph.D.	0-7645-0725-7	$24.99 US/$34.99 CAN
Travel Planning Online For Dummies®, 2nd Edition	Noah Vadnai	0-7645-0438-X	$24.99 US/$34.99 CAN
Internet Searching For Dummies®	Brad Hill	0-7645-0478-9	$24.99 US/$34.99 CAN
Yahoo!® For Dummies®, 2nd Edition	Brad Hill	0-7645-0762-1	$19.99 US/$27.99 CAN
The Internet For Dummies®, 7th Edition	John R. Levine, Carol Baroudi, & Arnold Reinhold	0-7645-0674-9	$19.99 US/$27.99 CAN

OPERATING SYSTEMS

Title	Author	ISBN	Price
DOS For Dummies®, 3rd Edition	Dan Gookin	0-7645-0361-8	$19.99 US/$27.99 CAN
GNOME For Linux® For Dummies®	David B. Busch	0-7645-0650-1	$24.99 US/$37.99 CAN
LINUX® For Dummies®, 2nd Edition	John Hall, Craig Witherspoon, & Coletta Witherspoon	0-7645-0421-5	$24.99 US/$34.99 CAN
Mac® OS 9 For Dummies®	Bob LeVitus	0-7645-0652-8	$19.99 US/$28.99 CAN
Red Hat® Linux® For Dummies®	Jon "maddog" Hall, Paul Sery	0-7645-0663-3	$24.99 US/$37.99 CAN
Small Business Windows® 98 For Dummies®	Stephen Nelson	0-7645-0425-8	$24.99 US/$34.99 CAN
UNIX® For Dummies®, 4th Edition	John R. Levine & Margaret Levine Young	0-7645-0419-3	$19.99 US/$27.99 CAN
Windows® 95 For Dummies®, 2nd Edition	Andy Rathbone	0-7645-0180-1	$19.99 US/$27.99 CAN
Windows® 98 For Dummies®	Andy Rathbone	0-7645-0261-1	$19.99 US/$27.99 CAN
Windows® 2000 For Dummies®	Andy Rathbone	0-7645-0641-2	$19.99 US/$27.99 CAN
Windows® 2000 Server For Dummies®	Ed Tittel	0-7645-0341-3	$24.99 US/$37.99 CAN
Windows® ME Millennium Edition For Dummies®	Andy Rathbone	0-7645-0735-4	$19.99 US/$27.99 CAN

Dummies Books™
Bestsellers on Every Topic!

GENERAL INTEREST TITLES

FOOD & BEVERAGE/ENTERTAINING

Title	Author	ISBN	Price
Bartending For Dummies®	Ray Foley	0-7645-5051-9	$14.99 US/$21.99 CAN
Cooking For Dummies®, 2nd Edition	Bryan Miller & Marie Rama	0-7645-5250-3	$19.99 US/$27.99 CAN
Entertaining For Dummies®	Suzanne Williamson with Linda Smith	0-7645-5027-6	$19.99 US/$27.99 CAN
Gourmet Cooking For Dummies®	Charlie Trotter	0-7645-5029-2	$19.99 US/$27.99 CAN
Grilling For Dummies®	Marie Rama & John Mariani	0-7645-5076-4	$19.99 US/$27.99 CAN
Italian Cooking For Dummies®	Cesare Casella & Jack Bishop	0-7645-5098-5	$19.99 US/$27.99 CAN
Mexican Cooking For Dummies®	Mary Sue Miliken & Susan Feniger	0-7645-5169-8	$19.99 US/$27.99 CAN
Quick & Healthy Cooking For Dummies®	Lynn Fischer	0-7645-5214-7	$19.99 US/$27.99 CAN
Wine For Dummies®, 2nd Edition	Ed McCarthy & Mary Ewing-Mulligan	0-7645-5114-0	$19.99 US/$27.99 CAN
Chinese Cooking For Dummies®	Martin Yan	0-7645-5247-3	$19.99 US/$27.99 CAN
Etiquette For Dummies®	Sue Fox	0-7645-5170-1	$19.99 US/$27.99 CAN

SPORTS

Title	Author	ISBN	Price
Baseball For Dummies®, 2nd Edition	Joe Morgan with Richard Lally	0-7645-5234-1	$19.99 US/$27.99 CAN
Golf For Dummies®, 2nd Edition	Gary McCord	0-7645-5146-9	$19.99 US/$27.99 CAN
Fly Fishing For Dummies®	Peter Kaminsky	0-7645-5073-X	$19.99 US/$27.99 CAN
Football For Dummies®	Howie Long with John Czarnecki	0-7645-5054-3	$19.99 US/$27.99 CAN
Hockey For Dummies®	John Davidson with John Steinbreder	0-7645-5045-4	$19.99 US/$27.99 CAN
NASCAR For Dummies®	Mark Martin	0-7645-5219-8	$19.99 US/$27.99 CAN
Tennis For Dummies®	Patrick McEnroe with Peter Bodo	0-7645-5087-X	$19.99 US/$27.99 CAN
Soccer For Dummies®	U.S. Soccer Federation & Michael Lewiss	0-7645-5229-5	$19.99 US/$27.99 CAN

HOME & GARDEN

Title	Author	ISBN	Price
Annuals For Dummies®	Bill Marken & NGA	0-7645-5056-X	$16.99 US/$24.99 CAN
Container Gardening For Dummies®	Bill Marken & NGA	0-7645-5057-8	$16.99 US/$24.99 CAN
Decks & Patios For Dummies®	Robert J. Beckstrom & NGA	0-7645-5075-6	$16.99 US/$24.99 CAN
Flowering Bulbs For Dummies®	Judy Glattstein & NGA	0-7645-5103-5	$16.99 US/$24.99 CAN
Gardening For Dummies®, 2nd Edition	Michael MacCaskey & NGA	0-7645-5130-2	$16.99 US/$24.99 CAN
Herb Gardening For Dummies®	NGA	0-7645-5200-7	$16.99 US/$24.99 CAN
Home Improvement For Dummies®	Gene & Katie Hamilton & the Editors of HouseNet, Inc.	0-7645-5005-4	$19.99 US/$26.99 CAN
Houseplants For Dummies®	Larry Hodgson & NGA	0-7645-5102-7	$16.99 US/$24.99 CAN
Painting and Wallpapering For Dummies®	Gene Hamilton	0-7645-5150-7	$16.99 US/$24.99 CAN
Perennials For Dummies®	Marcia Tatroe & NGA	0-7645-5030-6	$16.99 US/$24.99 CAN
Roses For Dummies®, 2nd Edition	Lance Walheim	0-7645-5202-3	$16.99 US/$24.99 CAN
Trees and Shrubs For Dummies®	Ann Whitman & NGA	0-7645-5203-1	$16.99 US/$24.99 CAN
Vegetable Gardening For Dummies®	Charlie Nardozzi & NGA	0-7645-5129-9	$16.99 US/$24.99 CAN
Home Cooking For Dummies®	Patricia Hart McMillan & Katharine Kaye McMillan	0-7645-5107-8	$19.99 US/$27.99 CAN

TECHNOLOGY TITLES

WEB DESIGN & PUBLISHING

Title	Author	ISBN	Price
Active Server Pages For Dummies®, 2nd Edition	Bill Hatfield	0-7645-0603-X	$24.99 US/$37.99 CAN
Cold Fusion 4 For Dummies®	Alexis Gutzman	0-7645-0604-8	$24.99 US/$37.99 CAN
Creating Web Pages For Dummies®, 5th Edition	Bud Smith & Arthur Bebak	0-7645-0733-8	$24.99 US/$34.99 CAN
Dreamweaver™ 3 For Dummies®	Janine Warner & Paul Vachier	0-7645-0669-2	$24.99 US/$34.99 CAN
FrontPage® 2000 For Dummies®	Asha Dornfest	0-7645-0423-1	$24.99 US/$34.99 CAN
HTML 4 For Dummies®, 3rd Edition	Ed Tittel & Natanya Dits	0-7645-0572-6	$24.99 US/$34.99 CAN
Java™ For Dummies®, 3rd Edition	Aaron E. Walsh	0-7645-0417-7	$24.99 US/$34.99 CAN
PageMill™ 2 For Dummies®	Deke McClelland & John San Filippo	0-7645-0028-7	$24.99 US/$34.99 CAN
XML™ For Dummies®	Ed Tittel	0-7645-0692-7	$24.99 US/$37.99 CAN
Javascript For Dummies®, 3rd Edition	Emily Vander Veer	0-7645-0633-1	$24.99 US/$37.99 CAN

DESKTOP PUBLISHING GRAPHICS/MULTIMEDIA

Title	Author	ISBN	Price
Adobe® In Design™ For Dummies®	Deke McClelland	0-7645-0599-8	$19.99 US/$27.99 CAN
CorelDRAW™ 9 For Dummies®	Deke McClelland	0-7645-0523-8	$19.99 US/$27.99 CAN
Desktop Publishing and Design For Dummies®	Roger C. Parker	1-56884-234-1	$19.99 US/$27.99 CAN
Digital Photography For Dummies®, 3rd Edition	Julie Adair King	0-7645-0646-3	$24.99 US/$37.99 CAN
Microsoft® Publisher 98 For Dummies®	Jim McCarter	0-7645-0395-2	$19.99 US/$27.99 CAN
Visio 2000 For Dummies®	Debbie Walkowski	0-7645-0635-8	$19.99 US/$27.99 CAN
Microsoft® Publisher 2000 For Dummies®	Jim McCarter	0-7645-0525-4	$19.99 US/$27.99 CAN
Windows® Movie Maker For Dummies®	Keith Underdahl	0-7645-0749-1	$19.99 US/$27.99 CAN

Notes

Notes